# Justice Belied

The Unbalanced Scales of International Criminal Justice

# Justice Belied

## The Unbalanced Scales
## of International Criminal Justice

Edited by
Sébastien Chartrand and John Philpot

Baraka
Books

Montréal

ISBN 978-1-926824-79-6 pbk; 978-1-77186-027-7 epub; 978-1-77186-028-4 pdf; 978-1-77186-029-1 mobi/pocket


Cover by Folio infographie
Book design by Folio infographie

Legal Deposit, 4th quarter 2014

Bibliothèque et Archives nationales du Québec
Library and Archives Canada

Published by Baraka Books of Montreal
6977, rue Lacroix
Montréal, Québec H4E 2V4
Telephone: 514 808-8504
info@barakabooks.com
www.barakabooks.com


Printed and bound in Quebec

Baraka Books acknowledges the generous support of its publishing program from the Société de développement des entreprises culturelles du Québec (SODEC), the Government of Quebec, tax credit for book publishing administered by SODEC, and the Canada Council for the Arts.

We acknowledge the financial support of the Government of Canada, through the National Translation Program for Book Publishing for our translation activities and through the Canada Book Fund (CBF) for our publishing activities.

Trade Distribution & Returns
Canada and the United States
Independent Publishers Group
1-800-888-4741 (IPG1);
orders@ipgbook.com

This book is dedicated to Jean-Paul Akayesu, an innocent man, and the first man convicted after trial at the ICTR. Prosecuted by the future American War Crimes Ambassador, Pierre Prosper, he was convicted after a modicum of a trial of genocide including rape. Virtually undefended by attorneys imposed against his will, he has been wrongly vilified in law schools in the West, in legal textbooks, in the jurisprudence in International Criminal Law, and on Internet.

# Contents

List of Acronyms     11

Introduction     13

## PART I
## International Criminal Justice in the Eyes of Africans and African Americans

1    African Court and International Criminal Courts: Discriminatory International Justice and the Quest for a New World Judicial Order • *Chief Charles A. Taku*    19

2    The Ailing Empire's Full Spectrum Dominance • *Glen Ford*    47

3    Victoire Ingabire: Chronology of a Pinochet-style Case of Repression • *Joseph Bukeye*    55

4    The Fabrication of Evidence before the International Criminal Tribunal for Rwanda • *Léopold Nsengiyumva*    67

5    Charles Taylor: The Special Court for Sierra Leone and Questionable Verdicts • *Chief Charles A. Taku*    77

6    The Seven Challenges for Truth and Justice in Rwanda *Théogène Rudasingwa*    91

7    The ICC and Kenya: Going Beyond the Rhetoric *Chief Charles A. Taku*    99

## PART II
## The *ad hoc* International Criminal Tribunals

8    The Heart of Dark Jurisprudence • *Philippe Larochelle*    115

9    Prosecutorial Failure to Disclose Exculpatory Material: A Death Knell to Fairness • *Beth S. Lyon*    127

**10**  Lessons Learned from the Bad Beginnings
of the International Tribunal for Rwanda • *André Sirois*          143

**11**  The Dubious Heritage of the International Criminal
Tribunal for Rwanda • *John Philpot*          161

**12**  The ICTR is war by other means—Ramsey Clark • *Phil Taylor*  179

### PART III
## Universal Jurisdiction... in a Single Country

**13**  Transitional Justice in Rwanda and Democratic Republic
of the Congo: From War to Peace? • *Jordi Palou-Loverdos*          189

**14**  The Kuala Lumpur War Crimes Tribunal: Interview with
Professor Michel Chossudovsky          211

### PART IV
## Justice for All?

**15**  And Justice for All? International Criminal Justice
in the Time of High Expectations          219
*Fannie Lafontaine and Érick Sullivan*

**16**  How the International Criminal Law Movement
Undermined International Law—Michael Mandel's
Groundbreaking Analyses • *David Jacobs*          239

**17**  International Criminal Law: An Instrument of United States
Foreign Policy • *John Philpot*          251

Conclusion          271

Contributors          277

Acknowledgements          279

# List of Acronyms

| | |
|---|---|
| AFRC | The Armed Forces Revolutionary Council |
| AFRICOM | United States Africa Command |
| AU | African Union |
| CDF | Civil Defense Forces (CDF) |
| DRC | Democratic Republic of the Congo (formerly Zaïre) |
| ECHR | European Court of Human Rights |
| FDLR | Forces démocratiques pour la libération du Rwanda (Democratic Forces for the Liberation of Rwanda) |
| ICC | International Criminal Court |
| ICRC | International Committee of the Red Cross |
| ICTR | International Criminal Tribunal for Rwanda |
| ICTY | International Criminal Tribunal for the Former Yugoslavia |
| JCE | Joint Criminal Enterprise |
| MICT | Mechanism for International Criminal Tribunals or International Residual Mechanism for International Criminal Tribunals |
| ODM | Orange Democratic Movement |
| OTP | Office of the Prosecutor |
| R2P | Responsibility to Protect |
| RPA | Rwandan Patriotic Army |
| RPF | Rwandan Patriotic Front |
| RUF | Revolutionary United Front for Sierra Leone |
| SCSL | Special Court for Sierra Leone |
| STL | Special Tribunal for Lebanon |
| UCK | Kosovo Liberation Army |
| UDF | Unified Democratic Forces (Rwandan opposition political party) |

# Introduction

The reality of International Criminal Law is virtually unknown to the general public. Yet International Criminal Law enjoys an aura of respectability—totally unwarranted in the eyes of many of our authors—and this aura creates an illusion that its judgments are reliable and at last tell us the "truth" about events in different parts of the world. The book you are about to read represents the first attempt by defence counsel, investigators, journalists, academics, attorneys, and experienced observers to shed light on the issues, problems, and injustices that International Criminal Law has raised, particularly over the past twenty years.

Judicial history can be written by the study of judgments, proclamations, tribunal statutes, and other tribunal legislation. We consider that the reality of International Criminal Law can be best understood and explained by those intimately involved, particularly from the defence point of view. The trials and tribulations of our clients, many of whom have been wrongly convicted, are at the heart of our work. We are all inspired by the high ideals of justice—the right to life, the right to full answer and defence, impartiality of justice where no one is above the law, where rich and poor, black and white are treated equally, and where guilt can only be determined when credible evidence overwhelmingly dictates the only verdict possible. Many of us are also inspired by a desire to bring about a better world that will respect all the world's peoples and their right to self-determination, thereby leading to an equitable sharing of wealth.

International Criminal Law has been overwhelmingly focused on— some would say foisted upon—Africa and Africans, yet rarely do we hear or read the points of view of Africans, be they from Africa or from the diaspora. The first section is thus entitled "International Justice in the Eyes of Africans and African Americans." Chief Charles Taku, an experienced defence counsel from Cameroun, addresses both problems of discrimination and serious legal problems raised at the International Criminal Tribunal for Rwanda and the International Criminal Court. In two other articles, he discusses the questionable practices and verdicts in the Charles Taylor case and then raises a red flag about the political consequences of the ICC's involvement in Kenya.

Glen Ford, a reputed African-American journalist and executive editor of the Black Agenda Report, takes on the taboo about the United States' dominant role in international law and politics in Africa.

Former Rwandan presidential candidate Ms. Victoire Ingabire Umuhoza, now in prison in Rwanda, has been compared to Mandela. Joseph Buckeye, former ICTR investigator, provides essential information on her trial and sentencing comparing it to "Pinochet-style" repression. Theogène Rudasingwa was Rwandan President Paul Kagame's Chief of Staff and also Rwanda's Ambassador to the United States. His paper focuses on justice and Rwanda over the long term. Leopold Nsengiyumva, an experienced ICTR defence investigator, sheds light on startling and much too common cases of fabrication of evidence at the ICTR.

Phil Taylor, journalist, broadcaster, and long-time ICTR investigator, provides sharp insight into the very nature of the ICTR, which Ramsey Clark has described as "war by other means." Whereas courts are expected to provide reliable jurisprudence and precedents for future cases, Philippe Larochelle, an experienced defence counsel, casts doubt on the reliability of the "dark jurisprudence" resulting from ICTR trials. André Sirois is an attorney and UN legal translator who was involved in what he describes as the "bad beginnings" of the ICTR. His observations will surprise readers. Beth Lyons, a leading ICTR defence counsel, addresses and analyses disclosure problems at the ICTR, which make final judgments both unfair and untrustworthy.

Jordi Palou Loverdos, from Catalonia, Spain, was one of the driving forces behind Spain's application of universal jurisdiction in criminal law and the development of alternative methods of reconciliation and peace following massive human rights violations. His article provides essential information and background on that initiative. Malaysia set up the Kuala Lumpur War Crimes Tribunal in 2006 based on the principle of universal jurisdiction. In an interview, Professor Michel Chossudovsky of the Centre for Research on Globalization and a founder of that Tribunal describes the challenges involved and the Tribunal's achievements.

In the final section entitled "Justice for All?" Professor Fannie Lafontaine and Erick Sullivan of Université Laval address the future of International Criminal Law and see some positive developments. On the other hand, Toronto lawyer and ICTR defence counsel David Jacobs offers readers a dedication to the late Michael Mandel, a pioneering scholar in international criminal law who passed away on October 27, 2013. Professor Mandel held that the international criminal law movement had delegitimised and marginalised the United Nations and effectively regulated, even legitimated, the use of violence in international affairs.

In two articles, John Philpot, defence counsel at the ICTR and the ICC, submits first that the ICTR's heritage is seriously flawed, and second that in general International Criminal Law tribunals are moulded to comply with, and aid and abet, United States foreign policy.

We hope this contribution based on our first-hand experience will be a useful tool to understanding the flaws in the International Criminal Law process and provide insight for the future and the creation of a just international order.

## PART I

## International Criminal Justice in the Eyes of Africans and African Americans

# 1

# African Court and International Criminal Courts: Discriminatory International Justice and the Quest for a New World Judicial Order

CHIEF CHARLES A. TAKU

## Introduction

The idea of establishing a standing international criminal court to investigate and prosecute international crimes as a significant component of the world's effort to safeguard world peace and security was first raised unsuccessfully by the Russian delegate at the first and second World Peace Conferences in 1899 and 1907. Africa was not then considered a subject of international law. To Western European imperial powers, Africa was a vast slave plantation that they apportioned among themselves at the so-called Berlin Conference in 1884. For that reason, Africa was not represented and its interests were not protected at the first and second World Peace Conferences.

Africa's situation did not change significantly during the long search for social, political, economic, and cultural stability conducted from 1899 to about 1960 when the so-called Western democracies granted her independence. Rather, the granting of independence to countries of the irrationally fragmented continent, without first accounting for the international crimes and the plunder of the continent's natural resources, left behind economically and politically unstable entities under the control of proxies and stooges who ensured that the flow of wealth to the colonial masters was unimpeded despite gratuitous claims to national sovereignty.

The creation of the League of Nations in 1919, the establishment outside the framework of the permanent Court of International Justice in 1921, as the principal judicial organ of the League, the creation of the United Nations in 1946, and the establishment of the International Court of Justice as its principal judicial organ had the ambitious goal of maintaining world peace and security. The promotion of human rights was recognised as a fundamental human value and an indispensable component of world peace, stability, and security.[1] This was followed in quick succession by the declaration of human rights[2] and the Geneva Conventions criminalising the crimes of genocide, war crimes, and crimes against humanity. These lofty goals were compelled by the devastating effects of the First and Second World Wars, in which Africans sacrificed their lives on the side of freedom and a new world order, and the need to hold perpetrators of international crimes accountable for their acts.

Despite stated claims to the universal reach of these instruments of international law, Africa and Africans were not contemplated as beneficiaries of the rights and freedoms flowing from them. At a time when the rest of the world made a solemn declaration of "never again" (in reference to the slaughter of millions of Jews in the worst crimes that shocked the conscience of humanity), the devastating effects of the egregious crimes perpetrated against Africa and Africans in their quest for independence were still visible.

Shortly after this pledge of "never again," some of the Western countries, which had put in place international laws to eternalise the spirit of the pledge to protect humanity against the scourge of war, conducted their own atrocious military campaigns in the colonial territories. International crimes of unimaginable proportions were perpetrated against millions of unarmed African children, women, and men; civilian settlements and villages were wiped from the face of the earth.

In 1948, the year the United Nations Declaration of Human Rights was made, France, a victim of German aggression in which war crimes of unfathomable proportions were committed against the French people, violently suppressed a peaceful nationalist campaign for independence in its French colonial territory of Cameroun. In the senseless slaughter of unarmed peasants and militant leaders that followed, hundreds of thousands of people were exterminated.

This punitive military campaign led to a civil war that lasted until 1959, during which French soldiers committed international crimes in parts of the territory, considered by many to include the crime of genocide. The same scenario took place in Algeria, Democratic Republic of the Congo, Angola, Guinea Bissau, South Africa, Zimbabwe, Kenya, Libya, and many others, where the pogroms and international crimes perpetrated by economic merchant colonialists went unchecked. In recent decades, international crimes have been perpetrated in Africa in which millions of civilians have been exterminated with weapons supplied by these so-called angels of death, the former colonial masters, either directly or through proxies. The killing and the maiming have continued unchecked under the watch of the United Nations.

## Selective and Discriminatory Justice in Context

The so-called international community has historically failed to demonstrate the same degree of interest and effort in resolving armed conflicts and bringing peace and reconciliation to conflict zones in Europe, Asia, and South America in comparison with African conflicts. It has hypocritically and timidly purported to employ the machinery of international law in African conflicts to handle politically volatile situations inflamed by the same international community. When the intervention and application of international justice in Africa became mired in controversy, discrimination, and selectivity, the international community turned its back once more on Africa in its time of need. This has impacted negatively on African conflicts and generated distrust among civilian victims in the affected countries and among a majority of Africans as regards the application of international justice on the continent.

Far from eradicating the culture of impunity that has fomented conflict and international criminality in Africa, the judicial institutions put in place to administer international justice have laid the foundation on which the very laws and values they sought to protect are invoked to perpetuate impunity and strengthen the hand of tyranny. The principles and standards of victors' justice were formulated and applied at the Allied Military Tribunals at Nuremberg and Tokyo against the vanquished in World War II; the application of these same principles in African conflicts has inflamed the conflicts rather than attenuated them.

The Rwandan Patriotic Front (RPF), for example, in search of political power, invaded Rwanda with the support of Uganda, the United States, and the United Kingdom on October 1, 1990, leading to the

slaughter of hundreds of thousands of Rwandan citizens and two presidents under the watch of United Nations' forces. The UN Security
Council, acting under Chapter VII of the UN Charter, established the
International Criminal Tribunal for Rwanda to investigate and prosecute perpetrators of the crimes that took place in that conflict. Despite
its mandate to investigate and prosecute the alleged perpetrators of the
crimes in a non-discriminatory and non-selective manner, the Tribunal
constituted itself into a victors' court in which the Tutsi-dominated
Rwandan Patriotic Front victors tacitly determined the fate of the vanquished Hutu. The application of this humiliating and unjust policy in
most African conflicts has resulted in frustration and resentment on
which impunity and criminality is grounded.

The success of this policy can best be explained and placed within
historical perspective. Africa in its present configuration was not a
creation of Africans but an imposition by Western imperial/colonial
powers at the treaty of Berlin in 1884. The African continent therefore
can at best be described as an imperfect product of Western European
imperialism. When the United Nations General Assembly proclaimed
the declaration on the granting of independence to colonial countries
and peoples, some of the significant beneficiaries of the slave trade
and colonialism abstained from voting in support of independence for
African countries.[3]

Several of the countries that abstained later played and are still
playing a major role in fomenting the conflicts that have led to the perpetration of the international crimes that gave birth to Africa's two international criminal courts on the continent. These courts are the United
Nations International Criminal Tribunal for Rwanda (ICTR) and the
Special Court for Sierra Leone (SCSL). Some of these countries have
significantly influenced the administration of justice in the courts. The
policies implemented by these colonial powers went against the spirit
and letter of the General Assembly Resolution 1514 (XV) of December
14, 1960, on the basis of which most African countries gained independence and became subjects of international law.[4]

To most Africans and official African observers, the political upstag-
ing of the two courts to the detriment of the lofty motivations for which
they were created was a cause of great anxiety.

When the Rome Statute, for example, heralded the creation of the International Criminal Court (ICC), African countries welcomed it with arms opened.[5] In embracing the ICC, they believed in its promise that the court would truly be "independent" and administer justice to all and sundry without any form of discrimination. As of July 21, 2009, thirty African states were parties to the ICC Statute.

African states did not anticipate that the administration of justice at the International Criminal Court, in particular within its first decade of existence, would be discriminatory, selective, and focused totally on Africa. This policy appalled African countries and fuelled conflict in parts of the continent. This and other reasons inform the decision by the African Union to determine to explore possibilities of conferring criminal jurisdiction on the African Court on Human and Peoples' Rights to investigate and prosecute international crimes perpetrated on the continent of Africa.

When the efforts evinced by the African Union materialise, it will afford Africa an opportunity to exercise sovereignty over the destiny of its people. The tortuous route that led Africa to this conclusion commenced with the assessment of the performance of the ICC and *ad hoc* tribunals in Africa and their largely mitigated performance in attaining their mandates.

## The International Criminal Tribunal for Rwanda: A Victors' Court

The International Criminal Tribunal for Rwanda was created by the Security Council acting under Chapter VII of the UN Charter by Resolution 955 (1994) at its 3454[rd] meeting on November 8, 1994.[6] The Resolution established that the crimes of "genocide and other systematic, widespread and flagrant violations of international humanitarian law" were committed within the territory of Rwanda, which continued to constitute a threat to international peace and security and that the "particular circumstances of Rwanda" warranted "the prosecution of persons responsible for serious violations of international humanitarian law" in order to "achieve and contribute to the process of national reconciliation and to the restoration and maintenance of peace."

This mandate of the ICTR specified in the Security Council Resolution is spelled out in Article 1 of the statute of the ICTR.[7] This

article gave the Tribunal the mandate to prosecute perpetrators of specified international crimes within the territory of Rwanda and Rwandan
citizens responsible for such violations within the territory of neighbouring countries.[8]

This mandate unequivocally applied to the crimes perpetrated by
all parties in the Rwandan conflict from all ethnic groups. It extended
to crimes by the Rwandan Patriotic Army and its political leaders, the
Rwandan Patriotic Front in the territory of Uganda (from where it
launched attacks against Rwanda as of October 1, 1990), the territory of
Tanzania, and the Democratic Republic of the Congo, where it pursued
and massacred hundreds of thousands armless Hutu civilians.

The Secretary General of the UN, in paragraph 12 of his report[9]
defined the subject matter jurisdiction of the ICTR broadly. He included
violations of customary international law as well as certain treaties inso-
far as they were binding on Rwanda at the time of the alleged crimes.[10]
In *Prosecutor v. Laurent Semanza*, the Appeals Judgment citing the
Čelebici Appeals Judgment at the ICTY, held at para. 170 "[t]hat the
Security Council when establishing the ICTR was not creating a new
law but was *inter alia* codifying existing customary rules."

To avoid doubt, the Security Council in its Resolution 1534 (2004) at
its 4935th meeting on March 26, 2004, resolved as follows in Article 2:
"Reaffirms the necessity of trials of persons indicted by the ICTR
and reiterates its call on all states, especially Rwanda, Kenya, and the
Democratic Republic of the Congo to intensify cooperation with and
render all necessary assistance to the ICTR, *including investigating of
the Rwandan Patriotic Army* and efforts to bring Félicien Kabuga and all
other indictees of the ICTR to surrender to the ICTR" (our emphasis).

From the above, it is safe to conclude that no rule of customary
international law or express mandate given to the ICTR by the Security
Council justified selective prosecution of only one side of the conflict
(i.e., targeting Hutu while ignoring the well-documented crimes perpetrated by the RPA).

Surprisingly, the Security Council failed to hold the prosecutor of the
ICTR accountable for the numerous promises he made to the council
to investigate and prosecute RPA crimes. The former prosecutor of the
ICTR, Carla Del Ponte, spoke out loudly about influence put on her by

the United States Ambassador-at-Large for War Crimes Issues, Pierre Prosper, to discontinue investigations of the RPA for unspecified reasons. Submitting to this political pressure, Prosecutor Carla Del Ponte decided to prosecute only Hutu alleged perpetrators. Her predecessor, Louise Arbour, commenced investigations against the RPF but quickly abandoned the investigations due to similar pressure.

Hassan Jallow, who succeeded Carla Del Ponte, repeatedly informed the Security Council in his annual reports that he was investigating the crimes committed by the RPF, before dropping the subject without explanation. The Security Council neglected to hold him to account for his failure to comply with the Security Council resolutions directing that all the parties should be investigated and perpetrated. This policy insulated the RPF from prosecution and gave tacit blessing to the culture of impunity with which it committed and continues to commit massive and widespread crimes against civilians in Rwanda and beyond its frontiers.

Prosecuting only one party to the conflict, based on political and ethnic considerations, violates the non-discriminatory provisions of the UN Charter under which the authority to establish the Tribunal emanated. As stated above, this violation has consistently been supported and encouraged by some world powers, in particular the United States, which from the very inception has influenced the direction the judicial process at the Tribunal has followed. This explains the reason and the impunity with which the ghosts of Nuremburg and Tokyo inspired the judicial process at the ICTR. This has serious consequences for the integrity and credibility of the ICTR and the international justice administered therein.

Although the ICTR has been touted as making valuable contributions to international criminal jurisprudence,[11] it has failed in its mandate to effectively "contribute to the process of national reconciliation and the restoration and maintenance of peace"[12] in Rwanda and the neighbouring countries to which its mandate extended. The UN found in two very damning reports that the escalation of conflict in the east of the Democratic Republic of the Congo was caused by the direct intervention of Rwanda and the RPA.

The responsibility for this escalation lies with the failure of the ICTR to properly execute the mandate assigned to it by the UN Security Council. The responsibility similarly lies with the Security Council for failing to exercise appropriate oversight of the ICTR to ascertain that its policy of selective, ethnic, and politicised justice did not encourage impunity and fuel a sense of exclusion by targeted ethnic groups, resentment, and further conflict.

It is safe to state that UN-sponsored justice at the ICTR has created a new concept in international law of "genocidal, ethnic-based justice." Rather than the crime of genocide being punished for the fact that alleged perpetrators targeted victims for extermination on the basis of ethnicity, the alleged perpetrators were prosecuted for genocide on the basis of their ethnicity. To the extent that this policy is discriminatory and selective, it violates the UN Charter and the mandates conferred on the Tribunal by the Security Council and the Statute of the Tribunal. This policy has encouraged impunity and reckless abuse of the international judicial process.

The most devastating consequence of the ICTR process is the branding of Hutu in Rwanda as "*génocidaires*" and the Tutsi as "victims." The decision of the Appeals Chamber of the ICTR taking judicial notice of the genocide of the Tutsi in Rwanda from January 1, 1994 to December 31, 1994[13] eternalised this stereotyping perception. The criminalisation of the Hutu ethnic group in the ICTR process aligns with the politics of the Rwanda judicial system that has expanded the jurisprudence of the ICTR on genocide to include crimes hitherto unknown in law. In the Gacaca Courts (its fundamental and organic law setting), Rwanda criminalised genocide ideology and divisionism and made the crimes and charges applicable to persons who were not born in April 1994 and potentially to generations unborn.[14]

The wide and ambiguous scope of the law on genocide ideology and divisionism limits free speech, freedom of association, and fundamental freedoms guaranteed by the International Covenant on Civil and Political Rights[15] and the African Charter on Human and Peoples' Rights that Rwanda adopted as part of its constitution. These laws are used to limit democratic space on the grounds of safeguarding national security. The arrest and politically motivated prosecution of Victoire Ingabire eloquently support these assertions; she is a politician who was not in Rwanda during the war or during the period the alleged crimes for which she is prosecuted were perpetrated.[16]

The statute of the ICTR guarantees fair trial rights to accused persons appearing before the Tribunal.[17] There are several provisions of the Rules of Procedure and Evidence that spell out the parameters within which these rights will be safeguarded in the conduct of trial proceedings, pre-trial proceedings, and proceedings after trial.[18] Despite these safeguards, the ICTR displayed unexplained reluctance and timidity in interpreting its own statute and rules of procedure and evidence in a manner that is fully consistent with the letter and spirit of its statute, international customary law, international human rights law, and the human rights regime of the United Nations.[19]

The human rights credentials of the ICTR were tested in the case of the *Prosecutor v. Jean-Bosco Barayagwiza*. In that case, the Appeals Chamber of the Tribunal found that the rights of Barayagwiza during his arrest and detention on an ICTR warrant were egregiously violated, quashed the indictment, and ordered his immediate release. Another panel of the Appeals Chamber reversed the decision of the Appeals Chamber, releasing Barayagwiza[20] on the basis of flimsy evidence of very doubtful relevance and credibility after Rwanda protested against the decision. This was later demonstrated before the Appeals Chamber in the Semanza interlocutory appeals.[21] After the decisions in Barayagwiza and Semanza, at the instance of prosecution applications, the Appeals Chamber quickly abandoned the standards set for appellate review in the Barayagwiza case and set higher standards that have made it difficult for applications by Tribunal convicts for review to succeed.[22]

The situation of acquitted persons at the ICTR has so far attracted little scrutiny from the international community. The arrest and detention of these victims by the Tribunal for several years without trial is a serious affront to fundamental human rights and the fair trial guarantees in the statute of the Tribunal; they have been prosecuted and acquitted but they are treated and abandoned as stateless persons in Arusha, Tanzania. The egregious nature of this violation was evident in a decision of a Trial Chamber of the Tribunal that denied the application filed by an acquitted person, Protais Zigiranyirazo, among others, to be returned to Belgium[23] where he was arrested with the cooperation of Belgium to pursue his pending application for political asylum as mandated by law.[24]

The inability of the Tribunal to recognise and protect the status of acquitted persons again justifies the allegation that justice at the ICTR is selective and makes victims of persons whose innocence it proclaims. It is a serious indictment of the Tribunal in its failure to enforce its own judgments of acquittal. It compromises the presumption of innocence and constitutes a serious affront to the fairness of the proceedings at the ICTR.

A dent on the legacy of the ICTR is the perception that the prosecution served as a lifeline with which the Rwandan Patriotic Front consolidated its grip on power, ensured its political survival, and settled political and ethnic scores. The intrusion of a number of associations aligned to the RPF in the proceedings before the Tribunal as well as an abundance of evidence of witness tampering by agents of the Rwandan government were repeatedly brought to the attention of the Tribunal, but no action was taken. In some cases, the Tribunal found selective credibility in the testimony of witnesses who confessed being suborned and coached to incriminate the accused on political, ethnic hatred and settling of scores, and relied on it to convict.

The establishment of an International Residual Mechanism for International Criminal Tribunals on July 1, 2012 by the Security Council, which put an end to new indictments at the ICTR, has deprived the Rwandan Patriotic Front of a significant tool it relied on to intimidate and blackmail political opponents and adversaries. This has at long last exposed the fragility of the RPF and led the government of Rwanda to seek a new security corridor through sponsoring armed groups in the East of the Democratic Republic of the Congo. While the ICTR exists, the RPF's political opponents, who include reneged Tutsi intellectuals and leaders, live with the fear of being denounced and arrested for their alleged participation in the genocide.

Through state cooperation it was always possible for Rwanda to seek the assistance of the ICTR to provide it with information gathered by its investigators to use against any persons it targeted for prosecution. With the end of the prosecutorial mandate of the ICTR, the RPF has lost a valued ally in its effort to silence political dissent, its fight against impunity, and the security of its political system.

## Backdoor Attempts to Eternalise Victors' Justice

With the impending closure of the ICTR, the West and the RPF have lost a valuable tool of their Great Lakes, East, and Central Africa geopolitical strategy. To mitigate the impact of the closure, the International Criminal Court has stepped up its intervention in the East of the Democratic Republic of the Congo by indicting Rwandan Hutu whose alleged cases previously fell under the jurisdiction of the ICTR.

Two concurrent UN and international human rights reports severely indicted Rwanda and its top military and civilian officials for perpetrating serious crimes amounting to genocide and other international crimes in that region.[25] The RPF and its military wing, the RPA, as well as its rebel proxy, the M23, bear the greatest responsibility for those crimes. The prosecutor's mission in this region of Africa is causing significant anxiety in the African continent. Many have concluded that the interest of the ICC is to shield warmongers, Western economic predators, arms dealers, and Western-protected promoters of the culture of impunity.

The calibre of alleged perpetrators against whom the ICC has so far filed indictments makes the assumptions made by the current prosecutor of the ICC, Fatou Bensouda, laughable. She claims that a cornerstone to her mandate is to defend the interests of victims wherever they may be threatened.[26] As the situations in Cote d'Ivoire, Libya, Democratic Republic of the Congo, and Central African Republic have demonstrated, the prosecutor has placed victims in categories: victims on the side of victors, who are protected, and victims on the side of the vanquished, who are denied protection.

On June 15, 2012, when she assumed office, all the situations Fatou Bensouda inherited came from Africa, namely, seven situations, fifteen cases comprising twenty-four indicted persons, most of them mid-level or marginal cases. Over the decade of the existence of the ICC, victims of war crimes, crimes against humanity, and other international violations have been crying relentlessly for prosecutorial intervention, from the streets of Gaza, the forests of Sri Lanka, the towns and villages of Iraq, the hills and villages of Afghanistan, to the forests of Columbia and Guatemala. These desperate appeals for intervention have been ignored. These situations are insulated by superpowers that are either involved in those conflicts or whose national interests are at best served by them. An investigation into these situations outside Africa would directly threaten the interests of these powers, and the prosecutor must not take a gamble by initiating one without the permission of these powers.

## The Special Court for Sierra Leone

The Special Court for Sierra Leone was a treaty-based court created by the United Nations and the Government of Sierra Leone. In his report on the establishment of the Special Court for Sierra Leone,[27] the Secretary General of the UN stated that it is "a treaty-based *sui generis* court of mixed jurisdiction and composition."

The Security Council, upon receiving the Secretary General's Report, by Resolution 1315 of October 4, 2000, established the Special Court with the following mandate:

> 1) To prosecute persons who bear the greatest responsibility for the commission of crimes against humanity, war crimes, and other serious violations of international humanitarian law as well as crimes under Sierra Leonean law within the territory of Sierra Leone.[28]

The Special Court, unlike the ICTR, prosecuted some of the opposing participants in the conflict that afflicted Sierra Leone for over ten years. This, however, belies the fact that perpetrators of some of the worst crimes during the conflict were left out.[29] Those prosecuted were some combatants of the Revolutionary United Front for Sierra Leone (RUF), The Armed Forces Revolutionary Council (AFRC), and the Civil Defense Forces (CDF, or Kamajors). Resolution 1315 recommended that the Special Court exercise jurisdiction over "those who bear the greatest responsibility for the commission of the crimes." That mandate limited the jurisdiction of the court to the number of persons by reference to their command authority and the gravity and scale of the crimes.

In exercising this mandate, the Special Court indicted Charles Taylor, then president of Liberia;[30] Corporal Foday Sankoh, the leader of the Revolutionary United Front for Sierra Leone; Sam Bockarie, alias Mosquito, Commander of RUF forces and interim leader when Foday Sankoh was detained in Nigeria; Issa Hassan Sesay, the Leader of the

RUF after the death of Foday Sankoh; Morris Kallon, deputy to Issa Hassan Sesay; and Augustine Gbao, the Security Chief of the RUF.[31] On the AFRC side, the list included Major Johnny Paul Koroma, the leader of the AFRC Junta; Alex Tamba Brima, alias Gullit, the leader of the AFRC after SAJ Musa and the disappearance of Johnny Paul; Bazzy Kamara, the deputy to Tamba Brima; and Santigie Borbor Khanu, alias 55, another deputy to Tamba Brima. Chief Hinga Norman, the former deputy Defence Minister under President Ahmad Tejan Kabbah and leader of the CDF was charged along two of his close associates, Moinina Fofana and Allieu Kondewa.[32]

Johnny Paul Koroma was never arrested and his whereabouts remain unknown. Both Foday Sankoh and Chief Hinga Norman died in detention. Sam "Mosquito" Bockarie is alleged to have been killed in Liberia. This therefore means that those who bore the greatest responsibility for the crimes perpetrated in Sierra Leone were never brought to trial as mandated by the Security Council Resolution and the Statute of the Special Court for Sierra Leone.

In his opening statement during the RUF trial, the prosecutor, American David Crane, promised to "dance with the devil" in prosecuting the RUF indictees. In that regard, he relied on the evidence of former combatants and perpetrators of some of the egregious violations that took place in Sierra Leone over a period of ten years as witnesses. Public opinion in Sierra Leone was divided over the indictment and prosecution of Issa Sesay, Morris Kallon, and Augustine Gbao due to their contribution to the peace process that brought an end to the war after the arrest of Foday Sankoh. The RUF was never defeated on the battlefront despite the heavy deployment of the United Nations Mission in Sierra Leone (UNAMSIL), engaged under Security Council Resolution 1270 (1999), ECOMOG (forces deployed by ECOWAS, the Economic Community of West African States), Sandline, and Executive Outcomes mercenary groups invited by President Ahmad Tejan Kabbah and sundry Liberian rebel forces like the United Liberation Movement of Liberia for Democracy (ULIMO).

Over the opposition of many of its senior commanders who were against the peace process but were later co-opted to testify against the trio, Issa Sesay and Kallon, taken on as interim leaders of the RUF, signed the Lome Peace Accord on July 7, 1999. The indictment, trial, and conviction of Charles Taylor have similarly been criticised due to his commitment and contributions to the Sierra Leone peace process. His conviction on secondary forms of participation also made him fall out of the category of those who bore the greatest responsibility for the crimes in Sierra Leone.

It must, however, be emphasised that peace and reconciliation in Sierra Leone were not brought about solely through the judicial process at the Special Court. They were enacted through the Truth and Reconciliation Commission that was established by the government of Sierra Leone, as well as the general amnesty that the successive governments of Sierra Leone granted to most of the perpetrators, some of whom were integrated into the army and security forces. By these courageous acts the government of Sierra Leone resolutely decided to put the past behind the country and focused on a development agenda that has placed Sierra Leone in an admirable position within a troubled continent.

The Special Court still has to find a solution to the predicament of its detainees that it transferred to Mpanga Prison in Rwanda. This must be done quickly within its Residual Mechanism. Officious observers have concluded that the cooperation agreement signed by Rwanda and the Special Court for its convicts to serve their sentences in Mpanga Prison failed to contain a clause safeguarding the sovereignty of Sierra Leone as a party to the treaty that established the court over its citizens. The winding down of the Special Court has focused the attention of the international community on this fundamental error. It is when the international community, in particular the donors, will no longer have the impetus to provide adequate funding to enable Rwanda to keep these convicts in its prison that the government of Sierra Leone, the donors, and the Security Council will appreciate the significance of this error.

Notwithstanding the shortcomings of the judicial process in Sierra Leone, it is safe to state that the combination of the international judicial and restorative justice process have brought enduring peace in Sierra Leone. Sierra Leone, like South Africa and Liberia, through the Truth and Reconciliation Commission has eternalised the virtues of the truth and reconciliation peace model, which is Africa's most valued contribution to international peace and security. Through this process, which should find its way into the constitutions and legal systems of "civilised" nations, a viable alternative to international criminal justice and the political motivations that have fundamentally derailed its mission on the African continent must assert its rightful place.

## The ICC: The Price of Selective and Discriminatory Justice

The International Criminal Court has come under serious criticism by African states for its unjustified focus on Africa during its ten years of existence. This focus has been reasonably explained by the fact that some of the superpowers that have opposed the ICC and indeed refused to ratify the Rome Statute have deflated the attention of the court towards Africa.

The provision in the statute of the ICC that the UN Security Council may make referrals or deferrals before the court[33] gives these world powers extraordinary authority to control the formulation, conduct, and execution of prosecutorial policy, in a manner that detracts attention from conflicts around the world that are sponsored by these powers either through proxies or as direct participants. To these superpowers and their proxies, the ICC has become a convenient conduit to effect regime change in errant regimes in Africa as well as to protect their strategic geopolitical interests.

The urgency with which the prosecutor of the ICC purported to have conducted investigations and filed indictments against Muammar Gaddafi and some of his close aides in Libya at the heart of the war, when NATO bombs were indiscriminately falling on Libya for eight months, surprised many in Africa. It was more amazing that when the ICC indictee Muammar Gaddafi was apprehended alive and murdered in cold blood, the media antics that characterised the tenure of Mr. Moreno Ocampo as the prosecutor of the ICC went dead. The next time we heard about him was when he was informing the world, invoking the principle of complementarity,[34] that the judicial system of Libya was well-equipped to try Islam Gaddafi, the captured son of Muammar Gaddafi held by rebels over whom the central governing authority in Libya has no control.

Paradoxically, the same prosecutor explained his intervention in the Kenya post-election violence on the grounds that no mechanism existed within Kenya for a credible trial of the indicted to be conducted. This decision to intervene in Kenya was made barely two months after the commencement of the post-election violence in 2007. Within the same period, the same Western powers that supported the position of the prosecutor towards the situation in Kenya were appealing to Kenya to prosecute within its judicial system pirates and perpetrators of international crimes against foreign vessels in the Indian Ocean.

The obsession to "baby-sit" Africa reached humiliating proportions when Mr. Ocampo, whose mandate was to oversee the fight against impunity at the global level, publicly displayed his implication in the politics of Kenya by singling out Kenya alone as the focus of his farewell address. It is demeaning and condescending neo-colonial posturing like this that finally compelled the African Union to stand up for the sovereignty, dignity, and interest of the African Continent and all black people the world over who felt insulted by this policy of humiliating selective focus on Africa by the ICC and international criminal justice in general.

The selective intervention in Côte d'Ivoire, the Democratic Republic of the Congo, and Rwanda through the proxy of the Congo[35] and elsewhere within the African continent is the most shameful event that has happened to Africa since the colonial wars of independence. Progressively, the African Union watched powerlessly as the sovereignty of its member states was taken away through constant intrusions by the ICC.

The African Union is concerned that the exercise of universal jurisdiction over a number of crimes perpetrated in Africa is unacceptably intrusive and degrading. The legal opinion provided by the African Court on Human and Peoples' Rights singles out the exercise of universal jurisdiction by France and Spain over a number of Rwandan senior officials as an example of the unwarranted, degrading intrusion.

The exercise of universal jurisdiction over alleged crimes committed within the territories of African countries must be put in perspective if the position of the African Union on the matter must be construed as principled. I must first remark that the exercise of universal jurisdiction by France and Spain in the cases concerning senior Rwandan officials contained in the African Court on Human and Peoples' Rights legal opinion arose because the individuals concerned were implicated in the murder of citizens of the two countries mentioned.

Citing these two cases in support of the AU decision to confer the African Commission on Human and Peoples' Rights is not helpful considering the duplicity surrounding the position of Rwanda on the matter. Where it advanced its interest, Rwanda encouraged, supported, and cooperated in the exercise of universal jurisdiction, even in cases where citizens of the country exercising universal jurisdiction were not the victims. The case of two Rwandan nuns convicted in Belgium with Rwandan support and cooperation is an example.[36]

Some confusion exists at the ICC and in Africa on the conceptual and practical application of the principle of complementarity. Some African member states conflate this principle and the related notion of universal jurisdiction regarding the alleged crimes perpetrated within their national borders and elsewhere in or out of the continent.

One case that aptly illustrates this confusion is that of the *South African Litigation Centre and Zimbabwe Exiles Forum v. National Director of Public Prosecutions and the Head of the Priority Crimes Litigation Unit, Director General of Justice and Constitutional Development and National Commissioner of the South African Police Service*.[37] The application before the court was brought under Section 6 of the Promotion of Administrative Justice Act (PJA) 3 of 2000 and the implementation of the Rome Statute Act of the International Criminal Court Act (ICC Act) 27 of 2002.

This application before the court concerned refusal or failure by the police authority to act in conformity with the ICC Act. A careful reading of the judgment which has since been confirmed by the Southern African Supreme Court reveals troubling legal misconceptions of these international criminal law concepts and their implementation. The judgment at pages 47 and 48 conflates or confuses the principle of complementarity with the principle of universal jurisdiction[38] and its practical application to the case that came before the court for determination. As a result, the court used a law intended to facilitate the implementation of the Rome Statute to make a judicial decision on universal jurisdiction.

## The African Court, the ICC, Universal Jurisdiction, and the Challenges Ahead

The creation of the African Court on Human and Peoples' Rights came at a time of increasing challenges caused by conflicts in which international crimes of unimaginable magnitude were perpetrated across the continent on a massive scale. As Africa faced the challenges of adapting to an uncertain world economic, social, and political future, the ghost of its colonial past continued to haunt it. Nowhere was this more visible out of the battlefield than the plethora of cases brought before the African Commission on Human and Peoples' Rights at Banjul, Gambia. A number of these cases directly challenged the injustices caused through inherited colonial territorial disputes. These are undoubtedly the cause of instability and conflict on the continent.

The African Commission made frantic attempts to adjudicate on some of these issues, although not comprehensively.[39] In a tacit attempt to avoid a controversial start, the African Court intended to avoid matters of such magnitude by taking a restrictive approach to access to the court.[40] A denial of the right of access to the majority of people in the continent has circumscribed the effectiveness of the African Court on Human and Peoples' Rights in providing binding remedies on the flagrant violations of people's rights on the continent.[41]

The reality of the factual, legal, logistic, and procedural problems afflicting the African Court in its present form has fuelled criticism that attempts by the African Union to confer criminal jurisdiction on the court, at a moment when it has displayed an alarming timidity bordering on irrelevance in granting access to a majority on the continent, may well be to shield African dictators from serious violations perpetrated against their own citizens. They have pointed to the reluctance of the majority of AU member states to sign on to the Protocol creating the court as well as the fact that the court has largely failed to be assertive in handling the matters brought before it.

That notwithstanding, the African Union has been very preoccupied by the image and future of the continent in view of the arrogant and humiliating focus by the ICC on Africa, and the effect of the unrestrained exercise of universal jurisdiction over a number of international crimes perpetrated in some African countries. To many observers, including Africans, some of the reported crimes are just too serious to ignore. Africa cannot close its eyes to these international violations. Doing so over the past decade or more has rightly or wrongly encouraged the culture of impunity providing justification for the controversial intervention of the international community and the ICC.

African heads of state finally decided to confront the problems during the Assembly of Heads of State and Governments in February 2009. During that assembly they took a decision requesting the African Union Commission, in consultation with the African Commission on Human and Peoples' Rights and the African Court on Human and Peoples' Rights, to examine the implications of the court being empowered to try international crimes such as genocide, crimes against humanity, and war crimes, and report thereon to the Assembly in 2010.

The Assembly of Heads of State underscored in their decision their determination to fight impunity on the continent. The Heads of State believed that conferring the African Court with criminal jurisdiction would help fight impunity as well as abuse of the use of universal jurisdiction. An Advisory Opinion provided by the African Court pursuant to this mandate recognised in particular the fact that conferring the African Court with criminal jurisdiction would surely provoke a risk of competition with the ICC.

It is clear that the decision to confer the African Court with criminal jurisdiction is an expression of lack of confidence in the ICC to exercise fairness in the fight against impunity on the African continent without submitting to the political pressures and agenda of neo-colonial interests. The African Union and most African countries were appalled by the fact that Mr. Ocampo, the perceived public face of the ICC, with each media outing turned the judicial process at the ICC into a media circus. He was perceived as acting more like a super-sheriff overseeing Africa rather than a minister of international justice in its fight against impunity.

Mr. Ocampo acted as though the respective African countries in which the ICC intervened had surrendered their sovereignty to the ICC. He conducted himself as if each intervention gave him the licence or fiat to superintend over the political affairs of African countries. For example, in his last address as the ICC prosecutor, he dedicated part of it to the upcoming elections in Kenya, a matter which did not fall within the mandate of the ICC.

This provocative arrogance explains in part why, towards the end of his mandate, Mr. Ocampo faced several court challenges from accused and suspects. The judgment in the Thomas Lubanga case, the only case he successfully prosecuted in his ten-year tenure, came with a serious rebuke by the Trial Chamber questioning his prosecutorial methods of using intermediaries in investigating and gathering evidence despite the budget available to him to conduct investigations and prosecute matters in total independence.[42] He was similarly rebuked by the Pre-Trial Chamber in the situation in Libya due to prejudicial press statements made by him that infringed on the suspects' rights to fair trial.[43]

The Appeals Chamber of the International Criminal Court did not rule on an application brought by Dr. David Matsanga recusing Mr. Ocampo from an investigation he initiated against him in the "continuing investigation in the situation in the Republic of Kenya" until his mandated ended. The message was clear; the end of his mandate must have come as a welcome relief to the ICC, the Assembly of State Parties, and International Criminal Justice.[44] Nevertheless, the Appeals Chamber considered the material submitted in support of the application to disqualify the departed Mr. Ocampo sensitive enough to be classified and kept in the records of the court as confidential.[45]

Despite the departure of Mr. Ocampo, the relations between the International Criminal Court, its African member states, and the African Union continued to deteriorate. A resolution initiated by the African Union before the Security Council for a deferral of the Kenyan Cases was defeated. That did not deter African State Parties initiating a similar request at the Assembly of State Parties Conference that took place in The Hague in November 2013, during which the Assembly of State Parties amended the rules of procedure and evidence to allay some of the concerns of the African Union.

There was high expectation that, on assuming office, the new prosecutor, Fatou Bensouda, was going to properly investigate persistent allegations made by Kenya and the African Union that Mr. Ocampo's intervention in the "Situation in Kenya" was politically motivated. It was alleged forcefully that Mr. Ocampo submitted to the influence of neo-colonial, geo-

political influence and relied on information provided by politically motivated activist groups to seek indictments against the accused. Africa addi-
tionally expected Ms. Bensouda to safeguard the global reach of the ICC
and extend its focus to other conflict areas in the world. She was expected
to make a meaningful and honest attempt to improve on the image of
the ICC as well as the professional quality of prosecutorial decisions.
Regrettably, these expectations have not been addressed.

African State Parties threatened but did not intend to take the opportunity of the decision of the African Union to initiate the process of
conferring criminal jurisdiction on the African Court to withdraw en
masse from the ICC, as opponents of its decision have feared. Rather,
the AU believed that its decision to initiate the process of providing
the African Court with criminal jurisdiction would operate as a rational basis for the implementation of the principle of complementarity
between the African Court and the ICC. The AU believed that conferring the African Court with criminal jurisdiction would provide the
ICC with enough time to take on crimes perpetrated elsewhere in the
world as its mandate demanded.

In its present context, the African Court has a mandate to combat
impunity on the continent.[46] However, the court lacks the jurisdiction
to try individual perpetrators of crimes and inflict penal sanctions. The
court is also inhibited by the fact that the Protocol limits the scope of
cases coming before it by citizens of countries that have not subscribed
to it. Challenges brought before the court to declare that Article 34(6) of
the Protocol that imposes this limitation or bar to access to the court is
inconsistent with articles 1, 2, 13, 26, and 66 of the African Charter on
Human and Peoples' Rights, and to that extent null and void and of no
legal effect, were dismissed by a majority of judges of the African Court.[47]

A powerful dissent filed by the vice president of the court, Justice
Sophia A. B. Akuffo (presently the president of the court), and Justices
Bernard Ngoepe and Elsie Thompson, held at paragraph 16 of their joint
dissenting opinion:

> To the extent that Article 34(6) denies individuals direct access to the court,
> which the charter does not deny, the Article, far from being supplementary
> measures towards enhancing the protection of human rights, as envisaged
> by Article 66 of the Charter, does the very opposite. It is at odds with the

objective, language and spirit of the Charter as it disables the Court from hearing applications brought by individuals against a state which has not made a declaration, even when the protection of human rights entrenched in the Charter is at stake.

Curiously, one of the judges who sided with the majority, Justice Fatsah Ouguergouz, in a separate opinion stated at paragraph 37:

Same as Mr. Falana, I am in favour of the automatic access to the Court by individuals and non-governmental organizations; it is my view however that it is a matter that comes up within the exclusive jurisdiction of Member States of the African Union. I hold the opinion that this important matter is more likely to be discussed by the Court as part of its advisory jurisdiction at the initiative of the entities mentioned in Article 4 of the Protocol or part of the procedure of amendment of that instrument considering the possibility availed to the Court under Article 35(20) to make proposals in that regard 'if it deems it necessary.'

The request made by African Heads of State and Government to the African Court and the African Commission thus provides an opportunity to review the contradictory provisions of the Charter and the Protocol that bars access to a majority of people on the African continent. The advisory opinion submitted by the African Court to the Heads of State and Government contains provisions for a profound amendment of the Protocol. In its conclusion and recommendations, the African Court, drawing from the framework essentially of the ICC, proposed profound amendments (para. 33) that will provide the court with the material, logistics, and the appropriate legal framework within which to function.

The resolve of the African Union to play a major if not controlling role in the battle against impunity on the continent, as well as fight what it calls abuse of universal jurisdiction, received a major boost in the International Court of Justice decision in the case of *Belgium v. Senegal*, where that court decided that Senegal, which was strongly supported by the African Union, would set up a Special Court with AU support to conduct the trial in Senegal of former Chadian president Hissene Habre.[48] It is discernible from the foregoing that the African Union has commenced an irreversible journey towards the fight against impunity using the indispensable weapon of international criminal justice.

The decision by the Assembly of Heads of State and Government to finally place this matter on their agenda with a sense of urgency gives some hope that at long last the humiliation of Africa through the disguised arms of international criminal justice may soon be a thing of the past. The cost and task that await the realisation of this project are enormous. Yet Africa cannot be that farmer that took the plough and looked back. To do so will be tantamount to adding salt to the injuries inflicted at the 1884 "Berlin Bazaar" which international criminal justice in its present context had sought to eternalise.

## Conclusion

In conclusion, it may reasonably be safe to state that although serious international violations have been committed on the African continent by Africans requiring urgent and serious response, the inability of international justice to prosecute these crimes within the standards defined by the UN Charter and the statutes of the courts has been very disappointing. There can hardly be any gainsaying that international justice in Africa is to a large degree an extension of international politics.

A majority of African victims have never benefitted from international justice. International justice in its present form neither addresses African crimes nor makes meaningful efforts to confront the culture of impunity. Significantly, it does not bring about reconciliation and justice to the afflicted communities in Africa.

The decision by African Heads of State and Governments to initiate the process of conferring criminal jurisdiction on the African Court to combat the perpetration of international crimes and the culture of impunity on the continent, although salutary, is still fraught with scepticism. It arises from the fact that some of the Heads of State and Government in Africa are the most responsible for the culture of impunity that oversees the senseless slaughter of innocent civilian victims whom they swore to defend.

For the initiative undertaken by the AU to be acceptable, African leaders must demonstrate that the court will be truly independent and all perpetrators of international crimes must have their day in court. This is the only condition in which international justice and foreign intervention will no longer make Africa and Africans guinea pigs on which to experiment new concepts in international law and international relations.

## Notes

1.  Art. 1(3) and 56(1) of the UN Charter.
2.  Universal Declaration of Human Rights, 1948.
3.  UN General Assembly Resolution 1514 (XV) on December 14, 1960: eighty-nine states voted for the resolution and none against. However, Portugal, Spain, Union of South Africa, United Kingdom, United States, Australia, Belgium, Dominican Republic, and France abstained.
4.  Article 1 of the said declaration states: "The subjugation of people to alien subjugation, domination and exploitation constitutes a denial of fundamental human rights, is contrary to the Charter of the United Nations and is an impediment to the promotion of World Peace and co-operation." Article 4 states: "All armed action or repressive measures of all kinds directed against dependent peoples shall cease in order to enable them to exercise peacefully and freely their right to complete independence and their integrity of national territory shall be respected."
5.  The Statute of the International Criminal Court was established in Rome on July 17, 1998.
6.  Based on the report of the committee of experts established pursuant to resolution 934 (1994) and the reports by the Special Rapporteur for Rwanda of the United Nations Commission for Human Rights (S/1994/1157) and the Secretary General's reports pursuant to resolution 935 (1994) of July 1, 1994 (S/1994/879 and S/1994/906). It is regrettable that similar circumstances that led to the creation of the ICTR and reports detailing more serious crimes perpetrated by the RPF and its leaders in the Democratic Republic of the Congo leading to the massacre of more than six million unarmed civilians have so far not attracted vehement intervention by the Security Council in initiating appropriate legal action to prosecute and punish those bearing the greatest responsibility.
7.  Article 1, ICTR Statute: "The International Criminal Tribunal for Rwanda shall have the power to prosecute persons responsible for serious violations of international humanitarian law committed in the territory of Rwanda and Rwandan citizens responsible for such violations committed in the territory of neighboring states between 1 January 1994 and 31 December 1994, in accordance with the provisions of this statute."
8.  See Articles 2, 3, and 4 of the Statute of the ICTR.
9.  UN Doc. S/1995/134, February 13, 1995.
10. See *Prosecutor v. Akayesu*, Trial Chamber judgment, paras. 604-607; *Prosecutor v. Kayeshema and Ruzindana* paras. 156, 158, 598.
11. For example, the recognition of rape as a war crime in *Prosecutor v. Jean-Paul Akayesu*.
12. UN Security Council Resolution 1315, Preamble, para. 7.
13. *Prosecutor v. Édouard Karemera, Mathieu Ngirumpatse, Joseph Nzirorera*, Case No. ICTR-98-44-AR(C), AC June 16, 2006. The Trial Chamber in the Case of General

Ndindiliyimana, Bizimungu, Nzuwonemeye and Sagahutu, Case No. ICTR-00-56-T on May 17, 2011, Judgment, para. 140 took judicial notice of the genocide of the Tutsi relating to the murder of Prime Minister Agathe Uwilingiyimana and ten Belgian UNAMIR soldiers, even though none of them were Tutsi.

14. Law No. 08/96 of August 30, 1996, to prevent the crime of genocide; Organic Law of May 26, 2003; and Organic Law No. 40/2000 of February 20, 2001, setting up the Gacaca courts.

15. See Articles 18 and 22 of the ICCPR.

16. See Chapter 3 below, "Victoire Ingabire: Chronology of a Pinochet-style Case of Repression."

17. Article 9 refers to the principle of *non bis in idem*; Article 12 deals with the qualification and independence of Judges; Article 15 deals with the independence of the Prosecutor; Articles 19 and 20 are fair trial provisions; Rule 14 of the Rules of Procedure and evidence refers to the solemn oath taken by judges professing their independence.

18. See in particular Article 20 of the Statute and Rule 47 of the Rules of Procedure and Evidence.

19. Articles 1(3) and 55(c) of the UN Chapter; Article 14 of the ICCPR.

20. Case No. ICTR-97-19, Art. 72.

21. *Prosecutor v. Semanza, ICTR- 97-20-A AC*, May 31, 2000.

22. See the decision on the review application in *Eliézer Niyitegeka v. The Prosecutor*, Case No. ICTR9614R; *Prosecutor v. Jean de Dieu Kamuhanda, Case No. ICTR-99-54A-R; The Prosecutor v. Kajelijeli, Case No. ICTR-98-44A-R*.

23. Protais Zigiranyirazo's application, Case No. ICTR-01-73-A, Decision of June 18, 2012.

24. Article 28(1) of the Statute of the ICTR stipulates: "States shall comply without undue delay with any request for assistance or an order issued by a Trial Chamber, *including but not limited to* (our emphasis); a) the identification and location of persons; b) the taking of testimony; c) the service of documents; d) the arrest of persons; e) the surrender or transfer of the accused to the international Tribunal" for Rwanda.

25. See significantly UN Second Joint Report of seven UN Experts on the situation in the DRC, A/HRC/13/63, March 8, 2010.

26. See *New African Magazine*, August/September 2012, pp. 12-18.

27. UN Doc. S2000/915, para. 9.

28. Paragraph 14 of the Security Council Resolution states: "The enumerated crimes against humanity included in the statute of the ICTY and the ICTR follow the pattern at Nuremburg. Violations of Common Article 3 of the Geneva Conventions and Article 4 of the additional Protocol II committed in armed conflict not of an international character have long been considered customary international law, and in particular since the establishment of the two international Tribunals, have been recognized as customarily entailing the individual criminal responsibility of the accused."

29. Forces of ECOMOG, soldiers of the Economic Community of West African states, Sandline, and Executive Outcome Mercenaries who perpetrated grave violations against the civilian population of Sierra Leone.

30. Case No. SCSL-03-1-T.

31. Case No. SCSL-04-15-T.
32. Case No. SCSL-04-14-T.
33. See Articles 13(b) and 16 of the ICC Statute.
34. See Article 17 of the ICC statute.
35. The unsuccessful attempt at indicting Rwandan political opponent and vice presi-
    dent of the FDLR, Callixte Mbarushimana, and the recent indictment of the FDLR
    Commander, Général Sylvestre Mudacumura, at the moment that Rwanda has
    been accused by the UN and world powers that have sustained the RPF in power
    for perpetrating war crimes, crimes against humanity, and genocide in the East of
    the Democratic of the Congo, has left many doubting the claims made by the ICC
    prosecutor that her focus is to protect victims of international crimes perpetrated
    on the African continent, in particular against women and children.
36. Two Rwandan Benedictine nuns were tried and convicted in Belgium even though
    the alleged crimes were perpetrated in Rwanda and the victims of the alleged
    crimes were all Tutsi nuns. The two accused were Sœur Maria Kizito, convicted
    and sentenced to 12 years, and Sœur Gertrude, sentenced to 15 years.
37. Case No. 77150/09, High Court of South Africa, North Gauteng High Court,
    Judgment, May 8, 2012.
38. See also pp. 54-56, 83-89. At p. 88, the Court incorrectly stated that Charles Taylor
    was prosecuted at the ICC pursuant to the exercise of the principle of complemen-
    tarity and Universal Jurisdiction exercised by the ICC.
39. In Application No. 004/2011, the African Commission on Human and Peoples'
    Rights requested and obtained provisional measures against the Great Socialist
    People's Libyan Arab Jamahiriya to stop the egregious violations that claimed
    thousands of victims leading to NATO and Western intervention that overthrew
    the government of Colonel Muammar Gaddafi. The Commission has since failed
    to exercise this broad mandate to seek access to the court in favour of millions of
    victims on the continent who have no access to the court due to the fact that their
    countries have not ratified the Protocol to the Court.
40. In Case No. 75/92, *Katangese Peoples' Congress v. Zaïre*, the ACPHR, confronted
    with the definition of "Peoples," underscored the sensitivity of African states
    towards stability of existing colonial borders and the potential of interpreting
    "peoples" to confer independence, decided that Katanga had a right to self-de-
    termination exercisable within the territorial sovereignty and integrity of Zaïre.
    However, in a demonstration of openness towards a case in which the evidence
    of alleged territorial claims to sovereignty was either weak or non-existent, the
    ACPHR, in the case of *Ngwang Gumne et al./Cameroon*, ACHPR Ordinary Session,
    Banjul, The Gambia, April 2009, noted the challenges made by Cameroon to the
    Statehood of the Southern Cameroons on behalf of whom the authors brought the
    Communication as well as the controversial nature of the issue due to the polit-
    ical connotation that it carried, paras. 169, 179. The Commission found that "the
    people of Southern Cameroon" qualifies to be referred to as a "people" because
    they manifest numerous characteristics and affinities, which include a common
    history, linguistic tradition, territorial connection, and political outlook. More
    importantly, they identify themselves as a people with a separate and distinct iden-
    tity. Identity is an innate characteristic within a people. It is up to other external

people to recognise such existence, but not to deny it.

41. The African Court, citing article 34(6) of the Protocol establishing the Court, declined jurisdiction in its first case in *Michelot Yogogombaye v. Republic of Senegal* (Appl. No. 001/2008, December 15, 2009; *Femi Falana v. The African Union (AU)*, Case No. 001/2011; *Atabong Denis Atemnkeng v. the AU*, Case No. 014/2001.

42. Judgment of Trial Chamber 1 in *Prosecutor v. Thomas Lubanga Dyilo*, March 14, 2012, Decision on Intermediaries, May 13, 2010.

43. ICC 011/11, Situation in Libyan Arab Jamahiriya.

44. Situation in the Republic of Kenya, public redacted version of Decision ICC-01-09-96, date of original filing July 11, 2012, date of redacted version September 6, 2012. Decision on request for the disqualification of the prosecution in the investigation of Mr. David Nyekorach-Matsanga, para. 18: "The Request for Disqualification seeks the disqualification of the Prosecutor from investigating Mr. Nyekorach-Matsanga." At the time that the Request for Disqualification was registered on June 1, 2012, the Prosecutor of the Court was Ocampo, and the Request for Disqualification is based on Ocampo's alleged direct and personal interest in investigating Mr. Nyekorach-Matsanga, para. 19. Mr. Ocampo's term in office began on June 16, 2003, and pursuant to Article 42(4) of the Statute, lasted for nine years. His term ended on June 15, 2012. With Mr. Ocampo having left office, the request to disqualify him has been rendered moot and must be dismissed as such.

45. See paragraph 10 of the public redacted version of the Decision.

46. Article 4(h) of the AU Constitutive Act.

47. See Application No. 001/2011, *Femi Falana v. The African Union*, Decision of June 26, 2012. See also *Atabong Denis Atemnkeng v. AU*, Case No. 014/2011.

48. 20/07/2012 – 2012/24, Questions relating to the Obligation to Prosecute or Extradite (*Belgium v. Senegal*), The Court finds that the Republic of Senegal must, without further delay, submit the case of Mr. Hissène Habré to its competent authorities for the purpose of prosecution.

## 2

# The Ailing Empire's
# Full Spectrum Dominance

GLEN FORD

The ailing empire situated not too far to the south of Canada once played a central role in delineating the rights of nations and of humankind, during a period when its economic hegemony was unquestioned. Today, the United States is in deep and, I believe, terminal economic, political, and cultural decline, with little to offer the planet other than its own ravenous appetite. This hyper-aggressive superpower now methodically dismantles humanity's most noble, civilising project: international law. It does so not brick by brick, one Geneva Accord at a time, but in a frenzy, as if in fear that the contradictions of late-stage capitalism will overtake the world's supposedly "indispensable nation" before the destruction can be completed.

The United States paves over the foundational principle of international conduct: respect for the sovereignty and rights of nations. If nations have no rights *as nations*, then peoples can have no rights as distinct peoples, nor do individuals have the rights of persons. It is all of a piece, and when you yank the thread, its human rights fabric unravels.

The United States is pulling the thread as hard as it can, to bring down the whole structure of law, and to substitute imperial fiat. Globally recognised rules of conduct that are the distilled lessons of bloody millennia are discarded like so much junk. Aggressive war is no longer a "crime against international peace," but a "humanitarian" obligation of the superpower and its servants. Resistance to aggression is no longer a right of nations and peoples, but a crime against humanity, prosecutable by the ICC—the *Imperial* Criminal Court.

The American Empire, ruled by bankers who create nothing and seek to monetise everything, has no further use for international law. Rather than trade, it favours coercion and blackmail, rigged markets, and derivative prestidigitation. In place of productive investment, it speculates and leverages. It is a vector of instability, which plays to US military advantage—its trump card.

*** 

The empire steals, and calls it foreign policy. They tried to steal Iraq. They stole Libya. They would like to steal Iran—again. And they have probably stolen Syria's chance for a future as a cohesive nation. They stole Haiti's sovereignty, and have no intention of ever giving it up. That which they cannot steal outright, they plunge into chaos. In Africa, they do both, stealing amid the chaos that they and their proxies created in the Democratic Republic of the Congo. Six million Congolese lives have been stolen since 1996, the greatest genocide since World War II. Yet the International Criminal Court protects the subordinate perpetrators of the Great Crime—the governments of Rwanda and Uganda—on orders of the Criminal Kingpin: the United States.

Such a bacchanal of criminality cannot co-exist with international law as it has evolved in our world. And so, the law must go—quickly, by imperial decree.

The United States is uniquely suited to exorcise law from the planetary body as if it were a demon. It is a nation that has been defined by aggressive war, from its invading white settler origins. Impunity is implicit in the divinely inspired conquests of a people who were, and whose cultural descendants remain, certain of the "manifest" nature of their destiny, no matter the millions that were snuffed out or plunged into perpetual servitude in the still unfinished journey.

How could such a "light unto the nations" not enrich the world through the constant expansion of American spheres of (full spectrum) dominance? Who better to act as the ultimate arbiter of disputes, than the world's "indispensable nation?"

The "humanitarian" version of US/NATO military intervention made its official debut in Bosnia under President Bill Clinton. "The fact is, America remains the indispensable nation," said the bomber of Belgrade. "There are times when America, and only America, can make a difference between war and peace, between freedom and repression, between hope and fear."

No America, no peace—America will make sure of that. The logic of self-proclaimed indispensability puts "justice" in its proper, conditional place, as well. "If we have to use force, it is because we are America. We are the indispensable nation," proclaimed Clinton's Secretary of State, Madeleine Albright (mentor to UN Ambassador Susan Rice, a collaborator in genocide).

Under Barack Obama, "humanitarian" intervention has become central to US foreign policy. If the US is indispensable to humanity's future, then all its interventions are humanitarian, by definition.

Most white Americans believe this, or behave as if they do. White liberals tend to feel as indispensable to the rest of humanity in their own way as Dick Cheney does in his. Mass belief in American indispensability is a collective expression of white privilege (to which both Obama and Rice subscribe). It is a deeply ingrained racial and national chauvinism that rejects out of hand the arguments of people like Prof. Danilo Zolo of the University of Florence, that humanitarian interventionism is in violation of "the United Nations Charter, the principles of the statute and the judgment of the Nuremberg Tribunal, as well as international law in general." Whether bombing other peoples to hell, or adopting babies from impoverished regions of the world, white Americans take for granted their rights of intervention and the humanity of their motives, as did the slaveholders and Indian-killers of another era.

Humanitarian intervention is the point of the spear of US aggression all across the planet, a blanket justification that compliments the so-called "War on Terror" and its drones. Invocation of the solemn "Responsibility to Protect," or R2P, cloaks the aggressor as the Samaritan and effectively strips the targets of all recourse to political, moral, or legal defence. They are outlawed, by the very forces that are busily tearing down the edifice of international law.

Libyan leader Muammar Gaddafi is defamed as a perpetrator of crimes against humanity and attempted genocide, although only a few score regime opponents died alongside a roughly equal number of soldiers and government supporters in the initial outbreak of violence in February 2011.

Hutus comprise at least eighty-five percent of the Rwandan population, but no Hutu can receive a fair trial in the court of western public opinion or at the International Criminal Tribunal for Rwanda, because the entire ethnic group has been damned as *génocidaires* by the minority Tutsi regime and its American sugar daddy.

European and American audiences seem positively eager to believe that Third Worlders are guilty of the ultimate atrocities, as if that somehow absolves their own nations and political cultures of five hundred years of crimes against the rest of humanity, including genocides without number. History is magically upended, the polarities of morality and guilt reversed, allowing Euro-Americans to imagine themselves entering the twenty-first century with a clean slate—a mandate to commit new crimes and to rewrite half a millennium of non-stop European plunder of the rest of the planet.

In Haiti, the predator dons the blue helmets of peace. The United States, having overthrown the democratically elected government of the world's first black republic in 2004, launders its crime through the compliant offices of the United Nations. Haiti is made into a kind of protectorate of the US, France, and Canada, masquerading as the "international community." United Nations troops are deployed as mercenaries to prevent majority rule from recurring. Democracy is suppressed, and cholera introduced, at the point of "peacekeepers'" bayonets. A former president of the conquering nation, Bill Clinton, is installed as the United Nations special envoy for Haiti, the equivalent of the League of Nations naming Heinrich Himmler as special envoy to Czechoslovakia in 1939. Haiti becomes a model for the non-sovereignty of nations. The UN acts as a rubber stamp for aggression—a self-nullification.

The US military command in Africa, AFRICOM, began its conquest of the continent at its inception in 2008. Building on bilateral "war-on-terror" agreements reached with countries in the Sahel after 9/11, the Pentagon's mission is best described as an "infiltration-in-force." One by one, and then in bulk, AFRICOM has subverted the militaries of virtually every member state of the African Union. Of the fifty-four African Union countries, only Zimbabwe, Eritrea, and Sudan remain outside AFRICOM's web of aid, training, and other entanglements.

Although AFRICOM has no formal headquarters on the continent, the whole of Djibouti is a US and French military base. AFRICOM routinely stages manoeuvres engaging the militaries of as many as thirty-five African nations, using command-and-control equipment and weapons systems supplied and serviced by the United States. In Africa, as nowhere else in the world, the US military has usurped a range of food and medical assistance functions usually performed by the State Department—part of the militarisation of the continent. AFRICOM brags that it has provided direct medical care to hundreds of thousands of African soldiers and their families. AFRICOM's "soldier-to-soldier" doctrine encourages the closest fraternisation between US and African military personnel: colonel to colonel, captain to captain, sergeant to sergeant, and so on through the ranks. The allegiance of many African militaries to their own governments, rather than their AFRICOM bene-factors, is seriously in question.

The African Union, itself, has become an annex of AFRICOM, rather than the armed expression of the continent's independence. The African Union's biggest operation, in Somalia, is a front for the United States. A recent *Los Angeles Times* article concludes that the 17,000-man Somalia mission is "largely a creation of the State Department and Pentagon, trained and supplied by the US government."[1]

Is it any wonder, then, that the African Union was pushed aside when the US and its NATO and royal Arab partners launched their air assault on Libya, with three African heads of state denied permission even to land on the soil of a brother African country? The AU does not collectively own Africa, or even the loyalty of its own soldiers. It is a vassal of the United States and, to a much lesser extent, France and Britain.

Kwame Nkrumah, the pan-Africanist Ghanaian leader, dreamed of "a single African military force, a single currency and a single pass-port," so that Africans could "move freely around the continent." In the twenty-first century, the dollar and the euro rule in Africa, and it is AFRICOM that moves as it wishes around the continent.

In June 2012, President Obama issued his statement on US policy in Africa. He warned that, "the United States will not stand idly by when actors threaten legitimately elected governments or manipulate the fair-ness and integrity of democratic processes." Africa, said Obama, "does not need strong men, it needs strong institutions." Yet, the strongest institution in Africa is AFRICOM.

A full combat brigade of US infantry will soon be placed on permanent duty in Africa. These 3,500 troops will not be housed in some sprawling US base, but billeted in what AFRICOM calls "safe communities"—meaning on the bases of collaborating African militaries. The American unit, now based in Fort Riley, Kansas, is called the "Dagger Brigade," and it's an apt name, because it will be a dagger in the heart of Africa, moving from country to country, subverting the loyalties of every African military unit with which it interacts. At least, that is the plan. We can only hope that the infinite arrogance of the Americans and their military will have the opposite effect on African soldiers.

\*\*\*

Late stage capitalism, with increasingly desperate, parasitical finance at the helm, demands a return to naked plunder and a kind of primitive accumulation in the face of rising economic powers in the formerly colonised world. In order to contain these peoples, the Lords of capital attempt to quarantine and stifle the productive forces of the world—an impossibility within the post-World War II international legal framework. Therefore, that framework must be destroyed.

President Obama is the first person that Norwegians have ever seen fit to award a Nobel Peace Prize *in advance* of the commission of a single peaceful deed. He has, instead, taken humanitarian aggression to new heights, leading ("from behind") the NATO *blitzkrieg* against Libya, an amazing mission in which 10,000 bombing sorties resulted in not a single civilian casualty acknowledged by NATO's high command.

Obama outdid NATO's generals; he redefined war itself. To avoid compliance with the War Powers Act, to which even his predecessor, George Bush, offered at least the formalities of respect, Obama promulgated a doctrine of hair-raising corruption. Henceforth and forever, the United States shall not be described as being in a State of War, or even of active "hostilities," unless Americans are listed among the dead. War equals dead Americans. No dead Americans, no war. The Nobel laureate—the constitutional lawyer!—in the White House has taken imperial impunity to its ultimate, insane logic, placing the US armed forces and presidency beyond the reach of human language.

Can anyone help but conclude that the United States is the most dangerous nation on Earth, the sworn enemy of not only international law, but of rational human speech itself?

What a great irony of history, that America's First Black President should become the perfect protégé of America's founding heroes: the Land Pirate, the Indian Killer, and the Slave Master. He stands on the shoulders of these evil archetypes.

## Note

1. *Los Angeles Times*, July 29, 2012.

# 3

# Victoire Ingabire: Chronology of a Pinochet-style Case of Repression

JOSEPH BUKEYE

In a report titled "Safer to stay silent: The chilling effect of Rwanda's laws on genocide ideology and sectarianism," Amnesty International reminds us that any Rwandan who dares criticise Paul Kagame's Rwandan Patriotic Front regime will be submitted to severe repressive measures. Victoire Ingabire is a telling example of that. Here is a chronology of her ordeal, which shows beyond doubt that any political dissent will be crushed by the regime, no matter if it is as peaceful and non-violent as Mrs. Ingabire.

Victoire Ingabire Umuhoza returned to Rwanda on January 16, 2010, after living for sixteen years in the Netherlands. Some believed that the regime would not brandish the spectre of the genocide to silence her. But they were wrong. It used pretty much the same methods as usual.

Mrs. Ingabire is the leader of the Unified Democratic Force (UDF), the main Rwandan opposition political party. In 2010, she had been mandated to register her party in Rwanda and to run in the presidential election to be held in August of that year.

Although the regime assured its financial backers, mostly English-speaking countries, that it was committed to a multi-party system, it perceived the arrival of Victoire Ingabire in Rwanda as a major threat to its twenty-year monopoly of power.

The great public interest for Victoire Ingabire as soon as she set foot in Rwanda prompted the regime to react strongly. It quickly started demonising her and accused her of spreading a genocidal ideology as well as promoting revisionism.

The regime needed a pretext to start the repressive action against Victoire Ingabire and it had to be quite creative to find one. One day, as Mrs. Ingabire was visiting the Gisozi Genocide Memorial, she was asked by the press what her feelings were. She answered that she wanted to pay tribute to the memory of the Tutsi victims of the genocide. She added that she regretted that nothing had been done to commemorate the other victims (i.e., the Hutus) of the Rwandan tragedy.

Simply evoking the crimes committed against Hutus was tantamount to a crime of *lèse-majesté*. Indeed, the sacrosanct dogma in Rwanda holds that one must never talk about the crimes committed by the ruling party, even if they are no secret today. The next day, Mrs. Ingabire was immediately torn to pieces by the media. The regime was setting the stage for her arrest. Quickly, the Rwandan police started tailing Mrs. Ingabire and had personnel constantly present in front of her house.

Mrs. Ingabire was summoned to the office of Kinyinya Sector on February 3, 2010, allegedly for administrative procedures. Upon her arrival, individuals ambushed her after obviously being informed of her visit to the office. The Sector's administrative manager, Mr. Shema, and the police officers on duty stood watching. With the help of a person who was accompanying her and who took the brunt of the assault and saved her, Mrs. Ingabire was able to get back to her vehicle. However, the aggressors stole Mrs. Ingabire's purse, which included her travel documents and other personal belongings.

The next day, the pro-government *New Times* published information on Mrs. Ingabire's Dutch passport and on her visa. The newspaper therefore had access to the stolen documents. A few weeks later, the police gave the documents back to Mrs. Ingabire but, strangely enough, did not arrest anyone for the theft. How did the police recover the documents?

During a press conference in his home village of Urugwiro on February 8, 2010, President Kagame launched a diatribe against Mrs. Ingabire. He threatened to use the whole Rwandan judicial arsenal to prevent her from "doing any damage."

Just two days after President Kagame's threats on February 10, 2010, Mrs. Ingabire was summoned by the Criminal Investigations Department of Rwanda. She was questioned, among other things, about her alleged links with the Hutu rebels of the FDLR (Democratic Forces for the Liberation of Rwanda).

The criminal police's allegations, widely reported by the media, were based on a report submitted to the UN Security Council, "Final report

of the Group of Experts on the Democratic Republic of the Congo"
(November 23, 2009). That report, however, only says that Mrs. Ingabire
attended a meeting of "inter-Rwandan dialogue" in Barcelona, where
representatives of the FDLR were also present. The "inter-Rwandan dialogue" meetings, which took place until June 2010 under the auspices
of Spanish and Rwandan associations, aimed at finding ways to resolve
peacefully the political crisis in Rwanda. Several hundred Rwandans,
Hutus, and Tutsis, of various political stripes, took part in those meetings, including some representatives of the Rwandan Patriotic Front,
President Kagame's party.

The UN report gives no further information about the alleged links
between Mrs. Ingabire and the FDLR rebels. But one thing is sure: given
the presence of the Rwandan Patriotic Front, the "inter-Rwandan dialogue" meetings were a less than ideal forum to plot against the Rwandan
regime.

The questioning sessions by Rwanda's Criminal Investigations
Department continued and became a form of psychological torture.
They took place once weekly until April 21, 2010.

The regime had switched into overdrive on March 23, 2010. As
Mrs. Ingabire was about to take the plane back to the Netherlands where
her family still lived, she was arrested at the airport in spite of not being
subject to any court order or other travel restriction inside or outside the
country. The police gave her no explanation and just told her that she was
not allowed to leave the country. Proactive and imaginative Rwandan
government officials even announced that she had been arrested while
trying to "flee" the country, and that she was being detained by the
police. Actually, no arrest or detention had yet taken place, but it was
clear from then on that the regime was out to get her.

Mrs. Ingabire was arrested and charged with propagating genocide
ideology, divisionism, and collaboration with a terrorist group on April
21, 2010. The accusations are clearly political in nature. Enacted in 2008,
the law criminalising the so-called genocide ideology and divisionism is
deliberately vague. According to Amnesty International, the law "constitutes an impermissible restriction on freedom of expression under
international law" (p. 14). Human Rights Watch says the law is used by
the regime against the political opposition.[1]

In one statement after another, regime officials continued harassing Victoire Ingabire. On several occasions, President Kagame attacked her personally and bluntly. On CNN, he stated that, "Mrs. Ingabire belonged in prison."

To represent her in court, Mrs. Ingabire requested the help of an American lawyer, Mr. Peter Erlinder, also a defence counsel at the International Criminal Tribunal for Rwanda in Arusha, Tanzania.

Peter Erlinder was also arrested on May 28, 2010, and charged with "denying and minimizing the genocide, and malicious spread of rumours that could threaten national security." In spite of being protected with immunity as a counsel in a UN tribunal, Mr. Erlinder's statements at the ICTR, for the defence of his client there, were held against him by the Rwandan prosecutor. The arrest of Peter Erlinder had only one purpose: to intimidate foreign lawyers and prevent anyone from defending Mrs. Ingabire.

Tired of being submitted to psychological torture, which was continuing in the office of prosecutor Bonaventure Ruberwa, on May 31, 2010 Victoire Ingabire told him that she would refuse his convocations. She asked for her case to be transferred to a tribunal where she would defend herself publicly.

On June 7, 2010, the Gasabo trial court rejected a request for temporary release of Peter Erlinder, in spite of guarantees that he could not evade justice. Pressured by an intense international campaign for the release of Peter Erlinder, with the involvement of the ICTR and members of the United States Congress, the RPF regime finally decided to release him on June 17, 2010 for "humanitarian reasons," while maintaining the charges.

Police officers were then deployed around Mrs. Ingabire's residence on June 24, 2010, to prevent her from going out. The police wanted to stop her from taking part in a protest against the regime's refusal to allow democratic election parties to take part in the August 2010 presidential election. During the protest, the police intervened with heavy-handed tactics, and members of the United Democratic Forces, Mrs. Ingabire's party, were beaten up and put in detention, including a man and a woman who held the positions of executive secretary and treasurer, respectively. It took almost a month for the police to release them, and they were told to distance themselves from the party.

While the justice system was harassing Mrs. Ingabire, the regime found other ways to torment her. For example, it pressured the owner of her house into cancelling her lease. She signed another lease elsewhere, but the regime used again the same tactic. Mrs. Ingabire had to move three times in two months!

On July 24, 2010, the police intercepted two members of the UDF at the entrance of Mrs. Ingabire's home, beat them up, and threw them in jail for "attempting to organize an unauthorized protest." Their crime was in fact that they were wearing t-shirts with a slogan: "We want democracy." In Rwanda, t-shirts depicting President Kagame or his party are well accepted, but wearing a t-shirt calling for democracy is a crime.

The presidential election was held in Rwanda on August 9, 2010. Paul Kagame won with ninety-three percent of the vote, after a campaign marred by violent events, including murders. Needless to say, Victoire Ingabire was not able to be among the candidates.

At 4 o'clock in the morning on October 8, 2010, the army cordoned off the neighbourhood where Victoire Ingabire lived, expelled the civilians who were patrolling as imposed by the authorities, searched the plainclothes police officers deployed in the area since Mrs. Ingabire's arrival and blocked all access to her home. The army gave no explanation for that and, the next day, gave the control back to the police, who then had officers positioned as close as the house doorstep.

Worried about the situation, Mrs. Ingabire called the police spokesman on October 9, 2010 to inquire about the object of the deployment around her residence. The spokesman reassured her that there was no reason to be alarmed.

Two days later, on October 11, 2010, Mrs. Ingabire directly phoned the official from the Prosecutor General's office who had questioned her in April 2010, when she was arrested. The official, by the name of Ruberwa, claimed he knew nothing about the operation and was in no way involved.

On October 14, 2010, at 12:50 p.m., a group of police officers rang the bell at Mrs. Ingabire's residence, arrested her, and took her to the Criminal Investigations Department. At the same time, the police spokeswoman justified this by saying that a new witness had just been arrested at the Congolese border, as he was trying to enter Rwanda to perpetrate terrorist acts.

However, various sources show that the arrested man, Vital Uwumuremyi, had been living in Kigali, Rwanda, since 2008. Undeniable corroborating evidence, such as photographs taken at the military camp in Rwanda where he was detained, is available publicly today. Besides, how did the police know, on October 8 when it lay siege to Mrs. Ingabire's residence, that it would arrest Mr. Uwumuremyi at the Congolese border, six days later?

In the evening on October 14, 2010, Mrs. Ingabire was transferred to the police jail of Kicukiro, after a suspicious detour in Rubirizi, in the suburbs of Kigali. The police subjected Mrs. Ingabire to a brutal incarceration regime, including keeping her handcuffed and forcing her to sleep on a wet floor, with no blanket, nor mattress.

Two lawyers were allowed to see Mrs. Ingabire in the police jail the next day on October 15. They found her still handcuffed and in a very poor condition. In spite of the lawyers protesting to the Criminal Investigations Department, who had ordered the detention, the handcuffs were not removed. In addition, the District Police Chief, Mr. Mutsinzi, decided to remove the mattress and the blanket. She had to spend the first seventy-two hours handcuffed and standing up.

On October 18, 2010, Mrs. Ingabire was taken to appear before a judge at the Gasabo district court, where all political opponents are prosecuted. In spite of assurances given by authorities about the way she was being treated, she appeared clearly in a poor condition, wearing the same clothes as at the time of her arrest. Her hair was not done and she was still wearing handcuffs. The numerous sympathisers who had come to watch the court appearance were kept outside.

That same day, during the night, Victoire Ingabire started feeling very bad. She asked to see her doctor. The police called their own doctor, and the diagnosis was acute hypotension.

On October 19, 2010, as Mrs. Ingabire's health had deteriorated, her counsel asked officially for her to be transferred to a hospital, but the police refused.

Meanwhile, a team from the International Committee of the Red Cross tried unsuccessfully to visit her. In order to confuse the issue, the intelligence service went as far as sending a false ICRC delegate to see her, but the stratagem was discovered.

Between October 18 and 21, 2010, Mrs. Ingabire was questioned by an official from the Prosecutor General's office, at the Gasabo district court, in spite of her health condition getting worse each day.

Early in the morning on October 21, 2010, the police had to call their doctor again, urgently, as Mrs. Ingabire was in great pain.

Nevertheless, in the afternoon, she was taken to the district court to be confronted with the key witness, Vital Uwumuremyi, an ex-rebel from the FDLR, who immediately said that he had been arrested in Rwanda and not at the Congolese border, as announced by the police. He added various confused and unsubstantiated accusations.

Mr. Uwumuremyi, supposedly an army major, stated that he was still an active member of the FDLR. However, a quick documentary research shows that he had abandoned that group in 2008.[2]

Mrs. Ingabire was subjected to harsh questioning and remained handcuffed the whole time, while Major Uwumuremyi, her co-accused and witness for the prosecution, was not handcuffed and was sitting comfortably.

Mrs. Ingabire's health condition worsened again on October 22, 2010, and she was examined by the police doctor.

The hearing took place at the Gasabo district court the next day on October 25, 2010,.

The following day the judge decided to continue her detention, even if the charges against her were exactly the same as when she had been arrested and questioned, in April 2010, and then released under a judicial restraint order.

As soon as the decision was made public, Mrs. Ingabire was transferred to the infamous Kigali Central Prison. Her head was shaved the same night, as a way to humiliate her. Before the decision, newspapers had already announced that a cell had been reserved for her. The hearing was a mere formality.

On November 12, 2010, the Supreme Court of Rwanda, to whom the defence counsels complained of numerous irregularities, rejected Mrs. Ingabire's appeal on her continued detention. The Supreme Court judges are all active members of the Rwandan Patriotic Front, Mr. Kagame's party. Their decision was based on multiple contradictory statements and on emails that were proven to have been forged.

On April 8, 2011, Mrs. Ingabire met with the Prosecutor General Martin Ngoga, who admitted that she had been arrested because the regime was afraid to lose control of the population.

Victoire Ingabire's trial opened at the Kigali High Court on June 20, 2011. The charges were:

1.  Genocide ideology
2.  Complicity in terrorist acts
3.  Divisionism
4.  Spreading rumours intended to incite the public to rise up against the state
5.  Creating an armed group
6.  Complicity in endangering the state through terrorism and armed violence.

Given the numerous gaps in the law against the genocide ideology, which the prosecutor was using against her, Mrs. Ingabire challenged the validity of the procedure before the Supreme Court. She asked the court if she could be prosecuted for events that occurred before the law was enacted. The law cannot be retroactive, and using it against Mrs. Ingabire was a violation of her rights and freedoms as guaranteed by the Constitution of Rwanda. Despite that, the Supreme Court stated that there was no problem with the law. But at the same time, a bill to amend the law was tabled in parliament.

On April 16, 2012, sickened by the harassment a key defence witness was subjected to after he had demolished the testimonies of the FDLR rebels-turned-informers, Mrs. Ingabire decided to boycott the court hearings.

The High Court found Mrs. Ingabire guilty of two of the six charges on June 30, 2012: 1) belittling the genocide; 2) threatening state security. She was sentenced to eight years in prison without parole. Even the European Parliament called the decision politically motivated.[3]

Two aspects of the judgment are quite striking:

1.  The crime of "belittling the genocide" was not included in the original indictment as filed by the prosecutor.
2.  The so-called threat to state security charge was based on allegations that Mrs. Ingabire had conspired with her co-accused

to establish the Coalition of Democratic Forces military wing. However, the so-called informants admitted themselves that the Coalition of Democratic Forces' armed group was a pure fiction.

The Fondation Jean Jaurès, the European Commission, Human Rights Watch, and even the European Parliament criticised the judgment.

On March 25, 2013, the Supreme Court of Rwanda started hearing Mrs. Ingabire's appeal in Kigali. During the appeal hearings, two important events occurred that left the prosecutor virtually without a case:

1.  The prosecution's main witnesses and co-accused, i.e., the ex-rebels from the FDLR, who had stated before the High Court that Mrs. Ingabire had initiated the establishment of the Coalition of Democratic Forces' armed group, retracted their statements and cleared her of any such wrongdoing. The prosecutor was so surprised to see his main witnesses tell the truth that he remained silent.

2.  A new defence witness confirmed the collusion between the prosecution witnesses and Rwandan security services.

Initially, the judgment of the Supreme Court was supposed to be announced on November 1, 2013, but it was postponed to December 13, 2013, therefore prolonging the detention and aggravating the anxiety for the accused. This also gave more time for the regime to try to neutralise Mrs. Ingabire's team. Her acting private secretary, who is the UDF treasurer, is wanted by the police. The General Secretary of the UDF was sentenced to two consecutive imprisonment terms of two and six years, plus a fine of one million Rwandan francs. His only mistake was to meet citizens in a café and to discuss with them the activities of his political party.

Finally, on December 13, 2013, the Supreme Court in its final appeal decision increased Victoire Ingabire's jail sentence from eight to fifteen years without parole. In addition to the two charges that the High Court had found Mrs. Ingabire guilty of previously (i.e., belittling the genocide and threatening state security), the Supreme Court also found her guilty of spreading rumours. It seems that Mrs. Ingabire deserved that further condemnation for having quoted documents that have been public for years. The regime is particularly annoyed at accusations of slaughtering Hutu populations, namely in the Democratic Republic of the Congo, even if the accusations against the Rwandan army are widely substantiated. Both the High Court trial and the appeal before the Supreme Court took place amid blatant interference by the executive branch. President Paul Kagame continually stated that Mrs. Ingabire was guilty. No judge would ever dare challenging such orders.

The trial was also marred by the following procedural shortcomings

1.  The authenticity of the prosecution witnesses' testimonies was not verified. The key witnesses were none but the co-accused. They had spent several months in detention in the notorious Kami military camp. Several reports from Amnesty International and Human Rights Watch revealed the torture inflicted on the prisoners by the army in order to force them to commit perjury.

2.  The Court dismissed the testimony of the defence witnesses. One of them, Michel Habimana, who had been in the FDLR with the co-accused, was forced to interrupt his testimony after he started talking about the dubious credibility of his ex-comrades whose testimonies were used against Mrs. Ingabire. The Court also did not pay much attention to the testimony of AA, even though that witness explained how the intelligence services had paid Vital Uwumuremyi for his false testimony.

3.  The civil rights of the accused were violated. In another case of similar violations (against two journalists, Saiditi and Mukakibibi), the Supreme Court discharged the accused. To continue detaining Mrs. Ingabire in spite of the abuse she suffered while others were released is a clear case of double standard.

4.  Mrs. Ingabire seemingly perpetrated the spreading of rumours, crime for which she was found guilty by the Supreme Court through her writings between 2000 and 2010. The Court was shown that every document quoted by Mrs. Ingabire was publicly available. She even quoted reports from International organisations, including some UN agencies. It is hard to imagine that the RPF might someday be suing UN agencies in Rwandan courts, for spreading rumours.

5. The sentences were completely unfair. While the co-accused recognised having attacked Rwanda at least on two occasions, they were given a sentence of only three to four years in prison. Some of them have already been released under obscure circumstances. On the other hand, Mrs. Ingabire was sentenced to fifteen years in prison even though she never was involved in any act of war.

Such a mixture of errors and bad faith proves that Victoire Ingabire's trial was politically motivated. Its purpose was to muzzle an opposition figure that refused to be compromised by the regime, whose usual methods comprise bribery and physical elimination

While today some countries regret having sacrificed Nelson Mandela for the sake of their economic interests in South Africa, it would be wise now to avoid creating, in Rwanda, a similar case of injustice by abandoning Mrs. Ingabire.

## Notes

1. "Opposition to government policies often led the government to accuse its critics of engaging in 'genocide ideology,' a vaguely defined offense established in 2008 that does not require any intent to assist, facilitate, or incite violence on the basis of ethnicity," Chapter on Rwanda in HRW World Report, 2010, http://www.hrw.org/en/node/87596.
2. R. OMAAR, *The Leadership of Rwandan Armed Groups Abroad with a Focus on the FDLR and RUD/Urunana*, December 2008.
3. See European Parliament resolution 2013/2641(RSP), adopted on May 23, 2013, http://www.europarl.europa.eu/sides/getDoc.do?pubRef=-//EP//TEXT+MOTION+P7-RC-2013-0243+0+DOC+XML+Vo//EN.

# 4

## The Fabrication of Evidence before the International Criminal Tribunal for Rwanda

LÉOPOLD NSENGIYUMVA

The past two decades witnessed the creation of several international tribunals: first the *ad hoc* tribunals like the International Criminal Tribunal for the Former Yugoslavia (ICTY) and the International Criminal Tribunal for Rwanda (ICTR); and tribunals such as the Special Tribunal for Sierra Leone, the Special Tribunal for Lebanon, and the Special Tribunal for Cambodia (also called Extraordinary Chambers in the Courts of Cambodia); and lastly the International Criminal Court (ICC). Being the only permanent court, the ICC is likely to inherit some experience and practices from the *ad hoc* and special tribunals that have already completed their activities or are in the course of doing so.

These tribunals have a considerable body of jurisprudence that customarily becomes part of international law, but the question being raised here is whether decisions rendered by these courts reflect the reality on the ground, namely, whether what these tribunals take as true, based on their own procedures and practices to ascertain the truth, is indeed true.

A major flaw regarding the disclosure of truth, which has never been addressed, haunts these international tribunals. Specifically, justice in international tribunals, contrary to the situation in domestic jurisdictions, takes place many miles from the crime scenes and often several years after the crimes were committed. This geographical, cultural, and temporal remoteness can have a significant impact on the outcome of the issue to be decided. Also, by their very nature, international courts are placed in an uncomfortable position of working with or relying on states that may have interests to protect.[1]

While those who framed the rules governing these tribunals have endeavoured to ensure that justice is served, they nevertheless, maybe in good faith, created some rules that opened important loopholes which unscrupulous interested parties could manipulate so that international justice would meet their own whims. At the ICTR, it would seem that those who framed the rules underestimated the possibility of such manipulation by an interested state, since the survival of the institution indirectly depended on the cooperation of the government of Rwanda.[2] Simply put, the government of Rwanda, a belligerent, was indirectly allowed to determine who should be tried and how they should be tried. There is, of course, no such authorisation in any statutes or rules, but some rules, principles of law, or practices were broad enough to bring about such results through manipulation, as is demonstrated below.

One loophole states may use to influence the outcome of judgments is the manipulation of witnesses. Such states, in an aim to consolidate their narrative of events, may attempt to feed the courts with pre-arranged witnesses. It is anticipated that judges have the capacity to discern this problem and make fair decisions. In theory everything is set to prevent this injustice but the theory seems to run afoul with the practice at the ICTR. It is my belief that before the ICTR, the Rwandan government was generally successful in influencing the outcome of judgments by meticulously feeding the court with manipulated witnesses; practices at the ICTR seemed to encourage such situations.

A quick look at ICTR indictments shows that the prosecutor had serious difficulties charging individuals. The indictment amendment rate is more than alarming since the initial charges do not correspond to the evidence gathered or invented later. On average, five amendments were made to indictments at the ICTR[3] with the result that a completely different case was brought against an accused after his or her arrest. The important point is that these amendments were very weak from a criminal proceeding perspective. They were made after several arrangements with freshly recruited witnesses who received considerable benefits for their testimony. Though rules regarding amendments are tough, they were flexible enough to allow the prosecutor to connive with unscrupulous individuals/states to defeat the noble goals of courts to make or render justice.

Mechanisms available in domestic jurisdictions to counter this abuse, such as public outcry or political punishment, do not exist and there should be some mechanism to rectify this trend at the international level.

It is not only states that can interfere with international justice; individuals can do so as well but the risk is not as great because individuals do not have the power of states. States can manipulate their internal laws and provide incentives to people; they can provide a wide range of rewards that individuals may not have. Interestingly, the ICTR has reacted harshly against individuals who were caught tampering with evidence but did very little or nothing to discourage the Rwandan government from interfering with the evidence.[4] In some instances the Tribunal is seen to encourage such practices.

## The Rwandan Law on Guilty Plea, Confession, and Forgiveness

This particular law was introduced in 2000 with minor subsequent amendments and provides for confession, denunciation of other accomplices, and apologies.[5] Article 61 gives the public prosecutor power to review the confession and determine whether it is complete or not, and take appropriate measures accordingly. If the confession is true and complete then the individual could be released.

On the face of it there is nothing wrong with the Rwandan government coming up with this idea and it is very normal in almost all jurisdictions for the prosecution to extend such favours to cooperative or confessing suspects. However, in the context of international justice, things should be double-checked. States may have an interest in extending these favours for ill motives, which is what happened with this Rwandan law. The Rwandan government has shown that it had an interest in protecting itself against possible prosecution for crimes committed by its own members during the hostilities. This was an opportunity to ensure that a narrative that takes into account this protection was affirmatively developed and repeated before the ICTR. The ICTR heard several witnesses explaining how this law was indeed used to fabricate evidence against detained people in Arusha. In many Rwandan prisons "Arusha wings" were created and those who confessed would be relocated to those wings where conditions of detention were better[6] and where several training sessions on how to testify were held. Witness CBP78 explained:

When somebody made confessions, they would be transferred to the Arusha wing and then would get more food. There was more room, more sleeping room. And so those who were in the Arusha wing lived under better conditions compared to those in the other wings of the prison.[7]

Completeness of a confession could mean anything from adding the name of someone detained at the ICTR as co-perpetrator to, in some instances, specifically creating a story that proved the prosecution case at the ICTR.[8]

It looks like witnesses were even warned not to mention how this manipulation took place. A prosecution witness reacted as follows to a simple question about whether he had met with authorities to record a statement:

> Mr. President, as I said at the very outset, it's because Defence counsel is inviting me to mention the name of Rwandan authorities with whom I have spoken. I think that if I go about mentioning their names, it will compromise my safety once I'm back in Rwanda, so I would like to beg you to allow me to stipulate the reasons leading me to decline answering this question.[9]

Lastly, as part of the same process, solidarity camps were introduced where all candidates to be released had to go to receive counselling on how to reintegrate into normal life. However, there was evidence suggesting that in these camps, the confessions were reviewed again and reworked to produce statements corroborating the prosecution theory at the ICTR. This practice of fabricating evidence by a state was commonly done in Rwanda to such an extent that witnesses behaved like envoys or representatives of the Republic of Rwanda at the ICTR. Witness FH is one such witness who went through the process and was paraded in several cases before the ICTR; he wrote to the Rwandan minister of justice asking for his provisional release and making it clear that one of the reasons he should be released was as follows: "I also wish to inform you that I was sent by the Government of Rwanda to the International Criminal tribunal for Rwanda located in Arusha to testify against the so-called *Abatabazi*[10] Government."[11]

Interestingly, those who testified for the defence and presented a narrative that differed from the one the government wanted were severely punished. Before Witness FH became the prosecution witness, he had testified for the defence at the ICTR at the very beginning of proceedings. When he went back to Rwanda he was put in prison[12] and the long process of fabrication of evidence began. From a defence witness in 1997, he went on to become a vocal prosecution witness. He testified that "moreover, for any detainee if anything can help to get released, a detainee would do it."[13]

Cases like that of FH are numerous, but the most interesting, which I find worthy to be mentioned here, is that of Mr. Fidele Uwizeye. He testified also for defence in the Akayesu trial. Upon his return to Rwanda, he was taken to jail and held incommunicado in very inhumane conditions. He was not charged with genocide, contrary to most people detained in the same situation, but was charged instead with "endangering state security."[14] After his release, he became one of the most virulent prosecution witnesses in Arusha and in all his testimonies he wanted to make sure that he was testifying for the prosecution.

There is a considerable body of jurisprudence indicating that the Tribunal would adequately deal with this situation and either disqualify such witnesses or question their credibility. However, the general trend has unfortunately been that those testimonies were believed, apart from rare instances where manipulated witnesses totally recanted their testimonies and were even indicted by the Tribunal for contempt of court.[15]

## Witness Protection

Witness protection is provided for in Rule 75 of the ICTR rules. It empowers a judge or a chamber, *proprio motu* (i.e., on his own impulse) or at the request of either party, the victim, or witness concerned, or of the Victims and Witnesses Section, to order appropriate measures for the privacy and protection of victims and witnesses, provided that they are consistent with the rights of the accused. Those measures include an *in camera* proceeding to determine whether it is appropriate not to disclose to the public the identity of a witness or his or her relatives, to expunge any identifying information from records, and to assign a pseudonym.

Again there is nothing wrong with this rule. The problem is how it was abused and simply used as an assurance that no one, least of all the public in Rwanda, would ever know that a false testimony was made against someone.

Also several professional witnesses who testified in numerous proceedings took advantage of such protection by adapting their stories/testimony according to the person charged. The prosecution and the defence have waged big fights over disclosure of these testimonies and in several instances the prosecution was caught not willing to disclose them. Incentives given to witnesses and condoned under the guise of protection have also been a problem.

Most important is the cultural meaning of what constitutes a testimony in Rwanda; publicity is needed because when it is done in secrecy it is no longer considered testimony in the eyes of Rwandans.

Finally, the rationale behind the protection given to some prosecution witnesses made no sense. Most of the prosecution witnesses enjoyed the protection of the Rwandan state while those testifying for the defence risked the wrath of the entire RPF government. *A contrario*, protection was overwhelmingly accorded to those prosecution witnesses coming from Kigali, and the grounds for protection cannot be reasonably justified. It has been argued that the accused, their families, and their supporters were likely to harm those testifying against them, but this argument is unfounded since the same witnesses were testifying in the open in Rwanda without fear. Furthermore, the protection accorded did not prevent the accused and their defence teams from knowing details about the person testifying. What, then, is the relevance of this ritual called witness protection?

The most shocking example is when witnesses testified in public in different open forums (e.g., Gacaca and various tribunals) or made public statements to media intended to be communicated to large audiences, and then requested protection for the same events while testifying about them in Arusha.

## Witness Proofing

Witness proofing can be described as allowing a witness to read his/her prior statements and then discussing any differences in recollection, as well as the questions and answers to be provided during the witness' testimony with the prosecutor. The prosecutor then inquires about additional information the witness may have.[16]

The International Criminal Court banned the practice in its decision of November 8, 2006, which held that the prosecution's practice of proofing its witnesses was not a widely accepted practice in international criminal law,[17] and that it was in fact prohibited in many national jurisdictions[18] (i.e., Brazil, Spain, France, Belgium, Germany, Scotland, Ghana, England and Wales, and Australia). The decision prohibited the ICC prosecution from proofing witnesses who were to be called at the confirmation hearing, holding that the principle within customary national practice was that witness proofing was not permitted.[19] However, both the ICTR and ICTY sanctioned the practice of witness proofing,[20] therefore it was accepted in some domestic jurisdictions (such as the US) but strongly opposed in others (e.g., most countries with a civil law tradition); similarly it was accepted by *ad hoc* tribunals but rejected by the ICC.

Without analysing the merits or demerits of the practice, it should be noted that, from the cultural perspective, this practice shocked Rwandans. In Rwanda, despite the strong tradition of the manipulation of messages or information,[21] there was also a well-established rule of evidence regulating how a witness should be produced in a court. Traditionally and well before the arrival of Europeans, a party calling a witness had simply to give his name and it was up to that person to appear before the court. There was no such thing as meeting your witness and discussing your case. Furthermore, rules existed to check the veracity of a testimony, and punishment for false testimony could be very severe,[22] which could go as far as substituting the wrongly convicted person by his accuser. In any case, these strict, archaic methods to check the truthfulness of a testimony have no place in modern law, but they tell us how testifying was taken very seriously.

Conversely, in Rwandan society, lying for fun occurs very frequently; it is as if they have "April Fools" on a daily basis. People generally accept such lies as they believe it is upon the other person to differentiate what is serious and what is humour. Once a story becomes grotesque, it is understood that anyone who believes in it does so at their own risk. For instance, a witness who had been implicated in several incidents of evidence fabrication explained that given his numerous prior statements on the subject matter, he understood that the truth should come to light even if he was personally bending his story to accommodate the person asking him to lie. The bench did not notice this warning and made him a credible witness afterwards!

> That is what he wanted, but I told him that that was not precise, but he insisted asking me to do so. But he knew that with reference to a previous testimony that I had given that the truth would ultimately come out because with reference to those dates, I had made many statements on the subject. And I said that even if I did bend to his request, it would come out in the end.[23]

In this case, to tell a Rwandan who culturally feared giving wrong testimony that you would test his memory to see if his recollection was good, but discuss what he told you previously and possibly adjust his testimony, especially in combination with the other practices mentioned above, effectively meant that testifying before the ICTR was a joke.

## Notes

1. For instance, in the Kenyan case, both president and vice president are indicted. In other situations such states are led by former belligerents who had an interest in seeing that their own crimes are not investigated; therefore they will make sure the Tribunal acquiesces to their own version of events.
2. When the ICTR released Jean-Bosco Barayagwiza, the government of Rwanda denied a visa to the chief prosecutor and vowed to stop any cooperation, bringing the Tribunal to its knees until Barayagwiza was treated as the government of Rwanda wanted.
3. For example in *The Prosecutor v. Édouard Karemera et al.* five amendments were authorised.
4. A defence investigator was prosecuted (*The Prosecutor v. Nshogoza*) and prosecution witnesses who recanted and denounced the Rwandan authorities were indicted instead.
5. Article 54 of that law says: "Any person who has committed offences aimed at in Article one of this organic law has right to have recourse to confession procedure and guilt plea. To be received as confession in the context of this chapter, the defendant's declarations shall contain: a) The detailed description on everything relating to the confessed offence, in particular the location where it has been committed, the date, the witnesses, the names of the victims and the damaged assets; b) The enquiries relating to co-authors and accomplices as well as any other enquiry use-

ful to the exercise of public action; c) The apologies offered for the offences that he petitioner has committed."

6. Benefits could include being appointed prisoners' representative, which meant access to some material benefits and conjugal visits. Even though conjugal visits are not permitted according to Rwandan law, those who confessed and agreed to testify in Arusha were capable of receiving conjugal visits at their request; this can be demonstrated by their wives' regular pregnancies. In the most extreme circumstances the Tribunal heard evidence that some were allowed to go back to their homes at their request and then report back to the prison, simply to show that they were still imprisoned.

7. *The Prosecutor v. Ndindiliyimana et al.*, ICTR-00-56-T, T., February 18, 2008, p.18.

8. For instance, in the Ndindiliyimana case, the court heard a defence witness who explained how a prosecution witness was trained to testify that he had received a weapon from Ndindiliyimana which he had used to kill (*The Prosecutor v. Ndindiliyimana et al.*, ICTR-00-56-T, T. February 18, 2008, p.24). The same prosecution witness GFR later recanted his testimony and explained that the prosecutor in Rwanda had coerced him to do so. (*The Prosecutor v. Augustin Ndindiliyimana*. ICTR-00-56, Trial Judgment, May 17, 2011, para. 183.)

9. *The Prosecutor v. Édouard Karemera et al.*, Case No. ICTR-98-44-T, Witness HH, 15/11/2006, p. 24.

10. *Abatabazi*, or literally "Saviours," was the nickname of the government sworn in just after the death of President Juvénal Habyarimana.

11. *The Prosecutor v. Édouard Karemera et al.*, Case No. ICTR-98-44-T, Exhibit DNZ322A p.2.

12. Id. DNZ 320, p.6.

13. *The Prosecutor v. Édouard Karemera et al.*, Case No. ICTR-98-44-T, Transcript 18/07/2007 p.49.

14. Amnesty International, "Rwanda: The Troubled Course of Justice," April 25, 2000, p. 21.

15. Witnesses GFA and GFR, who totally recanted their testimonies, were subsequently indicted. While it is perfectly fair to indict anyone who voluntarily attempted to mislead the court, the message sent to the community of people implicated in the scheme seems to be that "if you denounce us you will face the consequences."

16. *Prosecutor v. Dyilo*, No. ICC-004-01/06, Decision on the Practice of Witness Familiarization and Witness Proofing, November 8, 2006, paras. 16-17.

17. *Ibid.*, para. 33.

18. *Ibid.*, para. 37.

19. *Ibid.*, para. 42.

20. *Prosecutor v. Édouard Karemera et al.*, No. ICTR-98-44-T, Decision on Defence Motion to Prohibit Witness Proofing, December 16, 2006, para. 15.

21. It is generally advisable in Rwanda to twist your message before you express yourself and this generally leaves some kinds of lies culturally acceptable and even laudable. Some commentators call this phenomenon "the culture of lie."

22. One can say that they even have something akin to a lie detector: once a party complained of false testimony, they could swear in the witness over a very hot metal. This was done by calling in a blacksmith who could use his knowledge of melting metals, and a person was deemed to be telling the whole truth upon seeing

the threat of extremely hot metal. In other circumstances, "witchcraft" was used (wisemen/wisewomen who were believed to have techniques to read the minds of the witnesses and determine whether they were lying or not).

23. *The Prosecutor v. Édouard Karemera et al.*, ICTR-98-44-T, HH, November 17, 2006, p. 28.

# 5

## Charles Taylor: The Special Court for Sierra Leone and Questionable Verdicts

CHIEF CHARLES A. TAKU

### Introduction

Charles Ghankay Taylor, aka Charles MacArthur Dapkana Taylor, former President of the Republic of Liberia, was convicted by a Trial Chamber of the Special Court for Sierra Leone on May 18, 2012, and sentenced to a single prison term of fifty years.

He was convicted on eleven counts of crimes against humanity, violation of Common Article 3 of the Geneva Conventions, and other violations of international humanitarian law for aiding and abetting the Revolutionary United Front for Sierra Leone (RUF) and the Armed Forces Revolutionary Council (AFRC) in rape, murder, sexual slavery, enlisting children under the age of fifteen into armed forces, and pillage during the civil war in Sierra Leone.

He was specifically convicted under the modes of liability of planning, preparation, and execution of the operational strategy and therefore culpable in the crimes that were perpetrated. On October 24, 2013, the Appeals Chamber of the Special Court sitting at the Hague dismissed the appeal filed by Charles Taylor and confirmed his conviction and sentence.

The convictions in the Special Court have been praised for the length of sentences, accountability for the violent crimes that shocked the conscience of humanity in Sierra Leone, and the extreme brutality with which the crimes were perpetrated. Legal experts and keen observers have challenged the fairness of these trials and convictions.

This article points out some of the absurdities in the Taylor trial findings that were replicated in other trials before the different Trial Chambers of the Court and regrettably confirmed by the Appeals Chamber of the Special Court.

## Alleged Credible Examples for Future Trials

In his appeal, Charles Taylor alleged errors in defining "intent" to aid and abet by applying a "knowledge" standard rather than a "purpose" standard. The Appeals Chamber dismissed the defence's argument, holding that Mr. Taylor was knowingly involved in the planning, preparation, and execution of the RUF/AFRC operational strategy and was therefore culpable for the resulting crimes. The defence also alleged errors in evidence and reliability of witnesses.

The Appeals Chamber, however, held that the evidence proved that Charles Taylor had aided, abetted, and planned the crimes charged in the Indictment, and affirmed the sentence of fifty years imprisonment. The prosecutor of the Special Court, Brenda Hollis, commended the sentence, stating that "[t]his sentence makes it clear that those responsible for criminal conduct on a massive scale will be severely punished. No sentence less than 50 years would be enough to achieve retribution and deterrence, the primary goals of sentencing for international crimes."

The prosecutor then recommended that the judgment should set a powerful precedent for future international criminal cases to hold military and state leaders accountable for atrocities committed under their command, whether through direct orders or through knowing involvement in the planning, preparation, and execution of operations which led to horrific crimes against humanity.

A careful analysis of the evidential findings and application of legal principles to the facts reveal unprincipled and inconsistent bases for findings of credibility of material witnesses upon which the court relied to convict. It is therefore unsafe for international courts to rely on "precedent" generated from the trial and conviction of Charles Taylor and other judgments delivered by the court to inspire their legal and factual findings in cases that come before them. To apply this jurisprudence to any case anywhere will occasion a grave injustice due to the fact that the said judgment has been reasonably challenged for failing to meet international legal standards.

## Questionable Legal Justification of Evidential Findings

The prosecutor of the Special Court, Brenda Hollis, hailed the judgment as a "powerful precedent for future international criminal cases to hold military and state leaders accountable for atrocities committed under their command, whether through direct orders or through knowing." The world press joined the chorus enthusiastically, with the *Christian Science Monitor* venturing to suggest that Taylor "was the first head of state convicted by an international court since the Nazi trials after World War Two and the sentence set a precedent for the emerging system of international justice."[1]

While public opinion in Sierra Leone and Liberia was divided about the conviction and sentence for other reasons, lawyers and some experts associated with trials at the Special Court for Sierra Leone were pessimistic that this and other judgments delivered at the court would ever serve as reasonable precedent by the emerging system of international justice to combat impunity by persons in command and positions of power any time soon, or in fact at all. The reasons are many and I will venture to address some.

The Special Court for Sierra Leone was confronted with a situation where most of the witnesses who testified against the accused were accomplice witnesses. Several of them admitted under oath that they perpetrated all or most of the crimes about which they testified.

This was not surprising because, in his opening statement during the commencement of the RUF trial involving Hassan Issa Sesay (Interim leader of the RUF), Morris Kallon (deputy interim leader), and Augustine Gbao (Chief Security Commander of the RUF), prosecutor David Crane promised the Trial Chamber that:

> This case will be proven by witnesses, again, the brave and courageous people of Sierra Leone who stepped forward to meet and slay the beast of impunity with the righteous sword of the law. Additionally, we will bring in members of the inner circle of the Joint Criminal Enterprise who will testify against these war crimes indictees. In this situation, in some ways, we have to dance with the devil to put into proper context the complete, yet truthful picture. They too will come forward to face the good people of Sierra Leone and assist them in returning the rule of law to their country.[2]

The promise made by the prosecutor in the RUF case was replicated in all the other trials including the Charles Taylor trial. This means the Trial Chamber relied essentially on accomplice evidence to obtain convictions against Charles Taylor, just as other Trial Chambers did in the other cases. In so doing, the Chambers did not explicitly develop a consistent jurisprudence and a principled evidentiary threshold, on which they relied in finding evidence adduced from accomplice witnesses, which would be credible and safe to constitute a viable basis for conviction. As a result, highly self-incriminating evidence adduced through accomplice witnesses without indicia of credibility was relied on to convict.

A few examples appropriately highlight the questionable basis on which prosecution witnesses were found to be credible. Isaac Mongor, a Liberian citizen who was brigadier and one of the most senior commanders of the RUF, testified under the protection of an immunity granted by the prosecutor.[3] Although the Chamber found inconsistencies in his testimony, which it excused as minor, it observed at paragraph 273 of the trial that "Mongor maintained a calm demeanor throughout the entire trial and therefore found him credible."[4] There can be no gainsaying that this factor or attribute is not uncommon with persons trained and involved in combat, in particular senior commanders. The Trial Chamber did not provide an explanation of how his calm disposition was a reasonable basis for a finding of credibility, nor any authority to support the finding.

Witness TF1-516 came across as the very opposite of Isaac Mongor but was found credible nevertheless. At paragraph 283 of the trial judgment, the court found as follows in respect of this witness:

> TF1-516 was at times agitated, and tried to avoid answering questions… he refused to answer a question directly whether he agreed with his prior statement. Only after being pressed several times by the Trial Chamber did the witness then assert that investigators made an error. The Trial Chamber noted that the witness refused several times to answer the question whether General Tengbeh was one of the Special Forces. When pressed to do so, the witness replied that he did not know.

The Trial Chamber nevertheless accepted his response. It then went on to find as follows: "For these reasons the Trial Chamber finds TF1-

516 to be generally credible and will consider further matters relating to his reliability in context as they may arise."[5]

Particularly intriguing is that the trial finding upheld on appeal that a prosecution witness against Charles Taylor, named in the trial judgment as Bobson Sesay, was credible based on his confessed criminality spanning most of the crime bases in the national territory of Sierra Leone. The Trial Chamber found that:

> The witness [Bobson Sesay] admitted to having personally participated in numerous and a wide ranging array of crimes throughout the Indictment period, including raping two young girls in Kono and Freetown, training small boy units whom he instructed to amputate the hands of civilians in Yomandu and Tombodu, burning civilians in a house at Karina, abducting about 30 women in Karina, looting valuable property from civilians at Lunsar and Makeni in the implementation of 'Operation Pay Yourself', and participating in 'Operation Spare No Soul' as ordered by his senior commanders.[6]

Nevertheless, the Chamber decided, "for this reason the Trial Chamber finds TF1-516 to be generally credible given his detailed and coherent account, the candor with which he testified about his own complicity, and his lack of any motivation to lie."[7] In other words, the court considered testimony with self-incriminating confessions as a factor of credibility.[8]

## Findings in Other Trials

The RUF trial before the Special Court[9] affords a compelling example of how facts were mischaracterised or wrong principles of law invoked to justify wrong factual findings. The two trials were intrinsically, factually, and legally linked, to the extent that most of the witnesses that testified in the RUF trial testified in the Taylor trial. The RUF indictment and supporting material contain essentially the same allegations as the Taylor trial. There is little doubt therefore that the RUF facts adduced in the RUF trial were introduced into the Taylor trial and relied on to support the convictions.

From the outset the Trial Chamber sought to cure a defective indictment by invoking "the nature and scale of the conflict when evaluating the arguments of the accused with respect to the degree of specificity required in the indictment,"[10] and cited a plethora of jurisprudence of International Criminal Tribunals which considered the scale of the crimes perpetrated as opposed to the "nature of the conflict" as the critical factor.[11]

The Appeals Chamber endorsed this wrong legal standard that criminalised the ten-year conflict in Sierra Leone, as opposed to the crimes perpetrated during the temporary jurisdiction of the court that did not cover the entire conflict.

The Trial Chamber opted for, and relied on, the principle of "orality," thereby expressing a preference for the evidence adduced at trial to prior inconsistent statements during investigations disclosed to the defence.[12] The Trial Chamber also permitted the prosecutor to introduce "proofing notes" recorded during witness preparation and disclosed to the defence at any stage of the trial, including a few hours prior to the witness testimony.

Through these principles devised at trial and the judicial notice it took of relevant but contested facts, the prosecution's evidentiary proof was facilitated to the detriment of the defence.[13] The odds against Morris Kallon were insurmountable as the Trial Chamber repudiated his entire testimony on the grounds that he "failed to impress the Chamber as a truthful witness" and that it was of the opinion that "most of his responses and explanations throughout the trial proceedings suggested an attempt by Mr. Kallon to "align his testimony to the evidence presented during the prosecution case, including attempting to put himself in a favorable light by downplaying or accentuating his role in incidents described by prosecution witness. In many instances the evidence Kallon contradicts the weight of credible evidence presented by other reliable witnesses."[14] The Appeals Chamber sustained this gross transgression that occasioned a miscarriage of justice to Mr. Kallon and set the wrong standards for evaluating defence evidence, which it later applied in the Taylor trial and which facilitated his conviction, as it did with Morris Kallon.

In normal trials that meet international standards, the reasons advanced to "repudiate" the testimony of an accused that bears no burden of proof will not be that he "aligned his testimony to the evidence presented during the prosecution's case." That is exactly what reasonable accused parties will do in their own defence by addressing issues raised against them in the prosecution case, as Kallon did. Instead he was inflicted extreme punishment repudiating his entire testimony, without a formal justification.

Upon dismissing his testimony and reversing the burden of proof to facilitate his conviction, the Trial Chamber readily convicted on the basis of criminal liability of Joint Criminal Enterprise without specifying whether it was the basic form, the systemic form, or the extended form. In addition he was convicted on an expansive Joint Criminal Enterprise (JCE) covering the entire national territory of Sierra Leone, including crimes that were perpetrated in the district of Bo by soldiers of the Sierra Leone Army. The evidence disclosed that the Sierra Leone Army soldiers were court-martialed and executed prior the RUF rebels coming out of the bush and joining forces with the AFRC. The Appeals Chamber also cited and misapplied the jurisdiction of International Tribunals on the systemic form of Joint Criminal Enterprise in dismissing objections raised by the appellant concerning the application of wrong principles in convicting him that failed to distinguish properly the basic and the extended forms of JCE. The Appeals Chamber, for example, cited and relied on the Tadić Appeals Judgment at the ICTY, which was based on a systemic form of JCE, to dismiss the appellant's appeal on the massive and over-expansive reach of the trial judgment convicting him for crimes perpetrated in locations throughout the provinces of the national territory of Sierra Leone. The mental elements required for the systemic form of Joint Criminal Enterprise is the *mens rea* (or "guilty mind") that is shared with the perpetrators, whereas the third variant of JCE relies on the test of knowledge and foreseeability.[15]

In resolving Kallon's appeal on shared *mens rea* between the principal perpetrator and the appellant, and the legality of the so-called "tool theory"[16] developed by the Trial Chamber to convict him, the Appeals Chamber overturned a favourable finding that absolved him of criminal liability. It instead imposed an incriminating finding to enable it to supplement the constitutive element of the extended form of Joint Criminal Enterprise required to convict.

Although the prosecutor did not appeal the trial finding, the Appeals Chamber compromised its neutrality, fairness, and independence at paragraph 413 of the Appeals Judgment to find that: "The Appeals Chamber notes that the Trial Chamber did not make an explicit finding that mid- and low-level RUF and AFRC commanders" and "rank and file fighters" who carried out the *actus reus* (or "guilty act") of many of the crimes now at issue were not members of the Joint Criminal Enterprise. It merely found "insufficient evidence to conclude" that these individuals were JCE members. Therefore the Appeals Chamber considers it inappropriate to refer to these persons as "non-JCE members."[17] Instead, the Appeals Chamber will refer to them as "principal perpetrators" or "persons who carried out the *actus* of the crime" when considering the facts of this case.

The appellant in his appeal argued that the evidence adduced at trial did not prove (and the Trial Chamber did not find) that the principal perpetrators were members of Joint Criminal Enterprise, and thus a verdict of guilt, a conviction, and a sentence of thirty-eight years entered against him were not supported. The prosecutor did not appeal against the trial finding that the principal perpetrators who carried out the *actus reus* (guilty act) of the crime were non-members of the Joint Criminal Enterprise. The appeal as a matter of law should have succeeded on this ground.

Nevertheless, the Appeals Chamber concluded that in order to sustain a conviction based on the trial finding, the "principal perpetrators" or "persons who carried out the *actus reus* of the crime" must be found to have been members of the Joint Criminal Enterprise in which the accused participated.

The Appeals Chamber then concluded that the principal perpetrators were members of the Joint Criminal Enterprise and relied on that finding to confirm the conviction of the appellant. They pointed to no evidence on record, legal authority, provision in the statute of the court, or the rules of procedure and evidence to support this radical substitution of a factual finding concerning an essential element of the JCE to support the conviction imposed by the Trial Chamber.

This constituted a fundamental breach of the trust that the international community conferred on the Appeals Judges to render justice in all independence and fairness to the people of Sierra Leone. It was a violation of their oath and a serious affront to international justice, the rule of law, and civilised canons and tenets of credible justice. The judgment cannot and should not be invoked and relied on as precedent for the emerging international criminal law.

## Test of Judicial Scrutiny

The Charles Taylor trial and all other trials at the Special Court for Sierra Leone have been touted as breaking new ground in international criminal jurisprudence by criminalising and punishing conduct hitherto uncovered by international criminal law. The casual observer might concur. Yet a careful examination of the factual evidence in the trial and appellate records establishes an alarming factual deficit that supports neither convictions nor the jurisprudence developed.

Eminent scholars have produced compelling findings supporting this assertion. Their research is applicable to all the cases that were tried at the Special Court for Sierra Leone. Moreover, these findings explain how the convictions were facilitated by trial verdicts that favoured the prosecution in all the cases. In the Charles Taylor case, the Trial Chamber relied essentially on the evidence of witnesses who testified in the previous cases, particularly in the RUF case among the adjudicated facts established in those cases, judicially noticed facts adduced in those cases, and the jurisprudence derived from them to convict.

In her well-researched book titled *Fact-Finding Without Facts: The Uncertain Evidentiary Foundations of International Criminal Convictions*, Professor Nancy Amoury Combs details an alarming paucity of facts on the trial record to support the convictions at the Special Court for Sierra Leone.[18] Professor Combs elicited material and significant contradictions in prosecution witness testimony and their prior inconsistent testimonies. This should have raised reasonable doubts in favour of the accused or cast doubts on the credibility and reliability of the witnesses. However, the Chambers came to the rescue of the prosecution by deciding their preference for oral testimony presented in court over prior statements recorded during investigations or testimony given in other trials.[19] Professor Combs concluded that at the Special Court for

Sierra Leone, for instance, "54 percent of AFRC prosecution witnesses testified in a way" that she considered "seriously inconsistent with those witnesses' pre-trial statements. The prosecution was 53 percent in the RUF case and 35 percent in the CDF case."[20]

Professor Combs discussed some of the reasons that may account for these inconsistencies, but concluded nevertheless that "inconsistencies more than the testimonial deficiencies identified in Chapter 2 are equally likely to indicate that the witness lied—either while giving a statement or while testifying."[21] In Chapter 2, she discussed instances of significant testimonial deficiencies by prosecution witnesses, which the Chambers, despite their stated preference for oral testimony adduced at trial, failed critically to consider in evaluating the credibility of prosecution witness. Rather, the Chambers overlooked these internal inconsistencies and gave credit to the witnesses, and relied on their testimonies to convict most of the time.

Professor Combs explained that education deficiencies, cultural divergences, and translation errors stood as significant fact-finding impediments that certainly accounted for many of the confused exchanges and non-responsive replies that pervade many of the trials. She concluded that, "these inconsistencies, if attributable to witnesses, should call their testimony into considerable reasonable doubts." Regrettably, this did not happen in any of the trials that took place in the Special Court for Sierra Leone.[22]

In Chapter 7, Professor Combs is particularly concerned that:

> Although the problems identified in Chapters 2 through 5 are worryingly widespread and not easily remedied through other forms of evidence gathering, they need not impair the integrity of the Trial Chambers' legal judgments so long as the Trial Chambers recognized the significance of the fact-finding impediments and treat them with the requisite seriousness. However, much of the time, the Trial Chambers did neither.[23]

Professor Combs is not alone in expressing serious reservations on the quality of evidence relied on to support convictions at the Special Court for Sierra Leone.

In his research conducted at the Special Court for Sierra Leone, Tim Kelsall concluded that "although there seems to be an emerging consensus in international circles that the Special Court for Sierra Leone has been a relative success story, this article queries that view."[24] The author provides a critical "overview of some of the political, institutional and cultural ways in which the Court failed adequately to adjust to the context in which it found itself."[25]

As a political issue, the author criticised the fact that of the thirteen indictees, Foday Sankoh, the leader of the RUF, died in the Court's custody demented; Sam Bockarie, his right-hand man, was murdered in Liberia; Johnny Paul Koroma, the renegade Major who fronted the Armed Forces Revolutionary Council, disappeared; and Charles Taylor (then) found sanctuary in Nigeria.

By contrast, only inconsequential individuals were prosecuted, like Morris Kallon and Augustine Gbao of the RUF, and Santigie Borbor Kanu, Ibrahim Bazzy Kamara, and Alex Tamba Brima of the AFRC, all of whom lacked national profiles. Issa Sesay, the interim leader of the RUF who had been decorated by President Tejan Kabbah and three Civil Defence Forces members (among them Chief Hinga Norman, the ex-Deputy Defence Minister) for his contributions to the peace process were also indicted. The arrests of these peripheral individuals and that of the CDF indictees, particularly Chief Norman (considered a national hero), elicited much hostility towards the Special Court, which endures today.[26] The author raises serious concerns about how the Trial Chambers arbitrarily removed one of the key claims by the defence that the prosecution witnesses were "massaging or making up their stories and circumvented significant contradictions and inconsistencies in the prosecution witness testimonies 'by articulating a preference for oral evidence.'"[27] The judges also permitted the prosecutor to introduce statements at trial that were recorded during the process of "re-interviewing or proofing witnesses to correct their earlier inaccuracies in their inadequate statements... which permitted the prosecutor to expand his case against the accused."[28]

The transfer of the Taylor case to The Hague was a "serious blow to the Court's Record."[29] It was controversial and potentially inhibited the ability of the defence to secure witnesses while conducting trial in The Hague. The prosecution did not face the same obstacles due to the overwhelmingly disproportionate logistical advantage the prosecutor enjoyed over the defence.

The Trial Chamber explained the holding of the Charles Taylor trial at The Hague at paragraph 9 of the trial judgment thus: "Charles Taylor was arrested by Nigeria on March 29 [2006] at the request of Liberian President Johnson-Sirleaf to surrender to the Special Court for Sierra Leone." He was arraigned on April 3, 2006. Following unspecified security concerns about holding the trial in West Africa, the Security Council, by Resolution 1688, moved the trial to The Hague.

The reason provided in paragraph 9 of the trial judgment was another abuse of the Security Council's Chapter VII authority to foster a political objective. The mere expression of security concerns, short of serious threats to peace and security, is not sufficient for the Security Council to invoke Chapter 7 authority to transfer the trial to The Hague. The trial judgment does not indicate whether Charles Taylor was provided an opportunity to be heard prior to this change of venue, which had the potential to adversely affect his case preparation.

Dr. Kelsall is concerned that the "shamefully shambolic and compromised nature of the investigations at least in two of the cases" has the potential to compromise the legacy of the court.[30] The author laments that the end product of the case of Trial Chamber was "was extremely laborious and time-consuming with judgments that rested on very questionable evidential foundations."[31] The author criticises the court vehemently for completely ignoring the Sierra Leonean perspective which, if given due consideration, would have assisted in the interpretation of evidence adduced and the understanding of concepts that were relevant to crimes alleged, like recruitment of child soldiers and bush wives. To underscore the relevance of the hybrid nature of the court, the Trial Chambers were obliged to call and consider this evidence.

According to Dr. Kelsall, the Sierra Leonean traditional marriage takes a "clientelistic rural social order based on relations between families and the consent of the wife is immaterial," whereas the traditional rites of initiation prevalent in Sierra Leone "renders the traditional concept of adulthood in rural Sierra Leone different from those found in international legal instruments."[32] The author argues that ignoring the Sierra Leone concepts of childhood and wife and criminalising them to convict the accused occasioned grave injustice. The author concludes by stating that, "the court may have fallen short of high-minded aims to hold fair trials and embed the rule of law, but Sierra Leone remains at peace, and the country has partly the court to thank for that that."[33]

## Conclusion

The temptation for international tribunals and courts to draw inspiration from the Taylor trial and conviction at the Special Court as well as other previous trials may be great, considering political statements and press reports praising these convictions. Such a tendency is replete with potential landmines.

A critical examination and analysis of the evidence, law, and jurisprudence generated at the Special Court raises critical questions that required critical answers concerning the evidentiary basis of the lengthy convictions, the soundness of the jurisprudence established, and the questionable interpretation and application of international jurisprudence produced in other courts to the specific context of the Special Court. This raises the fundamental problem of the harmony of judicial decisions and judgments, and the consistency of decisions in international courts and tribunals. It is therefore unsafe for these tribunals to apply untested and unverified jurisprudence developed from a questionable evidential basis. Without scrupulous analysis, the jurisprudence of the Special Court for Sierra Leone in the Taylor case (or other cases before that court as demonstrated) have potential risks of rendering serious injustice to accused parties and to the integrity of International Criminal Justice.

## Notes

1. Thomas Escritt and Anthony Deutsch, "Former Liberian leader Charles Taylor sentenced to 50 years in prison," *Christian Science Monitor*, May 30, 2012, http://www.csmonitor.com/World/Latest-News-Wires/2012/0530/Former-Liberian-leader-Charles-Taylor-sentenced-to-50-years-in-prison-video.
2. Transcript of the opening statement of the Prosecutor of the SCSL David Crane, July 5, 2004, p. 28, paras. 6-11.
3. Paras. 269, 270 of the trial judgment.
4. Para. 274 of the trial judgment.
5. Para. 284 of the trial judgment.
6. Paras. 288 and 289 of the trial judgment.

7.   Para. 284 of the trial judgment

8.   Para. 289 of the trial judgment

9.   SLSL-04-15-I trial judgment dated March 2, 2009, appeals judgment dated October 26, 2009.

10.  Para. 329, RUF trial judgment.

11.  Footnote 608, RUF trial judgment.

12.  Para. 491, RUF trial judgment.

13.  See Judicial notice para. 520 of the RUF trial judgment.

14.  Para. 609 of the RUF trial judgment.

15.  Paras. 316, 317 (in particular para. 317), footnote 720, citing Brdanin Appeals Judgment, para. 431, Martić Appeals Judgment, para. 172. Krajišnik Appeals Judgment, paras. 283, 707, 800.

16.  Para. 395 of the Appeals Judgment, RUF case.

17.  The Appeals footnote refers to para. 1992 of the trial judgment.

18.  Nancy Amoury Combs, *Fact-Finding Without Facts: The Uncertain Evidentiary Foundations of International Criminal Convictions*, Cambridge University Press, 2010. Professor Nancy Amoury Combs is a Professor of Law at the William and Mary Law School where she is the 2009-2011 Cabell Research Professor and a 2008 recipient of William and Mary's Alumni Fellowship for teaching excellence.

19.  See numerous examples cited at pages 106—129 of Fact –Finding Without Facts.

20.  Pages 118 and 119. In footnotes 539, 540 and 541, the author provided a detailed explanation about how she arrived at the statistics she has cited to support her findings. She explains

21.  Page 128. cChapter 2 is found at pages 21-62,

22.  Pages 106-119; see in also detailed support for her findings provided in the foot-notes in those pages.

23.  *Ibid.*, p. 189.

24.  Tim Kelsall, "Insufficient Hybrid: Assessing the Special Court for Sierra Leone," *Critical Assessment of International Criminal Courts*, edited by Magda Karagiannakis, The Federation Press, 2009, pages 132-153. Tim Kelsall has taught politics at the Universities of Oxford and Newcastle and is former editor of African Affairs, the world's highest impact Africanist journal. He is author of *Culture Under Cross-Examination: International Justice and the Special Court for Sierra Leone*, Cambridge University Press, 2009.

25.  *Ibid.*, p. 132.

26.  *Ibid.*, pp. 133-134.

27.  *Ibid.*, p. 138.

28.  *Ibid.*, p. 138.

29.  *Ibid.*, p. 142.

30.  *Ibid.*, p. 143.

31.  *Ibid.*, p. 145.

32.  *Ibid.*, pp. 146-147.

33.  *Ibid.*, p. 149.

# 6

# The Seven Challenges for Truth and Justice in Rwanda

THÉOGÈNE RUDASINGWA[*]

I am here to talk to you about the challenge of the problem of justice both internationally, but in this regard I will also be talking about the problem of justice in Rwanda itself.

But I want to start by thanking the organisers of this conference, which of course has come at the most opportune moment; and in this regard, I want to start by thanking Mr. John Philpot who has graciously invited me and I suppose all of you to come and have a very sincere and serious deliberation on this question of justice.

In starting to talk about the problem of justice internationally, or even in Rwanda in particular, I want also to remember some of the words of a very pre-eminent philosopher, John Rawls, who once said that justice is actually fairness. And I think for us in Rwanda or for us as human beings across the world, and in history, we want to look at justice as fairness. He also says that truth, in philosophy, is what actually justice is in social institutions. And he went on to say that if something is forced, then we have an inclination to abandon it simply because it does not hold, especially as far as philosophers are concerned. He also says that if social institutions are unjust, then we should be inclined to abandon these institutions, even when we might say that these institutions serve as many people as possible.

So as our starting point in this discussion, I would wish to simply reiterate that *justice* is *fairness,* and that truth as well as justice is what underlies some of the endeavours that we as human beings are trying to achieve in the whole of human history or human civilisation.

\* Transcription of Speech by Theogène Rudasingwa at the Third International Conference on the Defence of International Criminal Law, "International Criminal Justice: Justice for Whom?" Montreal, Québec, September 29, 2012, translated by Carmen Nono.

Let me go now to the question of justice in Rwanda because I think if there is a society in contemporary time that poses this question in its very direct and stark terms, it is the question of justice in Rwanda.

## Five Burdens

If we had a movie that tried to capture the movement of Rwandan society over the ages, over history, we could try to look at this movie having isolated the role of the individual or the impact of what has being going on in society on the individual level. We could also try to look at the level of the family, the community, the nation, and the region—because Rwanda is nested in the region and it has impacted the region as much as impacted the country itself—and also look at it from a perspective of the African continent and yes, even look at it from an international perspective. Then in this movie we would look, for example, how Rwanda has been governed from the monarchy to the colonial regime in the twentieth century, to the post-independence or the post-colonial regimes, including those that were labelled Hutu regimes and the current one, the regime of the Rwandan Patriotic Front, which is of course labelled the Tutsi regime; and we would also pose the question, what next? And then when we look at this movie of Rwandan society over history, over millennia, over centuries, I have tended to look at five burdens that seem to weigh on the individual, the family, the community, the Rwandan Nation, the region, Africa, and the international community as a whole.

The first is the burden of history. Rwanda's history is quite burdensome because we tend to have so many perspectives. To many the history is that of kings in Rwanda; to many others it's the history of the colonial enterprise, I mean those who spent a lot of time trying to colonise Rwanda and who tend to look at themselves as the initiators of history, so that before them probably it was a dark history and after them probably something worse happened. And among the Rwandan people we tend to look at it differently. For example, after the RPF took over in 1994, history was such a challenging aspect of what we wanted to do that for many years, actually, the history of Rwanda was not taught to anybody. Because, what could we teach? How are we supposed to be teaching the history of Rwanda, when we tend to look at it in very, very different ways?

And so there is a burden of history. The kings, for example, believe that history ended in 1959. Those who initiated the Rwandan Revolution probably believe perhaps that history began in 1959. And ever since the RPF took over in 1994, it has tried to re-engineer history to sell its narrative. So there are all these competing narratives in Rwanda so that history has become a burden. Yet it is in history that we find ourselves, Hutus, Tutsis, and Twas, as a Nation, because Rwanda is a Nation that is centuries old, unlike many other entities on the African continent that would probably say that we are created by the colonial enterprise. So there is a burden of history.

The second burden is that of demography, which means we have the burden of the constituents of the demographic structure in terms of ethnicity and of region, and yes, even in terms of population pressures. When people look at Rwanda, many would look at Hutu, others might look at Tutsi, others at the Twa, others at the Hutu from the South or from the North, the so-called Bakiga/Banyenduga dichotomy. It is also a fact that we are a highly populated country. This in itself poses a challenge in terms of how we live together, and how we manage the country for the benefit of everyone. So this question of demography burdens us.

The third burden is that of the state. The ancient state, the pre-colonial state, was a state built by the kings, and they of course took their own advantage. When the colonial process began at the end of the nineteenth century and most of the twentieth century, the colonial state was super-imposed on the existing monarchical system. So some of the burdens that the king as a king and the people as subjects already inherited from many centuries, the colonial enterprise, over and above the king, created this kind of social language. Some of the king's excesses were pronounced during the colonial enterprise and of course were not abandoned after we got independence. So the state has been at the heart of some of the serious injuries and serious trauma that have been imposed or inflicted on the individual, on the family, and on the communities in Rwanda. This is in itself a burden.

There is also the burden of the Church, because for over a hundred years, we have been Christianised. We've become a special nation of Christians and probably over ninety percent of the people in Rwanda are Christians. This in itself is a burden in the sense that the Church in its life has also had sometimes very close (sometimes too close for comfort) relations with the state and sometimes there has been friction between the Church and the state. This has created some of the problems we have today.

Of course there has been the problem of the foreigners who have been coming to Rwanda for quite a while. Sometimes the foreigners have engineered and re-engineered our own ideas and our own practice to the extent that sometimes it has caused some of the problems that we still experience today.

So there is the burden of history, the burden of demography, the burden of the State, the burden of the Church, and the burden of the foreigners.

But the question which is important for today's discussion is what next, given this long history that has been a burden but in which there has been the good and the bad? How do we see the future? Because the current situation in Rwanda does not provide fairness, does not provide justice, and the institutions that we have in the country have not been seen as being fair. And therefore, it is the considered view of many Rwandans that we need to have justice in the country because there is no fairness in the country.

## Seven Challenges

Looking at the question of justice in Rwanda, I can simply say that there are probably seven challenges we need to be thinking about as we look forward. First, how do we stop the trauma? Because with all these burdens, and especially the burden of the state, Rwanda has indeed come to a situation where we could say that for so many decades the state has been at the heart of traumatising Rwandan individuals, Rwandan families, and the Rwandan community.

How do we stop this kind of trauma, which exists in several dimensions? We have the political trauma in the country, living with the closure of the political space. We have trauma in terms of many people who are in jail. We have trauma in terms of fear and daily haunting that take place within Rwanda. People are in jail in Rwanda, people are in jail in Arusha, and we have people in jungles of the Congo. We have refugees; we have civil society that has been denied a space to operate. There is no media that are able to operate as they should. And so we have immense trauma that has impacted on the people for a long time. How do we stop it?

Number two: how do we heal? It is simply not enough to stop the trauma that has been imposed on the individual. Even in usual medical terms, you also have to stop the trauma and help the person to begin to heal.

Number three: not only should we stop the trauma and heal, we should be able to unite the Rwandan nation, because the Rwandan nation has been ruptured. It has been traumatised to the extent that right now, we are a completely polarised nation in both ethnic and regional terms. So we need to figure out how do we unite this nation?

Number four: at the heart of this enterprise of stopping the trauma, of healing, of uniting the Rwandan people, we must put the individual Rwandan at the heart of whatever we attempt to undertake. As John Rawls would argue, you cannot sacrifice individual rights simply because you're saying that you want to do good for the community. I think there should be help about this, but at the very beginning of the process, the life of the individual, the rights of the individual must be protected and protected in a very strong way that begins to embrace the question of trauma, healing, and uniting the Rwandan people.

Number five: we must of course balance the individual versus community interests. Rwandans live on the hill, they live in these places where they have lived as communities for a long time. As Rwandans, they have not always killed each other as many historians make us believe, and so we would like this aspect to be understood. But the community interests must also be protected because that's where the individual finds himself or herself, and the community will also help the individual to heal. And if we have free individuals within a community, one will also suppose that the community will benefit a lot from these free individuals.

Number six: we have to redefine what people call the national interest. Until now, the national interest has been defined in terms of the interests of a small group of people. Whether it was the interest of the king and the Tutsi chiefs, whether it was the colonial enterprise with the few people who serviced the colonial undertaking or the post-colonial regimes, whether called the Hutu regime or the Tutsi regime, it has always been the person at the top with a few people who define what is called the national interest. And so we must begin to build the kind of institutions that really consider the individual Rwandan, the community interests of Rwandans (be they Hutu, Tutsi, or Twa), to be at the basis of what the institution should be. People in Rwanda must be able to look at themselves being represented in the institutions, and they must be sure that the institution promotes and propagates the rule of law so that all Rwandans know that they have equal opportunity and that they are equal before the law.

Finally, this also relates to international law, because much of what we know as international law has come to the forefront with the International Criminal Tribunal for Rwanda. We know now that the ICTR has tried so many people accused of having participated in the genocide, and literally most of them are Hutus. There has been a demonisation internationally, and it is still so because of the narrative in place for a long time. Actually this international law has not been fair; it has not been just because many Rwandans feel that it has been leaning towards favouring the Tutsi against the Hutu.

I think it's very important to understand that in the current regime there are Tutsi officers who committed crimes in Rwanda, who committed crimes in the Congo, including president Kagame himself, and all of these have not been held accountable for the crimes they have committed. So I think we must make sure that we struggle to make sure that international law serves the interests of all Rwandans without distinctions. By doing that I think it would be an immense contribution because Rwandans could also contribute to the development of international law. International law that really serves a faction of Rwandans does not help justice in Rwanda.

This would be the kind of round bargain that we should have on these issues of justice and fairness because we must go beyond ethnicity, we must go beyond narrow regionalism, and we must go beyond very beautiful laws and a brief constitution that elites are able to write and yet are unable to implement to ensure that justice and fairness are anchored in the interests of the Rwandan people.

I will conclude that this entire enterprise would be a grand bargain that would look at the interests of all Rwandans, and would support the individual, promote the community, and serve the nation as a whole. At the same time it would serve international law, and be served by international law, in a fair and just way. I think it must be finally anchored in truth, going back to John Rawls' question of truth. This is what I think is very important, because Rwandans in their vicious interests sometimes have been able to perpetuate falsehoods so as to champion the interests of the faction. For now we must challenge these falsehoods and begin to look at each other and begin to tell the truth so that we can find number two, namely healing. Another concluding remark is that in truth we can find forgiveness and in forgiveness we can also perpetuate the culture of truth among us, among the Rwandan people.

It boils down to a bunch of ideas. All these notions of justice, truth, and fairness, and the question of what history should do, the questions of demography, the state, the Church, the role of foreigners—somehow it has been a contest of ideas throughout history, throughout human history. Rwanda should cease to be the country where people die *because* of their ideas.

I think that Wole Soyinka, the famous writer from Nigeria, once said that in most African countries, including his own Nigeria, and especially in post-colonial history, it has not been a question of 'I am right and you are wrong'; no, it is 'if you're wrong, you must die.' We must contend with the idea of people suffering because of their ideas, since this is also part of the problem of Rwanda. We must understand that we as Rwandans, we and the international community, including the participants who were heard today, should understand that these are a bundle of ideas and occasionally people will suffer and die for what they believe in. I think this is how ideas have been propagated throughout history—that's how new ideas have come about, that's how negotiations have come about, and we must be able to contend with new ideas in our society especially if there are ideas that are propelling the society towards truth and justice in our country.

Thank you very much

# 7

# The ICC and Kenya:
# Going Beyond the Rhetoric

CHIEF CHARLES A. TAKU

## Introduction

In 2010, Professor Nancy Amoury Combs stated, "International criminal justice was, in sum, the subject of a great deal of soaring and inspirational rhetoric but in recent years, the glow surrounding international criminal justice has begun to fade."[1] Citing developments at the ICC, the International Criminal Tribunal for Rwanda, and the Special Court for Sierra Leone, among others, she concluded that, "many have begun questioning the ability of international criminal tribunals to achieve many of the goals that previously had been reflexively attributed to them."

Professor Combs asserted that recent research has called into question the ability of international criminal tribunals to advance reconciliation and peace-building efforts following large-scale violence. Despite the loss of faith in international criminal justice, in particular by Africa, the distinguished author concluded that, "even if they regularly fail to deter, rehabilitate, or reconcile, international trials have at least been considered useful mechanisms for determining who did what to whom during a mass atrocity."[2]

The developments in the *Situation in the Republic of Kenya* Pre-Trial at the ICC have provided a reasonable basis for the frustrations and indictment of international criminal justice in the terms depicted by Professor Combs.

## Beyond the Rhetoric

The prosecutor of the ICC, Fatou Bensouda, and a significant number of non-governmental organisations, special interest groups, human rights

organisations, and political activists in and out of Kenya have made public allegations about "unprecedented levels of interference" with prosecution witnesses and evidence by the Kenyan accused.[3] Bensouda alleged
the politicisation of the cases by the African Union and the government
of Kenya, and stated lack of cooperation by the government in supporting her numerous requests to gather evidence within the territory of the
Republic of Kenya. She cited the intimidation of protected witnesses and
their families as well as defence interference with witnesses, whom she
later withdrew in Case No. 1[4] and Case No. 2.[5] Challenged by the defence
to prove the allegations of the unprecedented levels of interference with
prosecution witnesses, the prosecutor responded by applying for a warrant for the arrest of one of its own intermediaries, Walter Barasa.[6]

There are significant underlying reasons that may explain why, notwithstanding these allegations, the Kenyan cases are falling apart. Some
arise from the prosecutor's theories of the cases and significant pre-trial
case management missteps. Key prosecutorial decisions taken at the
initial stages might also have contributed to the dire situation in which
the ICC finds itself regarding these and other ICC African situations.[7]

Beyond the rhetoric behind these allegations, the prosecutor made
a conscious decision to interject in a highly volatile political situation
and politicised the case from inception. The Pre-Trial Chamber was
concerned that the *proprio motu* (i.e. on their own initiative)[8] intervention in the *Situation in the Republic of Kenya* Pre-Trial could be politically motivated. In raising this problem at the earliest possible moment,
the Pre-Trial Chamber echoed the fears expressed by a number of state
parties during discussions leading to the Rome Statute in 1998. In this
regard, the Pre-Trial Chamber stated:

> Thus, it suffices to mention that, insofar as *proprio motu* investigations
> by the prosecutor are concerned, both proponents and opponents of the
> idea feared the risk of politicizing the Court and thereby undermining its
> "credibility." In particular, they feared that providing the prosecutor with
> such "excessive powers" to trigger the jurisdiction of the Court might
> result in its abuse.[9]

The Chamber struggled with this crucial problem and concluded
that in the exercise of its "supervisory role over the *proprio motu* initiative of the prosecutor to proceed with an investigation," it can fulfill

this function by "applying the exact standard on the basis of which the prosecutor arrived at his conclusion" and that there "is a reasonable basis to proceed with an investigation."[10]

In this decision the Chamber reasonably perceived that politics could complicate the case (as indeed they have), and unsuccessfully attempted to resolve the problem. Unfortunately, the legal threshold established by the Chamber in the confirmation of charges introduced considerable pitfalls in the cases which the prosecutor might not have anticipated or foreseen at the time. The Pre-Trial Chamber appropriately identified the potential political underpinnings of the prosecutor's *proprio motu* intervention, but failed to define or set the limits between the politics, the crimes, and the law of the cases. Rather, the Chamber compounded the problem by merely rubberstamping the very low threshold on the basis of which the prosecutor's application was grounded.[11]

In paragraph 52 of the confirmation of charges decision, the Chamber noted that, "the drafters of the Statute established... progressively higher evidentiary thresholds under articles [15], 58(1), 61(7) and 66(3) of the Statute." The Chamber, by deferring to Article 15 in this hierarchy of evidentiary thresholds, effectively endorsed the standard established at the authorisation of investigation for the confirmation of charges. In this regard, the Chamber specified that "the evidentiary threshold applicable at the present stage of the proceedings (i.e., 'substantial grounds to believe') is higher than the one required for the issuance of a warrant or summons to appear but lower than that required for a final determination as to guilt or innocence of an accused."[12]

The progression of thresholds established in this case led to the approval of the prosecution's applications and charges during the pre-trial proceedings. There can therefore be no refuting that the legal processes that occurred at the pre-trial stage of the Kenyan cases were not subjected to reasonable scrutiny. The failure in this regard might be haunting the trial processes as the prosecutor struggles to circumvent the pitfalls to which the cases were consigned at that phase of the proceedings.

This problem is not uncommon in international criminal tribunals. David Tolbert and Fergal Gaynor stated:

[T]he Statutes of the Tribunals require a judge to confirm an indictment brought by the prosecutor, applying a *prima facie* review standard as laid down in the ICTR Statute Art. 19(1). This requires a judge to be satisfied that the material submitted by the prosecutor provides a 'credible case,' which would (if not contradicted by the defence) be a sufficient basis to convict the accused on the charge.[13]

The application of this standard has inevitably resulted in the confirmation of the indictment and is seen in many cases as simply a "rubber stamp." The authors were concerned that the "Statutes of the Tribunals do not require judges to have any trial experience, nor is any judicial training mechanism in place for trial experience. Pre-trial judges should be more involved and make efforts to be familiar with the case to ensure that it is trial ready for trial."

Tolbert and Gaynor strongly advised:

[G]iven the seriousness of the charges in international tribunals, and the importance of the cases both to the charged persons and the victims, there is an argument that the standard should be set at a higher level and indictments subject to more intense scrutiny before confirmation. This may help in stopping weak cases from going forward, which result in lengthy pre-trial detention and where acquittals or low sentences result in disappointment to victim groups.[14]

Rubberstamping the prosecutor's "conclusion" in the decision authorising investigation in the post-election violence in the Republic of Kenya, the Chamber reasoned:

The Chamber, in turn, is mandated to review the conclusion of the prosecutor by examining the available information, including his request, the supporting material as well as the victim's representations collectively, the "available information" if, upon examination, the Chamber considers the "reasonable basis to proceed" standard is met, it shall authorize the commencement of the investigation.[15]

This low threshold established during pre-trial proceedings facilitated the admission without serious scrutiny of questionable evidence to confirm charges against the accused. Statements provided by Witness No. 4 in Case No. 2[16] and Witnesses Nos. 11 and 12 in Case No. 1[17] fell in this category. The defence provided compelling evidence during confirmation-of-charges proceedings that significantly undermined the credibility and reliability of these witnesses. The Chamber nevertheless proceeded to admit their testimonies based on this low threshold. The prosecutor has since established that these witnesses lied in statements they provided to the prosecutor during the pre-trial proceedings and therefore dropped them. Nevertheless the prosecutor is proceeding with the trials on the basis of charges that were confirmed using the false statements while alleging without proof "unprecedented levels" of interference with a number of prosecution witnesses, including these individuals.

The perception by victims and the public in Kenya that some legal representatives of victims participating in the proceedings were not acting as independent voices of the victims may have contributed to a loss of faith in the trial proceedings. Some of the legal representations have adopted controversial positions presented by the prosecutor at trial most of the time. Victims required independent voices to strongly present their cases independent of that of the prosecutor. Pre-Trial Chamber 1 defined the role of legal representative of victims in the Lubanga case as follows:

> In the Chamber's opinion, the Statute grants victims an independent voice and role in proceedings before the Court. It should be possible to exercise this independence, in particular vis-a-vis the prosecutor of the ICC so that victims can present their interests. As a European Court has affirmed on several occasions, victims participating in criminal proceedings cannot be regarded as either the opponent—or for that matter necessarily the ally—of the prosecution, their roles and objectives being clearly different.[18]

The perception that the supposedly independent voices of common victims' representatives have not been heard on a number of legal and evidentiary issues touching on the interest of victims has tainted public perception of the trials.

## Stepping on Sensitive Political, Ethnic, and Cultural Nerves

The prosecutor, Moreno Ocampo, chose the public media as a platform to lay out his cases from the moment he made known his intention to intervene in the *Situation in the Republic of Kenya*. In so doing, he made the media a legitimate arena for the litigation of the cases. This venue of choice attracted a plethora of participants, some intended, others not. The media has since influenced public opinion on the cases in ways unimagined.

A significant media influence arose from the decision by the prosecutor to recruit some media practitioners as intermediaries in conducting investigations. The evidence collected through this process was presented before the Pre-Trial Chamber for confirmation of charges against the accused and in the unfolding trials. Mr. Barasa, a journalist practicing in the Rift Valley against whom the prosecutor had secured a warrant of arrest and transfer to the court for witness tampering, was recruited by the prosecutor to help in gathering evidence against accused in Case No. 1. It is unclear how this suspect tampered with witnesses whom he had a prosecutor's mandate to recruit. It is hoped that the proceedings against him, when and if they occur, will open a window to the world about the manner and tactics the prosecutor used to collect the evidence she is relying on to pursue these prosecutions. It may reveal a consistent pattern of questionable prosecutorial tactics that a Trial Chamber of the ICC criticised and warned against in the Lubanga trial.[19]

In his public media statements and in public court documents, the prosecutor laid out his case in political, cultural, and ethnic terms,[20] which carried significant risks. An obvious risk was the possibility that alternative explanations might account for the existence of these factors during the election violence. The alternative explanations could undermine the prosecutor's theories of the cases.

The prosecutor disregarded the political trends and shifting political alliances that are known influential factors in Kenyan politics. Like past elections, these factors were present during the election in which the alleged crimes occurred. The presence of these unpredictable political trends significantly undermined the theoretical relevance of assumed ethnic allegiance and cultural homogeneity that were claimed as facilitators of the alleged crimes. Contrary to this theory, the political forces that existed during the elections transcended alleged ethnic and cultural compartments in which the purported crimes were locked.

All ethnicities in Kenya were active in all the political parties, fielded candidates in the elections, and reacted differently to victory and defeat in their respective constituencies. The fact that some of the parties commanded a majority within distinct ethnic and cultural groups in locations where the crimes were alleged to have been committed did not undermine this reality. This significant factor was not seriously considered, and where considered was not given the attention it deserved.

The prosecutor of the International Criminal Tribunal for Rwanda was confronted with a similar situation in the case of *The Prosecutor v. Augustin Ndindiliyimana, Augustin Bizimungu, Francois-Xavier Nzuwonemeye, and Innocent Sagahutu.*[21] In that case, the prosecutor struggled to explain every conceivable crime that occurred in Rwanda in 1994 in ethnic terms.

When the ICTR was established, UN investigative reports held the Rwandan Patriotic Front accountable for the crimes that led to the extermination of hundreds of thousands of Hutu, in particular in areas that were entirely under the RPF occupation throughout the war.

Unlike the ICC prosecutor, the ICTR prosecutor acknowledged that serious crimes were perpetrated against the Hutu and promised to investigate. Recognising the occurrence and magnitude of these crimes and undertaking to investigate at first gave the investigations a presumption of legitimacy. Regrettably, the tyranny of victors' justice left the ICTR prosecutor struggling to place the responsibility for the crimes that were perpetrated against Hutu victims (whom the prosecutor categorised as "moderates") on other Hutu whom she claimed to identify and categorised as "extremists."

At the trial, the prosecutor did not convincingly explain or establish the circumstantial categorisation of Hutu into "moderate" and "extremist." The prosecutor failed to account adequately for the massacre of hundreds of thousands of Rwandan citizens of Hutu and Twa ethnicity and to justify his inability to investigate and prosecute alleged perpetrators of the crimes. Like the ICTR, the inability of the ICC prosecutor to conduct proper investigations into all the crimes alleged significantly undermined her claims of seeking justice for victims and her supposed record of fighting impunity.

It may reasonably be discerned from Mr. Ocampo's numerous press statements that he intervened in the Kenya political arena when the perpetration of crimes was ongoing with a preconceived list of suspects and a case theory that perceived the crimes in ethnic terms. Once he sought and received permission of the Pre-Trial Chamber to open investigations, he found no need to conduct proper investigations to obtain credible evidence against all perpetrators of all crimes irrespective of ethnicity, or other discriminatory grounds. As a result, the cases he brought for trial lacked legitimacy in the eyes of a sizeable component of Kenyan citizens and victims. This may explain the lack of support the cases may be experiencing among the victims, witnesses, and the public at large. The alleged ethnic, cultural, and political foundations of the cases, both factual and theoretical, were therefore mired in serious controversy from inception.

On or about September 10, 2013, the prosecutor delivered her opening statement in Case No. 1. The statement was illustrated by, among other evidentiary material, videos of the Kalenjin elders in session performing traditional rites. The prosecutor, when laying out her case, failed to give serious consideration to the potential backlash that criminalising aspects of the Kalenjin and Kikuyu culture and traditions might cause. Alleging that Kalenjin initiation rites and protected cultural practices were used to perpetrate, or facilitate the perpetration of, crimes stated in the indictment was a serious misjudgment. The prosecutor came out, in the view of many Africans across the continent, as culturally insensitive. The misjudgment in this regard could potentially persuade some victims, witnesses, and their families to decide against participating in the trial process.

Evidence concerning sensitive aspects of the culture and traditions of victims, witnesses, and the public at large was treated with caution at the Special Court for Sierra Leone and the ICTR. Exposing to the world evidence on the initiation rites of a people and other aspects of their culture considered sacred is seen in most of Africa to be a serious affront to the cultural identity of the people. Alexander Zahar and Goran Sluiter[22] offered the following unpleasant opinion on a finding in the introductory section of the Akayesu judgment at the ICTR:

> In the introductory section of the Akayesu judgment, which offers a potted history of Rwanda, we are told that in the early twentieth century the distinction between Hutu and Tutsi was based on lineage rather than ethnicity. We are told not consistently that the demarcation line was blurred (one could move from one status to another).[23]

In footnote 11, the authors described this finding as "simplistic, tendacious, at times incoherent and full of inaccuracies."[24]

The safeguarding and protection of African cultures and traditions have been at the centre of African consciousness. Frantz Fanon decried the fact that "the indigenous population of Africa is discerned by the west as an indistinct mass."[25] Senghor wrote that the role of the intellectual has at least two responsibilities in his society: "First, to perceive what is good for his country, while holding intact the traditions of the past. The intellectual is one who must, in order to have a true national consciousness, be aware of his tradition and the sources of his past, a past which is still relevant even as he creates in reaction to it."[26]

Writing about advocates of African heritage, Wilfred Cartey and Marin Kilson stated:

> [T]o validate one's heritage, to explore one's culture, to examine thoroughly those institutions which have persisted through centuries is perhaps the first step in a people's search for independence, in their quest for freedom from foreign domination. Such a validation, such an exploration and examination is resolutely undertaken at the turn of the nineteenth and beginning of twentieth century by four Africans, Casely Hayford, Jomo Kenyatta, James Africanus B. Horton, and Edward Blyden.[27]

This spirit was and is alive in Kenya and most of Africa. It is the driving force of African renaissance and the ongoing struggle for freedom from the pervasive influences of neo-colonialism in the continent. The cultural sensitivities transgressed in these cases in laying out the prosecutor's case cannot therefore be minimised or wished away.

## The Political Card

It cannot be denied that prior to intervening, the prosecutor seriously considered the political implications of his decision. Some of the intermediaries whom the prosecutor relied on to gather evidence in these cases have been publicly identified as participants in the contentious elections that led to the violence in 2007-2008. They again participated in the last elections, which the accused and their supporters won resoundingly. Their involvement in the cases was bound to be problematic. This category of individuals has sustained the political spotlight and media frenzy on the cases.

The theory of the cases around the land disputes involving the different ethnicities in the conflict areas is not only a sensitive matter; it also carries a significant political implication. The problem is indisputably tied to Kenya's and Africa's colonial past with ongoing ramifications. Jomo Kenyatta, the first president of Kenya, spoke for his people but also for the entire continent when he aptly underscored the highly political nature of the land problem. On July 26, 1952, he did not mince his words during a rally organised by the Kenya African Union at the Nyeri Show Grounds attended by a crowd of thirty thousand people; Kenyatta decried the fact that in the Kikuyu country, nearly half of the people were landless and had an earnest desire to acquire land so they have something to live on. The Africans, Kenyatta said, "had not agreed that this land was to be used by white men alone." He went on, "Peter Mbitu is still in the UK where we sent him for land hunger. We expect a Royal Commission to quickly inquire the land problem."[28]

Bringing up the land issue as a factor and criminalising it in the 2007-2008 election gave the accused a talking point, which resonated with popular sentiment. It equally sparked tensions and mobilised opposition to the cases brought against the accused. The fact that during this period some surviving Mau Mau fighters were pursuing a longstanding case against the British government for the crimes Kenyatta denounced during the 1952 rally carried symbolic weight.

Considered separately or in aggregate, prosecutorial case management misjudgments and a limited knowledge of the political and cultural environment in which the alleged crimes were perpetrated provided an alibi for the charge of a neo-colonial conspiracy to have the accused jailed. The political, ethnic, and cultural foundations on which the prosecution is based has played to the fears of many people in Africa and Kenya, in particular given that the prosecutions are neo-colonial manoeuvres to deny them the benefit of credible leadership, which the accused secured the Kenyan peoples' mandate to provide. The charge of a neo-colonial conspiracy to use the ICC process to effect regime change has since become the rallying cry in the continent for those opposed to the ICC selective prosecutions targeting Africans.

Many vividly remember the prophetic premonition of Osagyefo Kwame Nkrumah, Ghana's founding president, concerning the vulnerability of many African countries and the threat posed to their sovereignty by neo-colonialism:

> This arrangement gives the appearance of nationhood to African territories but the substance of sovereignty rests with metropolitan power. The creation of several weak and unstable states in Africa, it was hoped, would ensure the continued dependence on the former colonial powers for economic aid, and impede African unity.[29]

The following statement by the late president of Tanzania, Mwalimu Julius Kambarage Nyerere, confirmed these fears and enjoined Africans to summon the values of the past to redress the challenges of the moment: "Although we do not claim to have drawn up a blueprint of the future, the values and objectives of our society have been stated several times."[30] The perception of insensitivity to these African values by the ICC prosecutor is a launching pad for the opposition to the ICC Kenyan cases on the African continent led by some influential progressive forces.

The politics of the ICC Kenya cases are further compounded by the controversial double standards established by other political actors involved in these and other cases at the ICC. An article in *The New York Times* on June 2, 2014, illustrates this point. US Ambassador to the United Nations Samantha Power expressed outrage against the Soviet Federation for vetoing a Security Council Resolution, referring the Situation in Syria to the ICC. Ambassador Power stated: "Our grandchildren will ask us years from now how we could have failed to bring justice to people living in hell on earth." According to the journalist, her remarks "were part of an unusual American push to widen the reach of the global tribunal." Emphasising the hypocrisy and political motivations surrounding this supposedly pro-ICC stand, the journalist stated:

> [T]hat perception could not come at a worse time for a court whose biggest challenge is to convince the world that its investigations are not directed by politics. It has been criticised for indicting a disproportionately large share of Africans. It has won only two convictions in the course of a decade. It has been unable to apprehend several men it has indicted-including the former Libyan dictator Co. Muammar el-Qaddafi's son, Seif al-Islam el-Qaddaffi, whose investigation the United States supported.[31]

## Conclusion

The Situation in the Republic of Kenya has dominated the agenda of the prosecutor of the ICC. This preoccupation has diverted the attention of the prosecutor from crimes falling within the jurisdiction of the Court in other parts of the world.

The extraordinary problems facing the prosecutor in these cases arose from significant misjudgments that occurred at the pre-trial stage of the proceedings. These were either overlooked or were not subjected to the degree of scrutiny required in cases where serious crimes are alleged.

The integrity of witnesses and significant aspects of the evidence they provided were called into question during pre-trial proceedings, requiring further investigation. The lack of cultural sensitivity and awareness has impacted negatively on the image of the ICC and the integrity of the cases. Alleged "unprecedented levels of interference" and the intimidation of prosecution witnesses and their families cannot reasonably be said to be the sole reason for the problems that the prosecutor is facing in these cases. Many of these problems were inherited from prosecutor Ms. Bensouda's predecessor, Moreno Ocampo. The prosecutor therefore has reasonable cause to seriously consider whether it is worthwhile proceeding with these cases under these circumstances.

## Notes

1.  Nancy Amoury Combs, *Fact–Finding Without Facts: The Uncertain Evidentiary Foundations of International Criminal Convictions*, Cambridge University Press, 2010.
2.  *Ibid.*, pp. 3-4.
3.  The accused in this highly politicised case include high profile personalities like the current president of Kenya, H.E. Uhuru Kenyatta and his deputy, William Ruto.
4.  ICC-PIDS-CIS-KEN-01-012/13, *The Prosecutor v. William Samoei Ruto and Joshua Arap Sang.*
5.  ICC-PIDS-CIS-KEN-02-010/11, *The Prosecutor v. Uhuru Muigai Kenyatta.*
6.  ICC-01-01/09-01/13, *The Prosecutor v. Walter Osapiro Barasa* (warrant issued on August 2, 2013 and unsealed on October 2, 2013).
7.  We cite for this purpose ICC-01/04-01/07, *The Prosecutor v. Germain Katanga*; ICC-01/01/11-01/11, *The Prosecutor v. Saif Al-Islam Gaddafi*; and ICC-02/11-01/11, *The Prosecutor v. Laurent Gbagbo.*

8. The prosecution has 'rights' to initiate investigations (on their own initiative) into a case where they deem it necessary and in accordance with the law. See for this purpose Article 15 of the Statute of the ICC.

9. ICC-01/09-19, Decision Pursuant to Article 15 of the Rome Statute, on the Authorization of an Investigation into the Situation in the Republic of Kenya.

10. Para. 24 *supra*, and para. 52 of the ICC-01/09-02/2012, *The Prosecutor v. Francis Kirimi Muthaura, Uhuru Muigai Kenyatta and Mohammed Hussein Ali, January 23, 2013.*

11. Para. 52 of the Decision, *supra*.

12. *Supra*.

13. *Prosecutor v. Haradinaj et al.,* 2007, para. 22 and *Prosecutor v. Popović et al.,* 2006. para. 36. These are both ICTY cases in which is reflected the *Prima Facie Review Standard* as embodied in Article 19(1) of the ICTR Statutes.

14. David Tolbert and Fergal Gaynor, Pre-trial: Greater Scrutiny Before Confirmation of Indictment; Pre-trial Management Use of Pre-trial Chamber or Judge, in *A Critical Assessment of International Criminal Courts,* Magda Karagiannakis, ed., La Trobe University Federation Press, 2009, p. 39.

15. Paras. 20 and 24 *supra*.

16. N. 9 *supra*.

17. N. 8 *supra*.

18. Para. 51, ICC, Situation in the Democratic Republic of Congo, Pre-trial Chamber 1, Decision on the Application for Participation in the Proceedings of VPRS 1, VPRS 2, VPRS 3, VPRS 5, and VPRS 6, January 17, 2006.

19. Judgment of Trial Chamber 1 in *Prosecutor v. Thamas Lubanga Dyilo,* dated March 14, 2012, Decision on Intermediaries, May 13, 2010.

20. The Prosecutor, Mr. Ocampo, was also rebuked by the Pre-Trial Chamber in the *Situation in Libya* due to prejudicial press statements made by him, which infringed on the suspects' rights to fair trial.

21. ICTR-00-56-T, *The Prosecutor v. Augustin Ndindiliyimana, Augustin Bizimungu, Francois-Xavier Nzuwonemeye, and Innocent Sagahutu.* The Trial Chamber entered a conviction and sentenced the accused to various terms of imprisonment. On appeal, co-counsel Beth Lyons and I obtained a reversal of the conviction of Major Francois-Xavier Nzuwonemeye and an acquittal entered in his favour, more than twelve years after he was arrested in France and transferred to the jurisdiction of the ICTR.

22. Zahar, Alexander and Sluiter, Goran, "Genocide Law: An Education in Sentimentalism: The Problem with the Group", in *International Criminal Law: A Critical Introduction,* Oxford University Press, 2008, p. 158.

23. *Supra*.

24. *Supra*.

25. Frantz Fanon, *The Wretched of the Earth,* New York, 1966, The Intellectual Elite in Revolutionary Culture, p. 126.

26. Wilfred Cartey and Martin Kilson, *The Africa Reader: Independent Africa,* "The role of the intellectual in independent Africa," Random House, New York, 1970, p. 124.

27. *Ibid.,* p 3.

28. Zahar *et al.*, *op. cit.*, p. 104.

29. Kwame Nkrumah, *Neocolonialism: Africa Must Unite*, 1964, p. 217, as reproduced in n. 3, p. 200-208.

30. Julius K. Nyerere, *Education for Self-Reliance*, Gov. Printer, Dar Es Salaam, March 1967.

31. Somini Sengupta, "Politics seen Undermining Credibility of a Court," *The New York Times*, June 2, 2014, http://www.nytimes.com/2014/06/03/world/the-hague-icc-politics-seen-undercutting-credibility-of-a-court.html?_r=0, accessed June 20, 2014.

# PART II

# The *ad hoc* International Criminal Tribunals

# 8

## The Heart of Dark Jurisprudence

PHILIPPE LAROCHELLE

To explore the Rwandan genocide through the ICTR jurisprudence is a traumatic experience. Only to probe into such an unfathomable event is a horrific encounter, but to discover the genocide through intimate involvement with the inner apparatus of the ICTR is not for the weak-minded. It is simply impossible to resist the sheer violence that engulfed Rwanda before, during, and after the genocide. Yet to work at the ICTR means to willingly embrace that violence, and to be immersed in it with the fellow lawyers and judges that erected the genocide jurisprudence shrine of the ICTR in Arusha, Tanzania.

Singling out the Rwandan genocide from the larger problems that have plagued the African Great Lakes area long before and after the 1994 genocide is in itself problematic. The disproportionate amount of resources put into the judicial response to the Rwandan genocide by the international community has contributed to occult a multitude of other serious violations of human rights in the region.

Finally, there is something completely artificial in reducing the Rwandan genocide to individual trials. There is very little room for some objective truths between the unreachable sufferings of the survivors on one end and the justified perception that the ICTR work has been completely manipulated from the outset on the other. The ensuing results of the court confrontation, be they among lawyers, human rights crusaders, champion deniers, or simply legal tourists, have a profoundly bitter aftertaste. That the ICTR has managed twenty years of survival between these two poles and repeated allegations of corruption and incompetence is a feat in itself.

The creation of the International Criminal Tribunal for Rwanda on November 8, 1994, by the United Nations Security Council, is probably the most significant effort by the international community to contribute to the end of impunity in the large-scale commission of crimes in Africa's Great Lakes region. A few months after the 1994 Rwandan genocide, it was believed that by prosecuting the persons responsible for the crimes committed in Rwanda during the genocide, the Tribunal would contribute to national reconciliation and restoration of peace. The Tribunal commenced its operations in 1995 in Arusha, Tanzania. During those early days of its operations, there is anecdotal evidence of defence lawyers meeting potential accused in Congo, Nairobi, and elsewhere, indictments being confirmed in hotel rooms, accused persons being transferred to Arusha and the Tribunal maturing into a much bigger judicial beast—one that operated for nearly two decades.

Save for a few outstanding judgments, the ICTR has nearly completed its mandate. On July 1, 2012, the Mechanism for International Criminal Tribunals (MICT) assumed the Tribunal's functions. The MICT's carefully worded statute prevents it from expanding the scope of its activities beyond the unaccomplished tasks of the ICTR.

During the Tribunal's two decades of activities, hundreds of lawyers and judges congregated in Arusha to participate in the drafting of fifty-four judgments concerning seventy-five accused (including one charge of false testimony). Out of these seventy-five accused, fifty have been convicted and fourteen acquitted. The eleven cases remaining are still under appeal.

Within the pages of these judgments, the ICTR bequeaths a substantial historical record of the genocide. One of the main complaints made by defence counsels and many scholars about the value of that record is that it does not create sufficient space for a fair assessment of the impact of Rwanda's socio-political landscape on the reliability of evidence emanating from that country. The Rwandan Patriotic Front won the war that was fought before and during the genocide, and seized power immediately after. Since July 1994, the RPF clutched on to power, using a range of well-documented illegal means to suppress dissent and remain in control of the country. The RPF has not been content with its dictatorial grasp over Rwanda; it has also invaded, occupied, and plundered the neighbouring Democratic Republic of the Congo with varying levels of intensity since 1994. Some of the suspicions lingering over the RPF even relate to crimes that should have fallen within the jurisdiction of the ICTR. In view of these circumstances, it is misguided for these judgments to refuse to factor in the prevailing legal, political, and sociological conditions of Rwanda.

Chief amongst these concerns is the danger that the historical record compiled by the ICTR was distorted by the RPF since its inception. This is not at all surprising considering that Rwanda reluctantly agreed to its creation after having resisted for various reasons, including the refusal of the Tribunal to impose the death penalty.[1] More importantly, negotiators siding with the United States recognised the fact that from the Tribunal's outset the RPF was insisting on a very limited temporal jurisdiction for the ICTR, aiming to ensure that their own liability for crimes under the statute would fall outside of the Tribunal's jurisdiction.[2] The RPF has indeed successfully evaded prosecution by the ICTR. The Tribunal's Registrar between 2001 and 2012, Mr. Adam Dieng, doesn't deny this fact, which he recognises as an issue that impacts the entire credibility of the Tribunal, while being a necessary evil since any indictment of RPF officers would effectively reach Paul Kagame himself, head of the RPF and current president of Rwanda, thus losing his indispensable cooperation.[3]

Now that the ICTR's judicial activity is winding up after almost two decades, the value of this legacy must be assessed. It is certainly no easy task to attempt to measure the Tribunal's output. While quantitative assessments such as the final price tag of each trial are interesting, this evaluation would only render a very partial view of the overall success, or failure, of such an institution. There are also intangible issues that are very difficult to price. For example, has the Tribunal contributed to eradicating impunity in Africa's Great Lakes region? Has it contributed to genuine reconciliation between the Hutu and the Tutsi in Rwanda? Such qualitative outputs are also of great interest and will most certainly be the object of years of academic study. Indeed, scholars will spend a considerable amount of time constructing a corpus of literature out of which some historical verdicts can be rendered.

## Highly Questionable Results

For those practitioners who have been intimately involved with the functioning of the ICTR, the quality of the evidence processed through

its chambers and the consistency and quality of the decisions and judgments issued by these chambers reveal a lot about the kind of justice the
Tribunal has delivered in many of the cases tried. Judges, prosecutors,
and defence counsels can offer first-hand knowledge, providing answers
to crucial questions concerning the quality of the justice rendered: Were
the trials fair? The judges unbiased and objective? The prosecutors firmly
but honestly pursuing conviction? To a certain extent these practitioners
can assess whether the Tribunal in its entirety has lived up to the expectations of the resolution creating it, namely providing national reconciliation and restoration and preservation of peace in Rwanda.

In answer to these questions, it is submitted that the ICTR has delivered highly questionable results, not only for those accused who were
paraded through its chambers, but more generally for Rwandans and
the international community as a whole.

In many instances the prosecutors have actually failed to act as officers of the court, and as a result they have seriously compromised the
mission with which they were entrusted. Furthermore, it appears that
the ICTR judges have not always been able to act as a safeguard against
such dishonest practices. As a result, the Tribunal potentially reflects a
sorely arbitrary form of justice.

An important criticism of the ICTR prosecution is the dereliction
of its duty to prosecute impartially.[4] The absence of RPF people from
the Tribunal dockets, despite converging and credible accounts of their
crimes, will remain forever an outstanding controversial feature of the
ICTR legacy, inasmuch as it can be said that the prosecutor's conduct
not only creates a problem of image, but gives serious credence to allegations that it colluded with the RPF to ensure the latter's impunity,
creating in the end what amounts to victors' justice.[5] The real problem
with Rwanda is that "victors' justice" not only conveys the notion that
the RPF is effectively shielded from prosecution for crimes committed *before* the creation of the ICTR, but also for prolonged and intense
international criminal activity throughout the existence of the ICTR.
Furthermore, it appears that the ICTR judges have not always been able
to act as a safeguard against such dishonest practices. As a result, the
Tribunal potentially reflects a sorely arbitrary form of justice.

## A Cloud of Secrecy

The better part of the ICTR's work is camouflaged by a cloud of secrecy, which makes it nearly impossible to comprehensively and exhaustively review it. While there may be well-founded reasons to remove some of the Tribunal's proceedings from public scrutiny, the confidentiality practices reflected by the ICTR's cases border on paranoia, and in many instances unnecessarily conceal material without which a full comprehension of the failings of the ICTR is made extremely complicated.

These confidentiality measures very effectively muzzle people who, by virtue of their work at the ICTR, have acquired a wider understanding and knowledge of the Tribunal's opus. These measures unfortunately have a very strong deterrent effect, and censor any leaning towards revealing Arusha's darker secrets.

*In concreto*, these confidentiality measures mean that the identities of the vast majority of the witnesses who testified before the ICTR are unknown to the public at large. These measures also cover a multitude of incidents where witnesses recanted or were threatened and intimidated. Therefore, to obtain disclosure of all evidence relevant to their cases, exculpatory or not, defence counsels were at the mercy of the prosecutor they were facing. On this point, it can safely be said that these prosecutors had varying levels of understanding of their duties. Therefore, large areas of the ICTR landscape are still only accessible to the prosecutor. The lethal combination of excessive confidentiality measures and reluctant prosecutors creates a smokescreen behind which very inconvenient truths must be brought to the open.

## The Case for an Independent Review: The East Timor Precedent

Following the completion of the work of the Special Panels of the Dili District Court, the hybrid international-East Timorese Tribunal created in 2000 in Indonesia, the Secretary General of the United Nations appointed a commission of experts to review the judicial processes through the work of these UN-sponsored judicial institutions.

Appointed in February 2005, the three members of the commission of experts rendered their report on May 26, 2005.[6] This report contains conclusions that would be equally applicable to the ICTR. The commission of experts goes as far as suggesting that cases should be reopened and that, "*de novo* trials take place and that indicted persons be retried in accordance with acceptable national and international standards."[7] The commission found that the prosecutor lacked a consistent prosecution strategy or focus, and was unable to function in a politically independent fashion.[8]

As daunting as this task may be, there are enough serious questions raised concerning the manner in which the ICTR has completed its mandate to warrant a similar exercise, particularly now that its mandate will soon be completed. In my opinion, the ICTR has failed to dispense justice in conformity with accepted international fair trial standards.

Indeed, one of the main reasons behind the incapacity of the ICTR to provide quality justice is the systemic failure of the Tribunal's prosecutor to effectively fulfill its disclosure duties. A good example of the prosecutor's dereliction of its duties is to be found in the Trial Chamber judgment in the case of *Bizimungu et al.*[9] of September 30, 2011, paragraphs 175 and 176:

175. The Prosecution's conduct in this matter is inexcusable. It failed to inform the Defence teams of exculpatory material, in some instances, for over a year. This material is clearly relevant, highly probative, and *prima facie* exculpatory of serious allegations upon which the Prosecution seeks conviction. The events, if proven, would also be highly relevant to the *mens rea* [guilty mind] of certain Accused. When one of the Defence teams communicated its inability to access this material, the Prosecution failed to ensure access for a period of almost five additional months. This conduct stands in stark contrast to the Prosecution's fundamental obligations and to the interests of justice.

176. Regardless of the root cause for the Prosecution's repeated failure to discharge one of its primary duties, this has materially prejudiced the Accused in this case. While the Defence teams should have raised this matter earlier, the reality is that the Prosecution only informed them of the exculpatory material once the Chamber was at an advanced stage in the process of drafting its judgement. Given this situation, the Chamber considers that the most appropriate remedy is to draw a reasonable inference in favour of the Accused from the exculpatory material.

That the prosecutor could be so severely warned in such an important a case[10] raises serious questions. This attitude could be explained not only by negligence, but also by recklessness, or even by deliberate attempts to withhold highly probative exculpatory evidence, thus calling into question the safety of *all* convictions rendered against other accused of this Tribunal to whom it may also have happened. In this context, it should also be remembered that the Tribunal's prosecutor is considered an undivided body.[11] The fact that the prosecutor in the *Bizimungu et al.* case could withhold, even for a single day, highly probative evidence regarding the innocence of a person who at the time had been in detention for twelve years is simply shocking. Certainly, the good faith of the prosecutor in discharging its disclosure obligations is disputable, considering that he did not provide any explanation to justify his failure to disclose this information for over a year, which leads to serious doubts concerning the integrity of the prosecutor before the ICTR.

The Trial Chamber in the *Bizimungu et al.* case also reminded the prosecutor that it had been advised by the Appeals Chamber at least twice in the past to establish procedures designed to ensure that such incidents would not occur.[12] Although that warning was given in 2005, many years later the prosecutor apparently still had not heeded that advice. This finding from *Bizimungu et al.* is troubling to say the least. This situation warrants a complete review of the entirety of the prosecutor's holdings by independent experts, with a view to ensuring not only that disclosure has been properly done but, more generally, to eliminate any doubts that any of the convicted persons have been wrongfully convicted.

## National Jurisdictions: To Disclose or Not to Disclose

Now that national jurisdictions are following in the ICTR's footsteps by pursuing genocide cases, they depend heavily on the cooperation of the prosecutor of the Tribunal to obtain from its vast holdings the material that may assist them in their work. It is therefore interesting to analyse the ICTR prosecutor's approach to its disclosure obligations since the approach the prosecutor takes will have a great impact on legal procedures regarding the Rwandan genocide being conducted in national jurisdictions.

A review of the emerging jurisprudence in this area is worrisome. It indicates that the Tribunal has condoned the prosecutor's very narrow approach in the matter of what evidence it will allow to be disclosed to national jurisdictions. As an example, in the *Mungwarere*[13] case in Canada and *Simbikangwa*[14] case in France, the MICT has refused to disclose the statement of witnesses testifying on the same facts for which Mungwarere and Simbikangwa are respectively accused. In the former case in Canada, the MICT refused disclosure to the accused, while in the other it refused disclosure to the judge responsible for the procedures in France. The refusal to disclose is unfair particularly because if Mungwarere or Simbikangwa had been accused before the ICTR, they would have been entitled to receive the material that they have unsuccessfully sought from that institution.

The chambers are in fact maintaining a very tight secrecy on the prosecutor's holdings. The MICT should contemplate the following argument: considering that the ICTR has primacy of jurisdiction with regard to Rwandan genocide cases, and to the extent that it is the institution that has gathered the most comprehensive database of material on the subject matter, it is clearly unfair to deprive accused of that material before other fora.

In light of the recurring admission of fabricated evidence, collusion between witnesses, and incidents of intimidation or bribery of witnesses, it is all the more crucial that all existing evidence on any given allegations be made available to related proceedings for those cases in which similar allegations have been made.[15] Instances where witnesses simply add the names of new accused as they are being investigated are too numerous to be coincidental. To prevent the risks of an innocent person being convicted on the basis of false, fabricated, and colluded evidence, it is imperative that ICTR material be made available to individuals tried in national jurisdictions, just as if they were facing a trial before the ICTR. The existing practice reflected in the ICTR's jurisprudence and the prosecutor's current regulation dealing with cooperation and communication of material—before the ICTR and the MICT—are simply unfair to third parties accused and they impair the ability of their counsel to effectively defend them. This injustice appears clearly from the text of those regulations under which only national authorities and international organisation can request assistance.[16]

The importance of making ICTR material available to accused before national jurisdictions is heightened by the fact that these national authorities are themselves intoxicated by false evidence. For example, in the Butare trial judgment rendered on June 24, 2011, [17] witness "QA" admitted that he had lied to the Canadian policeman in the case of Désiré Munyaneza, the first case of an accused tried for participating in the Rwanda genocide before the Canadian courts. Furthermore, witness "QA" specified in his testimony that he was encouraged to lie against Kanyabashi in the *Butare* case before the ICTR by influential figures within the administration of the Ibuka association and by the public administration of Rwanda in his home area.[18]

The credibility of Canadian authorities in their dealings with Rwanda should raise eyebrows. One must ask how the Canadian authorities can treat material received from that country as credible when Canada's own tribunals have already concluded that its ruler, the RPF, is an organisation with limited and brutal purposes, rendering its members *de facto* inadmissible because of the gravity of the crimes with which they are associated.[19]

In short, the ICTR prosecutor, on one hand, is jealously keeping its evidence in a tightly sealed box while national authorities, on the other hand, fail to insist on getting that evidence. Moreover, they completely disregard compelling evidence that would certainly warrant closer scrutiny of the material communicated by the RPF to initiate, launch, or start immigration or criminal proceedings against Rwandan people.

With regard to disclosure, a trial chamber of the ICTR has stated that proof contained in a statement that evidence had been fabricated in Ruhengeri prison against a person accused before the ICTR is of interest to other people accused, as well as the general public.[20] The prosecutor should heed that decision, and prepare a comprehensive and public record of the instances of fabrication that occurred in its cases, rather than maintain secrecy on that issue.

## Acquittals: A Double Standard Prevails

Another thorny question for the ICTR and its relations with national jurisdictions concerns the fate of people who have been acquitted or released after their sentence by the Tribunal. Whereas for a number of years now the ICTR has been begging countries to step forward and welcome the people who have been tried and acquitted, requests made by these people have been either arbitrarily denied or met with disdain. Arbitrary refusals are the current practice, including in France, which welcomed Ignace Bagilishema and Jean Mpambara, both of whom had been accepted following their acquittals. It now opposes an unjustified *fin de non-recevoir* to André Ntagerura and Gratien Kalibiligi, both of whose spouses live there. It remains to be seen whether Canada, the United States, or Belgium will follow in France's footsteps by responding arbitrarily. Some people acquitted have family in those three countries.

If the past is any indication of what the future may hold, there is cause for concern. ICTR history reveals that it is a spineless institution at times. The case of Froduald Karamira comes to mind: Mr. Karamira was sent to Rwanda where he was executed on April 24, 1998 at the Nyamirambo stadium despite attempts by the ICTR prosecutor to obtain his transfer since he was in transit at Addis Ababa Airport on his way from India. Later, Agnes Ntamabyariro, the only member of the interim government to be tried by Rwandan courts, was transferred to Arusha to testify before the ICTR in the Government II case. Mrs. Ntamabyariro claimed that she would be tortured if returned to Rwanda, and asked to remain under the Tribunal's guard rather than be returned to Rwanda. The ICTR shamelessly shipped her back to Rwanda without even assessing the torture risks.

## Conclusion

The exact nature of the cooperation between the ICTR prosecutor and the Rwandan authorities remains to be fully exposed. Rwandan authorities clearly have an interest in being fully apprised of ICTR investigations, not only because some are liable for prosecution under the ICTR, but also because the Tribunal represents a powerful tool for silencing many potential opponents at once.

In this context, it is interesting to take note of the RPF's eagerness to obtain the ICTR's archives. It is widely known that the ICTR conducted investigations into RPF crimes, and also that the investigations did not lead to prosecution following Rwanda's intense lobbying campaign at the United Nations, which was relayed and supported by the United States and the United Kingdom. Carla Del Ponte describes in vivid detail how Pierre Prosper, an ex-ICTR prosecutor turned Ambassador-at-large for the USA, pressured her intensely to transfer investigation of the RPF to Rwanda. She was ultimately stripped of her title as ICTR prosecutor.[21]

The RPF has been very successful at silencing its critics by labelling any questioning of the current imposed version of the 1994 genocide as "genocide denial." I therefore feel duty-bound to stress that there was indisputably a genocide in Rwanda, obviously involving victims and perpetrators. However I must add that, contrary to the idea force-fed to the international community by the RPF for years, it is completely false to suggest that all victims were Tutsis, and that the genocide was planned and prepared in a systematic fashion that involved every member of every level of the public administration of the country. This simplistic Manichean vision of the 1994 conflict that permeates the public discourse today has to be rejected.

On one hand, the biased jurisprudence of the ICTR reinforces the notion that all Hutus are guilty as such, a notion that Rwandan authorities strive to impose. On the other, it allows the RPF to remain unpunished, including for crimes falling under the ICTR's jurisdiction. To those victims of the RPF before, during, and after the genocide, the ICTR will remain forever a monument to impunity.

## Notes

1. Olivier Dubois, *Rwanda's national criminal courts and the International Tribunal,* International Review of the Red Cross, no. 321, December 31, 1997, http://www.icrc.org/eng/resources/documents/misc/57jnza.htm.
2. David Scheffer, *All the Missing Souls,* Princeton University Press, 2012, pp. 69-86, p. 81.
3. US Embassy Dar Es Salaam 000540, March 16, 2005, "ICTR Registrar Briefs Diplomats," para. 7 (obtained from WikiLeaks, http://wikileaks.org/cable/2005/03/05DARESSALAAM540.html).
4. See for example "Rwanda Tribunal should pursue Justice for RPF crimes," Failure to Act Risks Undermining Court's Legacy, December 12, 2008, Open letter from Human Rights Watch to the ICTR.
5. Filip Reyntjens, *Political Governance in Post-Genocide Rwanda*, Cambridge University Press, 2013, pp. 243-246.
6. "Report to the Secretary General of the Commission of Expert to Review the Prosecution of Serious Violations of Human Rights in Timor-Leste (then East-Timor) in 1999," May 26, 2005, S/2005/458.

7.  "Summary of the report to the Secretary-General of the Commission of Experts to Review the Prosecution of Serious Violations of Human Rights in Timor-Leste (then East Timor) in 1999," May 26, 2005, S/2005/458, para. 25.

8.  "Report to the Secretary General of the Commission of Experts to Review the Prosecution of Serious Violations of Human Rights in Timor-Leste (then East-Timor) in 1999," 26 May 2005, S/2005/458, para. 60-78.

9.  *The Prosecutor v. Bizimungu et al.*, Case No. ICTR-99-50-T, *Judgment*, September 30, 2011 ("*Bizimungu et al. Judgment*").

10. *Bizimungu et al.* was the trial of four Ministers of the Interim Government.

11. See for instance *Prosecutor v. Renzaho*, Case No. ICTR-97-31-T, *Judgment*, 14 July 2009, para. 48.

12. *Bizimungu et al. Judgment*, para. 177.

13. In *Re Ntakirutimana et al.*, Case No. MICT-12-10, *Decision in Respect to Jacques Mungwarere's Motions to Access Material*, January 18, 2013

14. In *Re Bagosora et al.*, Case No. MICT-12-26, *Decision in Respect to the Request for Access to Material Concerning Pascal Simbikangwa*, January 21, 2013.

15. See for example *The Prosecutor v. Karemera and Ngirumpaste*, Case No. ICTR-98-44D-T, *Decision on Callixte Nzabonimana's Motion for Access to Exhibit DNZ-461*, August 23, 2010.

16. Prosecutor's regulation no. 1, November 2008; Prosecutor's regulation no. 2, 2013, on requests for assistance by national authorities or international organisations to the Prosecutor (MICT/13), November 29, 2013.

17. *The Prosecutor v. Nyiramasuhuko et al.*, Case No. ICTR-98-42-T, June 24, 2011, paras. 200 and 334.

18. *The Prosecutor v. Nyiramasuhuko et al.*, Case No. ICTR-98-42-T, June 24, 2011, paras. 200 and 335.

19. *Rwiyamirira v. Canada (Minister of Citizenship and Immigration)*, 2004, RPDD No. 286 [*Rwiyamirira*], paras. 27-28.

20. *The Prosecutor v. Karemera and Ngirumpaste*, Case No. ICTR-98-44D-T, *Decision on Callixte Nzabonimana's Motion for Access to Exhibit DNZ-461*, August 23, 2010, para. 4, and exhibit DNZ-461.

21. Carla Del Ponte, *Madam Prosecutor: Confrontations with Humanity's Worst Criminals and the Culture of Impunity*, Other Press, New York, 2009, pp. 177-192, 223-241

# 9

## Prosecutorial Failure to Disclose Exculpatory Material: A Death Knell to Fairness

BETH S. LYONS

### Introduction

Most criminal courts and tribunals—at state, national, and international levels—have a rule obliging the prosecution to disclose to defence counsel material which is favourable to a criminal defendant.[1] This material is generally referred to as "exculpatory material" and affects the guilt or innocence of the defendant, or the credibility of the prosecution evidence, particularly witness testimony.

At the International Criminal Court, for example, the prosecution is mandated to "investigate incriminating and exonerating circumstances equally,"[2] and has the duty to disclose to the defence "as soon as practicable" any evidence which "shows or tends to show the innocence of the accused, or to mitigate the guilt of the accused, or which may affect the credibility of prosecution evidence."[3] Significantly, this exculpatory disclosure obligation is included under the Rights of the Accused, in Article 67 of the ICC's Rome Statute.

Whether a legal system is fair to defendants depends on prosecutorial compliance with disclosure rules. The problem, however, is that prosecutorial compliance is not assured by the rules' existence "on the books." In reality, defence litigation is required to make sure that these rules are fully implemented, so that exculpatory materials—and the rights of the accused—are not being buried.

\* \* \*

Many are familiar with the Innocence Project in the US, founded in 1992, which has been responsible for the freeing of 292 wrongfully convicted felons, including seventeen who spent time on death row. Much

publicity has focused on exculpatory DNA evidence, but other exculpatory evidence has included eyewitness misidentification testimony,
improper or invalid forensic science, false confessions, and incriminating statements from defendants as well as the use of informants.[4]

In July 2012, a California US criminal defence lawyer, Jeffrey Douglas,
sued Steve Cooley, the Los Angeles District Attorney (LADA); the Los
Angeles District Attorney's Office (LADA); Leroy Baca, the Los Angeles
County Sheriff; and the Los Angeles County Sheriff's Department
(LASD) for failure to comply with disclosure obligations under State
and Federal law, by adopting a formal policy which violated these laws.[5]
The Petition/Complaint[6] describes a formal policy—at multiple levels—
which resulted in the District Attorney's Office illegally suppressing
exculpatory evidence.

Under California State Law, the District Attorney is mandated to
disclose "any exculpatory evidence" to the defendant and his or her
attorney.[7] The California Supreme Court has held that this imposes
an obligation to disclose *all* exculpatory evidence before trial.[8] But the
LADA established a separate "*Brady* Compliance Unit" that operated
under Special Directive 10-06, under which evidence that was not exculpatory, based on a "clear and convincing" standard, would be excluded
from disclosure.[9]

At the level of the Los Angeles County Sheriff's Department, the
Petition/Complaint alleged that the official policies for filing inmate
complaints about deputies in the Los Angeles County jails violated the
California Penal Code, which requires the maintenance of all citizens'
complaints against officers for five years in their personnel files or in a
separate file. The Sheriff's Department *only* filed these complaints in the
inmates' files, so that the Department could not search for inmate complaints implicating specific deputies. Hence, in cases initiated by inmates
against the prison authorities for the use of excessive force, this practice
made it impossible for relevant complaints against specific deputies to
be disclosed either to the prosecution or a defence counsel because the
complaints could not be found, although they existed in the records.[10]

* * *

How do these prosecutorial violations of disclosure obligations happen? Are they rooted in prosecutorial negligence? Or in a prosecutorial intent to conceal? Or in a combination of both?

The reasons for this conduct may vary and be difficult to prove, but whatever the reason, it is my contention that the prosecution's failure to comply with its disclosure obligations to the defence—under any system—is a violation of fair trial and prejudices the rights of an accused or defendant so egregiously that it impacts on a court's adverse decisions and judgment(s) of conviction against a defendant.

Based on my experience litigating disclosure issues at the ICTR, I have concluded that objectively a policy of concealment is alive and well, which requires the defence to aggressively litigate in order for the prosecution to "play by the rules" and for the Chambers to implement the needed remedies for the prosecution's violations of the Rules, especially Rule 68 at the ICTR. But too often this occurs too late, resulting in fair trial violations that render judgments of conviction illegitimate.

### Rule 68: Does it "Level the Playing Field" Between Prosecution and Defence?

The ICTR's disclosure rule, Rule 68 (Disclosure of Exculpatory and Other Relevant Material) states: "The prosecutor shall, as soon as practicable, disclose to the defence any material, which, in the actual knowledge of the prosecutor may suggest the innocence or guilt of the accused or affect the credibility of prosecution evidence."[11]

Most salient in the rule's construction and jurisprudence is the broad and inclusive nature of the prosecution's disclosure obligations. Rule 68 is not narrow and limited.[12] In fact, in the *Karemera et al.* case,[13] the Appeals Chamber held that the prosecution violated its Rule 68 obligations since it did not disclose a document that contained some exculpatory material. In the Appeals Chamber's words, Rule 68 creates a "categorical obligation."[14] Often material such as prior prosecution witness statements may include some sections that exculpate the defendant, and others that contain some inculpatory material. To be covered by Rule 68, the material does not have to be one hundred percent (i.e., every word) exculpatory. Thus, the *possibility* that the material suggests guilt or innocence or affects the credibility of prosecution evidence is enough to trigger the prosecution's duty to disclose. The rule implies that it is up to the defence to decide whether and how to use the disclosed material.

However, even assuming that Rule 68 is a statutory, procedural mechanism which is intended to "level the playing field," the implementation of Rule 68 and its jurisprudence is potentially sabotaged from the beginning based on two factors: who initially decides what is Rule 68 material, and the timing of disclosure. The "what and when to disclose" are determined at the prosecution's discretion. There should be no problem, of course, with a prosecution that, in good faith, promptly and fully complies with the Rules. The fundamental problem, however, in the case of the ICTR prosecution (and usually replicated in too many prosecution offices elsewhere) is that its conduct is driven not by an agenda to comply with the rule of law and to apply it equally, but to exercise its discretion in a manner which is accountable to a "higher power," i.e., politics. Although the ICTR's founding resolution, Security Council Resolution 955 (1994), mandates the prosecution of both sides of the conflict, the ICTR prosecution has implemented a policy of selective prosecution: only persons on the losing side of the war, and, in fact, only Hutus. No members of the Rwandan Patriotic Front have been prosecuted despite earlier international arrest warrants issued in France in 2006 and in Spain in 2008, as well as the notable efforts of former Chief Prosecutor Carla Del Ponte. In fact, her career as ICTR Chief Prosecutor was cut short under pressure from the US and Rwanda for her "Special Investigations" into crimes of the RPF.[15]

In sum, the prosecution has total discretion on how, when, and for what material Rule 68 is implemented. A major obstacle to fairness at the ICTR has been that routinely and spontaneously, the prosecution does not fulfill its Rule 68 obligations. To my knowledge, there have been no ICTR cases where Rule 68 disclosure was not an issue to some degree or another which the defence has had to litigate, often over a period of years, at both the trial and appellate levels.[16] In this litigation, it is the burden of the defence to make a *prima facie* case as to why the identified material it is requesting should be disclosed. General defence requests are refused by the Court; the only chance of success, that is, for the Court to issue a compliance order to the prosecution is if the request is specific enough. This often requires resources for which the defence must apply to the Tribunal. The defence does not have limitless, available resources to conduct investigations, which regularly necessitate missions to Rwanda and other countries.

Finding resources for defence investigation is more difficult, if not impossible, after a trial is completed. If the defence receives information about a "lead" (namely, a witness who testified in a previous trial, but changed his or her story in a *gacaca* proceeding in Rwanda), it is the defence's burden to investigate and apply to the Appeals Chamber if there is Rule 68 material that should be disclosed by the prosecution. The bottom line is that the defence is simply not allocated sufficient means to investigate and track down Rule 68 evidence that is already in the possession of the prosecution.

The defence's discovery of Rule 68 material often requires a measure of luck. What usually happens is that the defence "stumbles" across potentially exculpatory material by accident in two ways:

- When a defence investigator is searching through material which has been disclosed, and she or he reads about another document which may be relevant and helpful to the defence; or,
- When a prosecution witness (especially a prisoner witness) responds "yes" to a defence counsel's query during cross-examination (e.g., have you given a statement about, or testified about, this same incident in another court, or to a commission?) and the statement is "missing" from materials previously disclosed to the defence by the prosecution under its Rule 66 obligation to disclose prior statements before the witness testifies at trial.[17]

However, the prosecution's Rule 68 disclosure obligation is a separate, distinct one from its other disclosure obligations under Rule 66. In the *Karemera et al.* case, the prosecution contested the Trial Chamber's holding that the prosecution has a "positive obligation" of disclosure under Rule 68, and appealed the Trial Chamber's decision.[18] The prosecution argued that its Rule 68 obligations were fulfilled "by making the prosecution evidence collection and other relevant materials accessible to the Defence through the EDS [Electronic Disclosure Suite]."[19] The Appeals Chamber dismissed the prosecution's appeal.

The Appeals Chamber unequivocally held that "[t]he Prosecution's obligation to disclose exculpatory material is essential to a fair trial."[20] It found that the EDS facilities cannot replace the prosecution's disclosure obligations under Rule 68.[21] In fact, the Appeals Chamber, affirming the Trial Chamber's finding that EDS fails to fulfill the "important and expansive obligations under Rule 68," explicitly stated that, "the Prosecution's Rule 68 obligation to disclose extends beyond making available its entire evidence collection in a searchable format. A search engine cannot serve as a surrogate for the Prosecution's individualised consideration of the material in its possession."[22]

"Accidental" discovery by the defence of Rule 68 material is neither the intent nor the jurisprudence of Rule 68 but, unfortunately, "accidental" discovery by the defence has been the norm.

## The "Military II" Case: Disclosure "As soon as practicable"??

Disclosure under Rule 68 is a continuing obligation, even after the appeal judgment.[23] The timing requirement of Rule 68(A)—"as soon as practicable"—does not mean that the "continuing" nature of the obligation is an "excuse" for late disclosure of material which has been within the prosecution's possession. It is obvious that the late timing of Rule 68 disclosures (for example, post-prosecution case or even post-trial judgment) effectively limits or even negates their use by the defence during trial. Their use, possibly, is also negated during the appeal stage, unless the Appeals Chamber grants a defence motion for additional evidence under Rule 115[24] and admits the material on appeal.

In the *Ndindiliyimana et al.* ("Military II") case, the prosecution was forced to disclose a massive quantity of Rule 68 material more than two years after it completed its case at trial. At the end of August 2004, the ICTR prosecution opened its presentation of evidence in the "Military II" case against four accused persons. The prosecution rested its case in December 2006. The four defence cases were presented between mid-April 2007 and December 2008.[25] The trial was conducted over a period of approximately four years and nine months, consisting of 395 trial days.

On February 4, 2008, on Trial Day 305, during the case of the second accused, the Trial Chamber issued an order to the prosecution to disclose Rule 68 material. The order was in response to the persistent defence litigation, which had been ongoing for years. To comply with the order, on February 29, 2008, the prosecution disclosed to the defence approximately 3,000 pages, including 140 unredacted witness statements, for the four defendants.[26] In March and April 2008, the prosecution disclosed some materials pertaining to the RPF.[27]

In September 2008, in a too rare decision, the Trial Chamber in the "Military II" case held that the prosecution's persistent violations of its disclosure obligation under Rule 68 violated the right of the accused to a fair trial.[28] It found that the prosecution "has shown a lack of diligence in the disclosure of exculpatory material."[29] The Chamber concluded that the accused were deprived of the opportunity to use exculpatory material to test the credibility of the prosecution witnesses, especially through cross-examination.

In respect to some specific statements disclosed in February 2008, the Chamber determined that the prosecution had "violated its obligation to disclose these statements 'as soon as practicable'—a requirement that is certainly not satisfied by disclosure several years after the trial has started."[30] The excessive lateness of these disclosures is illustrated by the fact some of the statements found by the Trial Chamber to be disclosure violations dated as far back as 1997.[31] It could be concluded, therefore, that these statements had been in the possession of the prosecution for than a decade prior to their disclosure to the defence.

In a highly unusual act, the Trial Chamber publicly scolded the prosecutor for "prejudicing all the defence teams in preparation of their defences."[32] Defence teams had requested a range of remedies, but the Trial Chamber rejected remedies it considered to be severe measures and basically granted the defence the right to some further cross-examination of selected prosecution witnesses and the right to call, if necessary, some additional witnesses.[33] Unfortunately, the Trial Chamber's remedies were incomplete and also late (especially considering that the Trial Chamber had notice from the defence teams of allegations of Rule 68 violations, in some cases, for years prior). Hence, the prejudice resulting from the Rule 68 violations to the defendants remained uncured in many respects.

As the chronology in the "Military II" litigation and also in other cases reveals, the granting of disclosure by the Chambers is not a routine or "rubber stamp" procedure. The defence most often loses, but occasionally, as in "Military II," we are able to claim a few "partial" victories.

* * *

What happened? Was anyone in the Office of the Prosecutor (OTP) looking for Rule 68 material? Did someone simply negligently miss something? Or, was it an intentional error?

Whatever the reason for late disclosure, the prosecution's interpretation and practices of "as soon as practicable" appear to ignore and objectively defy the well-settled jurisprudence that this obligation is essential to a fair trial. The results of these violations severely prejudice the rights of an accused to a fair trial.

Lastly, even when the Rule 68 material is disclosed and represented as what exists within the "actual knowledge" of the prosecution at that time, there is a nagging defence concern, based on experience and litigation, that there is "something missing" and that the material is incomplete. This has been the case especially for disclosure from the prosecution's "Special Investigations" of the RPF.

To summarise,

- Is Rule 68 disclosure a voluntary act of the prosecution? Most often it is not.
- If it does occur, can it be trusted to be complete? No.
- Is the prosecution penalised for violating the rule? Atypically, no.

* * *

Prosecutorial violation of Rule 68 obligations is a systemic problem. Of course, these violations are manifest in individual cases with individual prosecutors and prosecution witnesses. However, these Rule 68 violations are not unique to individual prosecutors, nor should they be viewed as "isolated" incidents or "lapses" in an individual's professional and ethical responsibility.[34] The Office of the Prosecutor is a single entity,[35] and these violations simply occur too regularly. It would be against the evidence (as well as naïve) to conclude that these violations did *not* constitute a pattern or policy, but were "aberrations" attributable only to negligence, or "honest" mistakes.

* * *

When these Rule 68 disclosure violations are combined with already deficient prosecution evidence on which the Trial Chambers rely, the deleterious effect of Rule 68 violations multiplies, rendering convictions illegitimate. These deficiencies in prosecution witness testimony are documented by Professor Nancy Combs in her invaluable book, *Fact-Finding without Facts: The Uncertain Evidentiary Foundations of International Criminal Convictions*.[36] Combs concludes that the tribunals she analysed—the ICTR, the Special Court for Sierra Leone, and the Special Panels (in East Timor)—"operate in a fact-finding fog of inconsistent, vague, and sometimes incoherent testimony that leaves them unable to say with any measure of certainty who did what to whom."[37] Based on a review of ICTR convictions through 2005, Combs found that about fifty percent of the cases featured prosecution witnesses whose testimony and statements had serious discrepancies.[38] Some examples would include a witness who testified that the defendant was at a crime scene, but failed to mention his presence at the same crime scene in a prior statement (which was taken many years closer in time to the events of 1994). Or the witness "forgot" a major "detail" when prosecution investigators spoke to him in 2000, but suddenly "remembered" it in 2003 when he was testifying in Arusha. Or there are discrepancies between a witness's account of his own actions during the events of 1994 in his statement to the Office of the Prosecutor and his testimony to the Trial Chamber.

Judgments should be based on legally sound evidence, but it is apparent from reading judgments that the attitude of the judges towards this "fact-finding fog" is not uniform. Combs found, for example, that in cases of acquittal, there was also more scrutiny of prosecution witness inconsistencies and rigorous application of the beyond a reasonable doubt standard.[39]

Can disclosure of exculpatory material remedy the wrongs of judgments of convictions based on deficient evidence? Not necessarily. There is no question in my mind that Rule 68 implementation will be a crucial step in fairness but alone, it is not enough to make international justice a fair process. Fairness is a legal issue, but it is also an issue of human rights and is not decided in a political vacuum. We have to use what rules exist in judicial fora, however, and insist that they be fully complied with by the prosecution.

* * *

The defence must continue to pressure the Tribunal to hold the prosecution accountable for its violations that prejudice the fair trial rights of the defendant. Rule 68 violations are a major trigger for post-conviction remedies. The continuing obligation of the prosecution, post-trial and post-appeal, to disclose exculpatory and other relevant material under Rule 68[40] provides the legal basis to continue the fight for truth and justice, and against illegitimate convictions.

Even if a defendant loses the appeal of his trial conviction, there is still the possibility, under Rule 120, to request that the Appeals Chamber review the final judgment based on the existence of a "new fact" which was not known and could not have been discovered through due diligence at the time of the trial or appellate proceedings.[41] It should be noted that the statutory language contains no deadline or time limit for defence requests, but the prosecution must make its request for a review of the judgment within one year of the final judgment.[42]

The potential bases for post-conviction remedies are growing with the increasing number of recanting prosecution witnesses. These witnesses may have inculpated the accused in their trial testimony, but have had a change of heart and memory. This change may be triggered by the fact that the witness is now living in exile outside the country and feels "safer" to tell the truth. In the case of recanting prosecution prisoner witnesses who have been released, the incentive to commit perjury in Arusha in the expectation of a lesser sentence or lower penal classification in Rwanda is no longer operative.

One can also point to the parade of prosecution "professional" witnesses who testify in multiple cases on the same events, at the ICTR and perhaps in Rwanda or elsewhere. The problem is that each prior statement on the same event is not exactly the same, and often there are discrepancies on major points. Under the Rules, all statements of a prosecution witness should have been disclosed to the defence prior to a witness's testimony, but this does not always occur. Even if there is just one instance of an undisclosed statement, this prejudices the defendant because the defence cannot fully cross-examine the prosecution witness and test his or her credibility. All of these prosecution witnesses potentially have Rule 68 evidence that challenges the credibility of the evidence adduced at trial and on which a conviction may have been based.

Lastly, the continuing discovery of undisclosed Rule 68 evidence in files in the Office of the Prosecutor after the trial judgments may provide fertile grounds for the defence to challenge convictions, based on prosecution evidence tainted with its fair trial violations.

The sheer quantity of these examples transforms this situation into an urgent issue for international justice. No convicted person should be denied his or her rights because of negligence or intent of the prosecution, which results in Rule 68 violations, prejudicing the right to fair trial, but under the current legal regime it is difficult for a convicted person to discover this exculpatory material, especially after the appeal judgment has been rendered. There is no automatic "right to counsel" for convicted persons, nor is there an automatic "right to investigate" claims of recanting witnesses. The convicted person has to apply to the Appeals Chamber to be given legal assistance. If the Appeals Chamber is convinced that the *prima facie* legal standard has been met, and that "exceptional circumstances" exist, where it is "necessary to ensure the fairness of the proceeding," it will assign legal resources for a limited period.[43] The Tribunal, *as a matter of right*, needs to provide defence counsel and other investigative resources in order for convicted persons to litigate the fair trial violations that are identified in the post-conviction stage.

\* \* \*

The International Residual Mechanism for Criminal Tribunals[44] must address these continuing Rule 68 violations as a systemic failing in the international tribunals. Its Rules of Procedure and Evidence, adopted

June 8, 2012, contain the ICTR Rule 68 provisions under its Rule 73 on
Disclosure of Exculpatory Evidence and Other Relevant Material.[45]
Under both Rules, prosecutorial discretion controls the initial disclo-
sure process.

The Residual Mechanism must address:

- What body within the Mechanism, and after the Mechanism,
  will monitor and hold the prosecution accountable for its continuing Rule 68/73[46] obligations; and,
- When and how convicted persons will be provided with a right
  to counsel to rectify the Rule 68/73 (and other) violations of the
  prosecution.

The Mechanism must adopt affirmative and aggressive policies
whose objective is the enforcement of prosecutorial implementation of
Rule 68/73.

The responsibility of the Mechanism as the "guardian" of Rule 68/73
is more urgent because the overwhelming majority of defence counsel
are not in Arusha once their cases have been completed. The institutional contact between their clients, who are serving sentences in various countries, and the ICTR, which is still responsible for the convicted
persons,[47] is minimal and is never a substitute for legal representation
by defence counsel. As a group, the convicted persons have effectively
become a "forgotten" entity within the ICTR structure, with no statutory
right to legal assistance when it is still urgently needed—at the post-conviction stage, especially in cases with "newly disclosed" Rule 68 material.

\* \* \*

Location, access, and use of the Archives are key related issues. The
Mechanism is responsible for the preservation and management of the
Archives. With the establishment of the Mechanism in Arusha, the
Archives have also been located there. It is important that they be held
permanently in a UN-recognised facility, controlled by the UN, not by
a sovereign individual state.

At Security Council briefings on the status of the "Completion
Strategy" of the Tribunals, Rwanda has pleaded to house these Archives.

The Archives are a trove of a wide range of material covering almost two decades. They include transcripts of proceedings as well as documents related to investigations, indictments, the detention of accused persons, protection of witnesses, and enforcement of sentences and the ICTR's relationships with states, other law enforcement authorities, international, and non-governmental organisations and the public. The Mechanism's Statute, Article 27, ensures the continued protection of confidential information.

Although it is not possible to determine with absolute certainty that the Archives will contain exculpatory material, this likelihood is a safe bet. This conclusion is based on the demonstrated inability of the prosecution, over well more than a decade, to identify and disclose Rule 68 material in its possession "as soon as practicable." In addition, if the Archives were eventually to become inaccessible to the defence, whatever material exists would be useless to the defence. Such would be the case if, in the future, the Archives were re-located to Rwanda.[48]

\* \* \*

The prosecution's obligation to disclose exculpatory material is essential to a fair trial.[49] The prosecution's violations of its obligations prompt the query: do these violations compromise the fair trial rights of the accused so as to render judgments of conviction illegitimate?

The answer will determine not only the legacy of the *ad hoc* tribunals, such as the ICTR and ICTY, but whether international justice is compromised, to the point of illegitimacy, because of the prosecution's failure to comply with the rules to disclose *all* the evidence in the search for justice and truth.

A trial is a search for truth, not a game of hide-and-seek.[50] Prosecutorial disclosure under Rule 68 has been a game of hide-and-seek. Whether this game is allowed to persist, in the ICTR or any other international court or tribunal, will provide a litmus test for fairness in international justice. Prosecutorial disclosure of exculpatory material must be a central focus for those of us who fight for fairness in international justice.

## Notes

1. The terms "defendant" and "accused" are used interchangeably.
2. Rome Statute of the International Criminal Court, Article 54(1)(a).
3. Rome Statute of the International Criminal Court, Article 67(2). Article 67(2) also states: "In case of doubt as to the application of this paragraph, the Court shall decide." Under Rule 83 (Rules of Procedure and Evidence), the "Prosecutor may request as soon as practicable a hearing on an *ex parte* basis before the Chamber dealing with the matter for the purpose of obtaining a ruling under article 67, paragraph 2."
4. More information on the Innocence Project is available at www.innocenceproject. org.
5. *Douglas v. Cooley, et al.*, Superior Court of California, County of Los Angeles, July 9, 2012; *See* Martha Neil, "Defense Lawyer, Backed by ACLU, Sues Los Angeles DA, Says Exculpatory Evidence is Often Withheld," July 11, 2012, http://www. abajournal.com/news/article/defense_lawyer_backed_by_aclu_sues_los_ange-les_da_says_exculpatory_evidence/ (includes links to Petition/Complaint and newspaper articles); Updated information on *Douglas v. Cooley, et al.* is available at www.aclu-sc.org.
6. Verified Petition for Writ of Mandate and Complain for Injunctive and Declaratory Relief ("Petition/Complaint"), July 9, 2012.
7. California Penal Code, §1054.1.
8. Petition/Complaint, para. 23.
9. Petition/Complaint, paras. 31-51.
10. Petition/Complaint, paras. 52-56.
11. Rule 68(A), ICTR Rules of Procedure and Evidence, 2009.
12. Note: The title is "Disclosure of Exculpatory *and* Other Relevant Material" (italics added).
13. *Karemera et al.*, Case No. ICTR-44-AR73.13, Appeals Chamber, Decision on Joseph Nzirorera's Appeal from Decision on Tenth Rule 68 Motion, May 14, 2008.
14. *Ibid.*, paras. 12-14.
15. Ms. Del Ponte's contract as ICTR Chief Prosecutor, which expired in mid-September 2003, was not renewed in August 2003 by the UN Security Council due to her refusal to stop the "Special Investigations" of the RPF and the pressure from President Kagame. Del Ponte "had no doubt Mr. Kagame's calls for her resignation were made as a result of her investigations into possible RPF atrocities." Steven Edwards, "Del Ponte Says UN caved to Rwandan Pressure," Global Policy Forum, September 17, 2003. See Carla Del Ponte and Chuck Sudetic, *Madame Prosecutor: Confrontation with Humanity's Worst Criminals and the Culture of Impunity*, Other Press, New York, 2009 (English edition), Chapter 9 (account of US/Rwanda-led pressures on Del Ponte to drop the "Special Investigations" of the RPF).
16. Rule 68 decisions are listed under each case and are available at www.ictr.org. See, especially the *Nzirorera* case, where Lead Counsel Peter Robinson filed seventeen Rule 68 motions, also available at www.peterrobinson.com.
17. Rule 66, ICTR Rules of Procedure and Evidence, mandates Prosecutorial disclosure of witness statements for witnesses it intends to call at trial. Rule 66 material

most often is disclosed to the defence through a searchable electronic format, the EDS (Electronic Disclosure Suite).

18. *The Prosecutor v. Édouard Karemera et al.*, Case No. ICTR-98-44-T, Trial Chamber, Oral Decision, T. February 16, 2006, pp. 2-10.

19. *Karemera et al.*, case no. ICTR-98-44-AR73.7, Appeals Chamber, Decision on Interlocutory Appeal Regarding the Role of the Prosecutor's Electronic Disclosure Suite in Discharging Disclosure Obligations, June 30, 2006, para. 8.

20. *Ibid.*, para. 9.

21. *Ibid.*, para. 10.

22. *Ibid.*, para. 10.

23. Rule 68(E) reads: "Notwithstanding the completion of the trial and any subsequent appeal, the Prosecutor shall disclose to the other party any material referred to in paragraph (A) above."

24. Rule 115, ICTR Rules of Procedure and Evidence, details the requirements and procedures governing additional evidence.

25. In mid-April 2007, the first of the four accused, General Bizimungu, presented his defence. The second accused, General Ndindiliyimana, completed his case in June 2008. The third accused, Major Nzuwonemeye, completed his case in October 2008. The fourth accused, Captain Sagahutu, completed his case in December 2008.

26. *Ndindiliyimana et al.*, Case No. ICTR-00-56-T, Trial Chamber, Decision on Defense Motions Alleging Violation of the Prosecutor's Disclosure Obligations Pursuant to Rule 68, 22 September 2008, para. 2.

27. *Ibid.*, para. 4.

28. *Ibid.*, para. 59.

29. *Ibid.*, para. 59.

30. Ibid., para. 38.

31. *Ibid.*, paras. 38, 46.

32. *Ibid.*, para. 59.

33. *Ibid.*, paras. 59-64. Defence requests for sanctions against the prosecution were rejected, as were remedies such as dismissal of charges, exclusion of evidence, and a stay of the proceedings. There was further litigation as to which witnesses would be recalled for cross-examination and the requests for additional witnesses.

34. Prosecutors "should promote principles of fairness and professionalism," and "assist the Tribunal to arrive at the truth and to do justice for the international community, victims and the accused." Prosecutor's Regulation No. 2 (1999), Standards of Professional Conduct [for] Prosecution Counsel, available at www.ictr.org.

35. *Bagosora et al.*, Case No. ICTR-98-41-T, Trial Chamber, Certification of Appeal Concerning Access to Protected Defense Witness Information, July 29, 2005, para. 5.

36. Nancy Amoury Combs, *Fact-Finding Without Facts: The Uncertain Evidentiary Foundations of International Criminal Convictions*, Cambridge University Press, 2010. See Beth S. Lyons, "Enough is Enough: The Illegitimacy of International Criminal Convictions: A Review Essay of *Fact-Finding Without Facts: The Uncertain Evidentiary Foundations of International Criminal Convictions* by Nancy Amoury Combs", *Journal of Genocide Research*, 2011, 13(3), September 2011, pp. 287-312.

37. *Ibid.*, p. 174.
38. *Ibid.*, p. 120.
39. *Ibid.*, pp. 222-223, 229, 254, 362.
40. Rule 68(E).
41. Rule 115 concerning additional evidence is based on similar legal criteria.
42. Rule 120(A).
43. *Kamuhanda v. The Prosecutor*, Case No. ICTR-99-54A-R, Appeals Chamber, Decision on Motion for Legal Assistance, July 21, 2009, paras. 17, 20; *Kajelijeli v. The Prosecutor*, Case No. ICTR-98-44A-R, Appeals Chamber, Decision on Request for Extension of Time, March 30, 2010, para. 3.
44. Under Security Council Resolution 1966 (2010), the International Residual Mechanism for Criminal Tribunals (IRMCT, and also referred to as "MICT") was established to complete the remaining tasks of the ICTR and ICTY, and maintain their legacies. The Mechanism commenced operations for the ICTR on July 1, 2012, and for the ICTY on July 1, 2013. The initial mandate for the Mechanism is four years and is subject to biennial review.
45. There is one minor difference: Rule 73(B) removed the clause "Where possible and with the agreement of the Defense" found in Rule 68(B).
46. The Mechanism generally continues the rights and obligations of the ICTR and ICTY Statutes (IRMCT Statute, Article 1[1]), hence the references in this section to Rule 68/73.
47. Rule 104, ICTR Rules of Procedure and Evidence, states: All sentences of imprisonment shall be served under the supervision of the Tribunal or a body designated by it.
48. For more problems about the MICT, see article by Philippe Larochelle above, Chapter 2.2.
49. *Ndindiliyimana et al.*, Case No. ICTR-00-56-T, Trial Chamber, Decision on Defense Motions Alleging Violation of the Prosecutor's Disclosure Obligations Pursuant to Rule 68, September 22, 2008, para. 12.
50. Verified Petition for Writ of Mandate and Complaint for Injunctive and Declaratory Relief, *Douglas v. Cooley, et al.*, Superior Court of California, County of Los Angeles, July 9, 2012, para. 1.

# 10

## Lessons Learned from the Bad Beginnings of The International Tribunal for Rwanda

ANDRÉ SIROIS

When John Philpot suggested that I write a text on the International Tribunal for Rwanda[1] (also called the International Criminal Tribunal for Rwanda (ICTR)), my response was to propose a short text describing the beginnings of the Tribunal, particularly in Kigali. For a few simple reasons, it could be of interest to some researchers and lawyers; I can bring testimony, and nothing seems to have been done so far about that.

Several articles and documents have been published about the Tribunal, generally ordered or subsidised by it or written by academics that have a vested interest in appearing "positive" if they want to maintain their access and their contacts at the United Nations. Nothing is available from the immediate actors of the beginnings of the Tribunal, either because they cannot talk if they want to pursue a career at the UN, or simply because they devote their time and energy to something else. This is also true of other international UN tribunals, like the Khmer Rouge Tribunal (the Extraordinary Chambers in the Courts of Cambodia), where I also served as a consultant. Hence texts on these tribunals seem so far from reality that they appear to be fiction.

The studies that have already been published ignore completely the numerous investigative reports, particularly those of the Office of Internal Oversight Services (OIOS) of the UN, which condemn the administration of the Tribunal (even though several of these reports are public),[2] the judgments rendered against the Tribunal,[3] and numerous newspaper articles about the issue. The result is a very favourable but completely fictitious image, often at odds with reality, where many actors of the Tribunal are at a loss to recognise their experiences. Nothing is known about the internal functioning—or dysfunction—of the Tribunal, nor of the impacts they may have had on the administra-

tion of justice, the choice of cases to be prosecuted, the quality of the
trials, and the value of the judgments. In short, the facts are not known
and therefore it is impossible to make a critical analysis of the Tribunal's
work. This leaves plenty to do and, without claiming to cover everything,
I will attempt to provide some elements for further study and analysis.

***

I was recruited by the Tribunal in February 1995, at its inception, after
a job interview with the then deputy prosecutor and the director of
investigations. I then had to convince them that, as the statutes of the
Tribunal provided for two languages, English and French, and as the languages commonly spoken in Rwanda were French and Kinyarwanda, the
Tribunal would need some language services (namely, legal and judicial
translation and legal and judicial interpretation). It was quite surprising
to have to convince them of what was evident and simply logical, and
inscribed in the provisions of the statutes of the Tribunal, especially since
the deputy prosecutor spoke only French and the director of investigation
spoke only English. Moreover, as the interviewee, I had to interpret my
own interview, questions, and answers for the benefits of the two inter-
viewers who were still not convinced of the necessity of an interpreter.

Later on, when the deputy prosecutor phoned to announce that
the Tribunal was hiring me, he said that the Tribunal had decided to
"afford itself the luxury of one translator." (Later, despite its humble
beginnings, the Language Services had difficulties handling the work-
load with nearly a hundred translators and interpreters.) For his part,
the attorney responsible for the establishment of the Tribunal, the first
head of the administration, assured me that we should have nothing
to fear in Kigali since the UN would "assign each of you a bodyguard
and an armoured car." (One could claim that this was a condition of
employment, never fulfilled needless to say.) All this just to show that
the way I was recruited already smacked of total improvisation and that
this would unfortunately prove to be the constant characteristic of the
Tribunal's administration.

I am still amazed at the state of the office of the deputy prosecutor of
the Tribunal on my arrival in Kigali. The situation can be summarised

in four words: Ignorance. Incompetence. Improvisation. Incoherence. Except for the content—quite theoretical—of the statutes, there was no way to know the administrative structure of the Tribunal, its organisation, its objectives, and its work plan. In practice there was nothing. We had to improvise constantly.

## Disorganisation and Causes of Conflict

As the Tribunal was in its infancy, it was not necessarily surprising that there would be no orientation session for its new employees. That would come later, no doubt, though it never came. The needs, however, were already desperate: employees came from very different countries and legal cultures and had only vague notions of Rwanda and what had happened there; lawyers and investigators who were trained in law knew only their national legal systems, which conflicted with the training and experience of others. Moreover, they had no idea of the role planned for the Tribunal, if there was any, and the statutes and regulations of the Tribunal, which had been improvised and patched up overnight, could not be of much help. In addition, with the exception of some French-speaking employees, the vast majority of the staff, including investigators and prosecutors, did not speak any of the languages used in Rwanda, which were necessary to do any investigation or prosecution. (This problem of language would only worsen thereafter, as discussed below.) In addition, the employees were told at the same time both that they must comply with UN regulations that they did not know, and also that they did *not* have to comply with them because the registrar, Andronico Adede, considered the Tribunal to be an independent body. More accurately, the rules did not apply when they did not fit him.

## Power Struggles

One would have expected that those who were supposed to establish the Tribunal had an idea of what they were supposed to do. This was not the case, either. Most improvised from day to day according to their personal interests and with the greatest contempt for the most basic rules of law and public administration.[4] In addition, Registrar Adede was very busy taking absolute control of the Tribunal in order to impose its own form of administration, described as follows by the United Nations Administrative Tribunal (UNAT):

> There is no doubt that a strange, despotic and capricious form of organi-
> zation was put in place by the Registrar and the Chief of Administration,
> ICTR, but far from justifying the activities undertaken with respect to the
> Applicant, that form of organization was severely criticized in their deal-
> ings with Office of Internal Oversight Services (OIOS) by the Director of
> Finance, the President of the Tribunal and the Judges. In the OIOS report,
> annexed to the report of the Secretary-General on the Activities of the
> Office of Internal Oversight Services (A/51/789 of 6 February 1997), the atti-
> tude of the Registrar, who had usurped full powers and imposed his own
> authority, not to say his authoritarianism, was highlighted.[5]

The result was that from its inception, the Tribunal was a free-for-
all where it was totally impossible to know who had the real authority.
Regardless of what the statutes of the Tribunal said, it was open war
between the president, the deputy prosecutor, and especially the registrar. To their dismay, several employees became pawns and victims of
that administrative war, which could paralyse almost all the work of the
Tribunal day after day.

## Racial and Ethnic Internal Conflicts

The Tribunal was a battlefield with hierarchical, linguistic, and even
racial conflicts. The registrar, the president, the chief administrative
officer, and the chief of human resources, all black Africans, wanted the
Tribunal to be exclusively black African (which, *inter alia*, would allow
them more leeway for favouritism and nepotism), despite a clearly contrary decision of the Security Council on this issue. In order to succeed,
they wished openly to replace all white employees by black Africans and
targeted them with constant discrimination and harassment. European,
Canada, Australian, and American lawyers and investigators reacted
strongly on the basis of the decision of the Security Council and on the
basis of their independence, their competence, and their rights, as well
as the fact that it was their countries which were largely financing the
Tribunal.

At the same time, major struggles between the Hutu and Tutsi employees occurred, but fearing being accused of discrimination, the authorities of the Tribunal forbade asking local applicants if they were Tutsi or Hutu, with the result that the managers, who did not verify identities and had even hired candidates under false names, did not know who they were dealing with or what was really going on between these two groups. Tragically, one of the consequences was that finally some local employees were killed or disappeared permanently, as a former special representative of the Secretary General attested.[6]

## Absence of Working Tools

The simplest and most essential working tools were missing: the vast majority of employees had no desks, no chairs, no computers, no codes, no law books, no Rwandan laws, and there was no legal library. Nothing. Investigators did not have enough cars to go out on investigations. We were assured repeatedly that this was ordered or promised, but nothing arrived, or sometimes what had arrived had been stolen directly at the airport by some Tribunal employee.

Moreover, it soon became very difficult to get supplies locally. The Tribunal had quickly earned itself a reputation as a very bad debtor. Not only did the Tribunal not pay its phone bills, it also failed to pay local suppliers, small entrepreneurs who were trying to revive their businesses after the massacres. Funds were diverted as soon as they were deposited in the local account of the Tribunal and suppliers never received their due; some were even driven to bankruptcy. So many were affected that finally, in desperation, some staged a very threatening demonstration in front of the Tribunal building, which made us realise that these malpractices could endanger the very lives of the entire staff of the Tribunal.

## Complaints, Denunciations, and Requests
## for Investigation by Families of Victims

The mandate of the Tribunal, experience, simple logic, and respect for victims should have made the Tribunal immediately set up an information and registration service to receive complaints from victims and

families of victims, and open investigation files. Not only was absolutely nothing of the sort done, but neither in Kigali or elsewhere did
the Tribunal have a single receptionist who could greet Rwandans in
one of the two languages of that country at the time, Kinyarwanda or
French. The receptionists could only answer in English; if occasionally
they could speak another language, their mother tongue, it was not one
of the languages of Rwanda. They could not take a single complaint or
even understand enough to transfer the call.

This shows that the Tribunal never really bothered to directly collect
complaints of the victims or their families. Relations with the victims or
their families were nonexistent. This was evident daily in the meetings
of the Tribunal where the word "victim" was never uttered and seemed
taboo. Files and cases were generally opened on the basis of complaints
selected and imposed by certain non-governmental organisations, without any knowledge of what these organisations were exactly or what
interests they served. A lot could be discovered from a serious study of
the control and roles of some NGOs in the creation and manipulation
of international tribunals. Some lawsuits also appeared monitored and
controlled by mysterious characters, usually American, who showed up
occasionally in the office and moved around accessing computers and
files without us being able to determine what they were really doing or
who they were (except for a couple who were identified as being CIA).

## Problems of Language and Communication

Communication problems were many and constant and they only aggra-
vated the general situation. This was particularly the case in investigations services and translation services. Not only did the investigators
and attorneys not speak the languages spoken in Rwanda, some of them
spoke English so poorly that it was very difficult to understand and
interpret what they said, which made it quasi impossible to use them.
A huge amount of work had to be done in translation or interpretation,
even in double translation (from a third language and to it, in which
cases the risk of errors and misunderstandings is greatly accrued). In
addition, it appeared at one point that investigators, who were of various
origins and would sooner or later be replaced by investigators of other

nationalities, took their notes and established their files in their native languages (Dutch, for example) which would render these files unusable when they left the Tribunal.

As regards translation, only one translator had the necessary competence and was officially certified as a judicial translator. Competence at hiring was not monitored, nor was quality controlled thereafter, not even for simple revisions. When I performed a quality control of translations in January 1996, I discovered that the content of translations and typing, done by local Hutu or Tutsi employees, were extensively manipulated and modified from one step to the other, and apparently not accidentally, with the result that we could theoretically have for the same statement or the same interview up to three manuscript versions and three typewritten versions (in Kinyarwanda, English, and French), that is to say, six versions that did not correspond one with the other. The witness could challenge each of them, sincerely pleading that none of them was really what he or she had said. (I remain convinced that some defendants could and should have been acquitted, at trial or on appeal, just on these grounds).

It was not much better in terms of judicial interpretation, all done by unqualified personnel, with the result that one interpreter made this comment: "You know, these Africans are really much too talkative. They talk, talk, talk. One must summarise. I have to cut, cut, cut." I should add that this interpreter was talking about evidence that could entail a very long prison sentence. Of course, this comment goes against the most basic rules of legal and judicial interpretation.

### Communications

At the beginnings, the Tribunal had three offices: one administrative base in New York, an office in The Hague for the prosecutor (who was also prosecutor for the ICTY that was based there), and another office in Kigali for the deputy prosecutor and his attorneys and investigators. A little later, the Tribunal would have its headquarters in Arusha, Tanzania.[7] So the Tribunal had three, and then four, offices.

As it was the beginning of the Internet, the Tribunal's work depended mostly on telephone and fax, operated by satellite, hence very randomly.

Moreover, on several occasions the registrar refused to pay the phone bills of the office of the prosecutor in Kigali and categorically forbade employees to pay them with their own money, which of course resulted in service interruptions, paralysing all work. That did not prevent him from ordering the tapping of the office of the prosecutor in Kigali, including investigators and lawyers, and demanding to be sent a copy of everything that was faxed from that office. According to some, this tapping and the leaks that resulted had the effect of paralysing or undermining several investigations, and even allowing some potential defendants to be warned of their coming arrest thus enabling escape.

## Recruitment

With this hierarchical infighting, nepotism, and favouritism, recruitment was a source of considerable problems. It was impossible, even for personnel managers, to obtain résumés and to know the real training and work experience, if any, of candidates. So it went from surprise to surprise. The Tribunal had many so-called attorneys who had never taken a single law course and who had never been enrolled in a bar, and some others who had been enrolled in a bar but had been disbarred for serious professional misconduct, even for common crimes (two for murder, one for forgery and tampering with evidence, etc.). Yet it was generally impossible to make the necessary checks since the official position of United Nations human resources authorities and of the Tribunal is—curiously—that bar membership is to be considered personal information and cannot be disclosed. It was thus impossible to know who was really a lawyer and who was not, or to complain about the conduct of a lawyer to his or her professional order. (The UN should get rid of this nonsensical rule in order to meet the very purpose of the existence of professional orders.) Furthermore, contrary to current beliefs, anyone who takes the trouble to check the résumés of judges, which are published, will be surprised by how little experience most of them had at the time of their appointments.

The Tribunal staff was clearly divided into two distinct groups: a minority, usually professionals on loan from their governments who mostly had the required skills and experience, sometimes even more, and a vast majority of employees, too many of whom had been hired for unknown reasons, who were of an appalling incompetence, and who could not and would not do any work. That was another source of constant conflict.

In the recruitment of local staff, two officials had established a network of bribes, kickbacks, and extortion, subjecting to it absolutely all local employees, and which turned out to be very difficult to abolish. In addition, members of the same family did not necessarily carry the same family name and that allowed the chief of personnel and some other authorities to hire members of their own families or ethnic background in contravention of UN rules.

## Government Pressure

Adding to these problems were the attempts by the Rwandan government to control the Tribunal and the pressure and intimidation measures that the government put on the staff of the Tribunal in all sorts of ways, including physical beatings of some investigators by the military. In addition, at the inception, the office of the prosecutor was forced to concede one of its offices to a military officer, an "observer" of the Rwandan government, and it took over a year to put an end to this situation, given that repeated death threats were made every time the Tribunal showed some willingness to correct the situation. The Rwandan government had its inputs and exercised control at all levels. A local employee who was the concubine of one of the heads of the Tribunal, and who claimed to be at the same time the mistress of an important general of the local army, circulated around making death threats to employees who dared to defy her orders or just displeased her. One could see her often very early in the morning checking all offices and computers of investigators and lawyers.

Several staff of the Tribunal took their orders from the government by complacency, by fear or for personal sympathy. Others were doing so for bribes plain and simple, and eventually one of the leading attorneys for the prosecution had to be fired for that very reason, the case having become too public.

That helps explain why the investigations covered only crimes allegedly committed by Hutu against Tutsi. It was clear that if the

Tribunal ever tried to investigate crimes of the Rwandan Patriotic Front (RPF), we would be lucky if the government expelled us immediately and did not throw us in jail for an indeterminate length of time. Prosecutor Louise Arbour understood that very well and she quickly put an end to the investigations of prosecution investigator Michael Hourigan, who had already found out too much about those responsible for the attack against the plane of President Juvénal Habyarimana,[8] which triggered the massacres of 1994.

Similarly, later, when Carla Del Ponte, who had succeeded Louise Arbour, attempted to investigate RPF crimes, she was forced to come to Kigali and apologise to Kagame. She then lost the post of prosecutor of the Tribunal for Rwanda (although she was maintained in her position of prosecutor of the ICTY). This is a far cry from the mandatory independence of the judiciary.

## Financial Administration and Corruption

What quickly became very intriguing was the alleged financial administration of the registrar and the chief administrative officer. Under the pretext of lack of funding, the Tribunal could not have the staff or offices or cars or equipment it needed. For the staff, the solution seemed obvious: we could ask for increased loaning of staff from Member States and international organisations, and that is what should have been done. Convinced of this, I decided to do just that to solve personnel problems in my service. With just a few phone calls I got promises of staff loans representing more than three million dollars per year.

To my amazement, this initiative was not well received at all, and it was roundly rejected by the registrar, who absolutely did not want to hear about personnel loans. The reasons seemed manifold: (a) the staff on loan was often much more competent than their superiors who were permanent UN administrators, which created discomfort and conflict; (b) by definition, such a staff member was independent and could not be subjected to internal pressures of any kind; (c) the staff on loan took jobs that could have been awarded by favouritism and nepotism; (d) the staff cost nothing, so it did not entail any "management" of funds, thus no possibility of embezzlement; (e) staff on loan would generally work and provide results, which would have gone against the dream of the registrar and his henchmen, which was to ensure the longest possible existence for the Tribunal. Therefore, the registrar was strongly opposed to such a measure and the Tribunal never took advantage of the offers of free collaboration that I had gathered.

## Waste

One should also examine the multitude of lavish and extravagant expenses—considered normal—even when the Tribunal could not afford thirty US dollars for a phone bill, pay for gas, or buy the necessary supplies and equipment. Two cases illustrate this point.

In the first, at the departure from the Tribunals of the first chief prosecutor, Judge Richard J. Goldstone, the authorities of both the ICTR and ICTY decided to have a farewell party in his honour at the office in The Hague. The registrar of ICTR decided to go with his mistress; the deputy prosecutor did the same with his wife. In accordance with UN rules, all four travelled business class from Arusha and Kigali to The Hague, round trip. With the hotel stay and all incidental costs, this represented more than a whopping 10,000 US dollars per person, totalling more than 40,000 US dollars for a party of a few hours, not counting the cost of the party itself.

In the next example, one should examine the use of the Tribunal plane, considered the private toy of a privileged few, which the deputy prosecutor used for a weekend in Nairobi with his wife and his secretary (who was on board simply to buy some shrimp in Nairobi), while at exactly the same time the Tribunal had to pay for plane tickets for some investigators who had to travel to Nairobi on duty. Keep in mind that this was done with public funds and taxpayers' money, allotted following the most terrible massacres.

## Embezzlement, Theft, and Corruption

It was impossible to ignore the widespread corruption present in the boldest and most extravagant forms. There was enough to write a good book on the subject. Here are two examples:

1. Many of the heads of the Tribunal managed to obtain payment of a monthly allowance based on the evacuation of the United Nations Assistance Mission for Rwanda (UNAMIR) to Nairobi during the massacres of 1994, evacuation that had taken place more than a year earlier. One should know that the Tribunal did not even exist at the time of this evacuation; that the Tribunal was never evacuated; that the employees in question were not even working for UN at that time; that they were therefore never evacuated; and, once again, that the evacuation had ended more than a year earlier. How was it possible to justify the payment of these monthly evacuation allowances under such circumstances? Impossible to know.

2. The Tribunal's budget had two main sources: the regular UN budget and a Special Fund, as often exists in UN missions. The Special Fund then amounted to about seven million dollars, and one could legitimately wonder why the registrar did not want to use one single dollar from the Fund even as he was begging and pleading for more money and arguing that the Tribunal was paralysed by its lack of resources. I finally learned, from an absolutely reliable source in finance at the UN Office of Nairobi, that the Registrar was at the very final steps of transferring the entire content of the Special Fund to some personal accounts in a bank of West Africa. Something had to be done.

## Complaint to the Secretary General and Request for Investigation

Such corruption could not go on. This fraudulent farce had to stop. In agreement with some brave employees who did the same, I wrote to the Secretary General and to OIOS to request an investigation into embezzlement, theft, bribery, kickbacks, nepotism, favouritism, and general mismanagement of the Tribunal.[9]

## Results and Consequences of the Investigations

Several investigation reports were drafted, some confidential, some public. They all confirmed that the Tribunal was hopelessly mired in incompetence, corruption, and internal conflict. Then the Member States, including Norway, as well as some international NGOs began to lobby increasingly strongly to have the situation corrected and for the Tribunal to show some results, especially since rumour already estimated the costs of the Tribunal at more than 350 million US dollars. For the Tribunal, in practice, this meant that trials had to be undertaken immediately and expeditious convictions obtained at all costs. The very existence of the Tribunal and too many very profitable careers depended on that.

The first victim of this panic was the presumption of innocence. Under this kind of pressure, the first accused, whoever they were, had no chance of benefitting from the presumption of innocence and getting a fair trial, much less being acquitted. They were doomed from the start. Who cared? The justification was already found. It was repeated like a mantra: "Even if there are some problems with evidence, it is sure that they are guilty." One could not deny the presumption of innocence more clearly.

That is, in my opinion, what happened to the first man accused, Jean-Paul Akayesu, whose conviction would have amazed me if he had not been the first accused. I participated in the investigation about Akayesu; I went to Taba Commune with some Dutch investigators to interview so-called witnesses who had been described to us as solid and interesting elements for the prosecution. Not only did the team come back empty-handed, because the witnesses had nothing to say or were not providing reliable evidence, but one of the interviewees turned out to be an excellent potential witness for the defence with a remarkable presentation of the statements, actions, and behaviour of Akayesu during the period in question. I was shocked to learn that years after this investigation, the prosecution had "discovered" new witnesses against Akayesu. Then I reminded myself that investigators had found out that at the time anyone could hire a brigade of six false witnesses for twenty-five US dollars ready to give a sworn statement about anything.

\*\*\*

Given the impact of the media campaign and of the publication of some of the investigation reports of OIOS,[10] all exceptionally damning for the administration of the Tribunal, as well as some increasingly strong pressure from donor countries to the Tribunal, the Secretary General decided that he had no choice but to demand the resignation of the registrar and of the deputy prosecutor, which he obtained and announced with a statement and a press release. These forced resignations and their announcement were absolutely unprecedented in the history of the United Nations,[11] which gives an idea of the scale of the scandal.

With the forced resignation of Registrar Adede and of the Deputy Prosecutor Rakotomanana, all the senior management of the Tribunal was transferred to other UN departments. However, it was impossible to replace each and every incompetent staff member appointed by favouritism and nepotism; there were too many and it would have depleted the Tribunal. Unfortunately, the UN seems to have an absolute rule, unwritten but absolute: the administration never goes back and never corrects its mistakes or its flawed administrative decisions. Hence one should not believe that all the problems of corruption and incompetence were thus corrected and solved. Far from it, as it would appear later.

## And the Good Staff?

One should not conclude that all Tribunal employees, all its lawyers, and all its judges were dishonest or incompetent; it would be very unfair for a minority who fought day after day to achieve professional, honest, and competent work, and to ensure that justice was rendered for the victims, all the victims, and for the accused to have fair trials. Unfortunately for them, the rule that the UN applies to its judgments and investigative reports is to never disclose the names of those concerned, including the names of those found guilty. The appalling result is that when there is a conviction, one cannot distinguish the honest employees from the dishonest ones, and also that all honest employees are included in this conviction just like those whom they have condemned and denounced. What is worse is that incompetent and dishonest employees can take advantage of the anonymity to keep their functions and avoid any punishment, or even obtain promotions. That rule, clearly, must be changed. There were multiple examples of this at the Tribunal itself.

One should not forget the brave employees who risked—and lost— their jobs for having denounced mismanagement and embezzlement by the Tribunal authorities in accordance with the obligation imposed on them by UN rules. If the Tribunal could be re-launched on a better footing later, it is due to their unselfishness and their sacrifice. Unfortunately, contrary to official US government claims about its own practices, the UN does not encourage whistleblowers; it punishes them instead of rewarding them, even when their actions save millions of dollars to the UN as was the case in the aforementioned instance.[12] The UN would benefit greatly, financially and administratively, if Member States corrected that situation by following the US example.

It must be recognised that for too many people in the Rwandan tragedy, the creation of the Tribunal has given rise to political mystification that has served as a springboard for their career plans or, worse yet, that it represented a great opportunity for personal promotion and enrichment on the backs of the victims. This was very far from the duty of respect and remembrance owed to victims. Too often, also, it was far from the diligent search for truth and the most elementary justice.

The same problems of incompetence, embezzlement, and mismanagement were also endemic in some other international Tribunals, including the Khmer Rouge Tribunal where I was consultant.[13] The duty of remembrance and the respect due to the victims require us to demand a serious, critical, and independent examination of the functioning and working of the International Criminal Tribunal for Rwanda and other international tribunals, in terms of both administration and justice, in order to draw lessons which would go beyond the flattering mystification that is now offered to us about these Tribunals.

## Notes

1. S/Res/995, 1994.
2. A/51/789 of February 6, 1997, and several other investigation reports from OIOS concerning the Tribunal.
3. See for example: *Sirois v. The Secretary General of United Nations*, ATNU, Judgment No. 1135; *Goddard v. The Secretary General of United Nations*, ATNU, Judgment No. 1132; *Lacoste v. The Secretary General of the United Nations*, ATNU, Judgment No. 1159.
4. An example of the result of this improvisation relates to the sometimes very significant adverse effects of certain important political or procedural decisions made by the Tribunal. For example, the Tribunal decided that it would concern itself only

with the "big fish," those who were accused of having killed at least 10,000 people. In practice this meant that those accused of the worst crimes were guaranteed a much better treatment and fate than the "small fish" who were accused of "only" a few murders, even just a single one. Those accused of the worst massacres were guaranteed not to risk the death penalty, contrary to the "small" accused, who would be tried in Rwandan courts and run the risk of the death penalty. In addition, pending their trial, the worst accused were assured of the best conditions of detention in Africa, if not the world, while the "small" accused were languishing in conditions so harsh that they might die before their trials. Worse, if convicted, these «worst criminals» were assured of living conditions so good that their life expectancy became instantly one of the best in Africa, certainly better than if they had never killed anyone and remained quietly at home. It could be argued that there are surely people in Africa or elsewhere who would be willing to sacrifice their freedom for such living conditions. A premium for massacres?

5. *Sirois v. The Secretary General of United Nations*, ATNU, Judgment No. 1135.

6. Shaharyan M. Khan, *The Shallow Graves of Rwanda*, I. B. Tauris, London, 2000.

7. This location was chosen after a long night of debate in the Security Council; Tanzania was picked mainly because, unlike all other embassies in Kigali, the Tanzanian embassy remained open during the time of the killings and courageously kept trying to be of some help.

8. See *inter alia*: Robin Philpot, *Rwanda and the New Scramble for Africa: From Tragedy to Imperial Useful Fiction*, Baraka Books, Montreal, 2013; Ann Garrison and Robin Philpot, "Legacies: Michael Hourigan and the International Criminal Tribunal for Rwanda, Who was behind the Assassination of the Rwandan and Burundian presidents in April 1994," Global Research, April 7, 2014, http://www.globalresearch.ca/legacies-michael-hourigan-and-the-international-criminal-tribunal-for-rwanda/5361083.

9. Simultaneously, in order to make sure that OIOS did not stifle the case, I made my denunciation widely known within the Tribunal and the UN thus discouraging the looting of the Special Fund; then I launched a media campaign using local and international media. This is now considered the first whistleblower campaign about the UN.

10. A/51/789, February 6, 1997, and several other OIOS investigation reports about the ICTR.

11. However, the Registrar was allowed to come back to his former office at the Tribunal for more than six months (under the pretext of «cleaning up» his files). He then was able to have retaliatory actions taken against those who had denounced him and requested the investigations and, *inter alia,* prohibited the renewal of my contract (and that of the director of finance and of the Tribunal spokeswoman), despite the pressing representations of Louise Arbour against such a baseless decision, citing the "excellence" of my services and despite the fact that he had no authority to make such a decision. He did not have any grounds either but, as the Administrative Tribunal later concluded, the registrar ordered some staff to withdraw from my personnel file all that was favourable to me and replace that by false, unfavourable documents that he ordered to be fabricated. I then sued the Secretary General and, seven years later, received a terse, unprecedented judgment

from the UN Administrative Tribunal concluding totally in my favour and harshly criticising the administration of the ICTR, granting me the maximum of damages allowed, i.e., two years' salary, or about twenty percent of what I had lost in this affair. By the same occasion I obtained two other judgments against the ICTR for similar cases that I had filed for colleagues, judgments that also condemned the administration of the ICTR very severely.

12. Steven Edwards, "Honesty doesn't pay at UN, staff say in survey," *National Post*, June 16, 2004; Barbara Crossette (Chief of *The New York Times* UN Office), "The Cost of U.N. Whistleblowing," U.N. Notebook, in *The Atlantic*, February 9, 2004, https://www.theatlantic.com/past/docs/foreign/unwire/crossette2004-02-09.htm.

13. Some day someone must examine seriously the importance of bribery and the abysmal incompetence of too many in relation to the administration of justice within the Khmer Rouge Tribunal.

# 11

# The Dubious Heritage of the International Criminal Tribunal for Rwanda

JOHN PHILPOT

Since the creation of the ICTR in 1995, the prosecutor has tried seventy-four men and one woman, all members of the vanquished majority and no one from the invading force, which called itself the Rwandan Patriotic Army. One of the alleged aims of the ICTR was to contribute to the process of national reconciliation and charge both sides.[1]

The glaring injustices arising from the work of the International Criminal Tribunal for Rwanda and addressed herein include:

- Guarantee of impunity for the leaders of the Rwandan Patriotic Front/Rwandan Patriotic Army and Paul Kagame, and the sustainability of their government aided by the removal of the ICTR prosecutor and the referral of ICTR cases to Rwanda.
- The perpetuation of dishonest myths including that of a planned genocide of the Tutsi by the Hutu, which is contradicted by its own judgments denying planning and the related murder of Juvénal Uwilingiyimana and of a dishonest version of history with decisions on judicial notice.
- Biased and unfair application of review proceedings: the cases of Jean-Paul Akayesu and Jean-Bosco Barayagwiza.
- Mistreatment of acquitted persons and unreasonable time delays.
- Anomalies such as the prejudicial behaviour of former Judge Navanethem Pillay and result-oriented law.
- Failure to encourage reconciliation in Rwanda.

## Impunity

The crimes of the Rwandan Patriotic Front and its army have been fully documented. They include the wanton massacre of Hutu following the invasion of October 1, 1990; the assassination of the two Hutu Presidents, Juvénal Habyarimana and Cyprien Ntaryamira, respectively of Rwanda and Burundi on April 6, 1994; the scorched-earth policies in the east of Rwanda in 1994 and the massacres of thousands of Hutu refugees and Congolese between 1993 and 2003 documented in the 550-page 2010 United Nations Mapping Report;[2] and the continuation of these policies up to the present.

The Kagame government is also well known for its international crimes: invasion of the Congo; the murder of dissidents and its enemies such as Theoneste Lizinde and Seth Sendashonga in Kenya, Patrick Karegeya in South Africa, Juvénal Uwilingiyimana in Brussels, Pasteur Musabe in Cameroun, University of Dar es Salaam Law Professor Jwani Mwaikusa in Dar es Salaam; and the three recent attempts in South Africa on the life of former RPF founding member Faustin Kayumba Nyamwasa.

None of these crimes has been brought before the ICTR or any other international court. The ICTR has ignored these crimes, many of which lie within its 1994 jurisdiction.

This impunity tends to legitimise the minority RPF leadership while removing all legitimacy from the previous Rwandan leadership, almost entirely Hutus, whom the ICTR has charged and demonised.

## Firing a Wayward Prosecutor

The ICTR prosecutor has the power to charge any persons responsible for serious violations of international humanitarian law including, of course, the victorious RPF. Yet despite the professed intention to charge all parties to the conflict, the ICTR prosecution has been faithful to the governments that sponsored it (the United States and the United Kingdom) by ensuring impunity for members of the Rwandan Patriotic Front and only charging the losers in the war. According to Article 15 of the ICTR Statute, the prosecutor is "independent" and receives instructions from no government. The facts prove the contrary: if you don't follow instructions, you will be fired, as Prosecutor Carla Del Ponte learned.

From 1996 until 2003, the International Criminal Tribunal for the Former Yugoslavia (ICTY) and the ICTR had a single joint prosecutor.

The ICTR prosecutor had overwhelming evidence of crimes committed by the RPF. In early 1997, prosecution investigator Michael Hourigan and other investigators in the National Team had uncovered convincing evidence that the RPF had assassinated President Habyarimana. Prosecutor Louise Arbour terminated the investigation and put an end to the career of Mr. Hourigan.[3] In 2000 and 2001, the new ICTR prosecutor, Carla Del Ponte, considered prosecuting leaders of the RPF. The prosecution files had sufficient evidence to convict many RPF leaders, including Paul Kagame. To counter this threat, the Rwandan Government blocked the transfer of witnesses to testify at the ICTR in 2001.

Del Ponte showed some signs of independence. In 1999 and early 2000, Carla Del Ponte had been carrying out an investigation of NATO for war crimes committed in the course of the NATO airstrikes on Yugoslavia committed from March to June 1999. The war was illegal and produced massive civilian casualties and the illegal destruction of the infrastructure of Serbia.[4] During the investigation of NATO, Del Ponte was *persona non grata* in Washington since the US Government was totally opposed to the investigation of NATO.[5]

Del Ponte was open to charging both sides in the Rwandan conflict. She had stated publicly in 2000 that, "if it is the RPF that shot down the plane, the history of the genocide must be rewritten." She also stated it would be within her jurisdiction to investigate the downing of the plane if the prosecutor had evidence or concrete suspicion that the assassination of the president was an act related to the genocide and if true the investigation would be reopened.[6]

In her book titled *The Hunt: Me and My War Criminals (La caccia. Io e i criminali di guerra)*,[7] she wrote that Rwandan authorities already controlled each stage of their investigations and that the Office of the Prosecutor knew that Rwanda's intelligence service had received equipment from the United States used to monitor phone calls, faxes, and the Internet. The Office of the Prosecutor suspected that the authorities had also infiltrated the Rwandan computer network and placed agents among the Rwandan interpreters and other members of the team in Kigali.[8]

Washington mistrusted Carla Del Ponte and undertook to remove her as prosecutor of the ICTR.

Based in Arusha at the seat of the ICTR, American prosecutor Michael Johnston suspended the "Special Investigations" of the RPF in September 2002 without the knowledge of Del Ponte. In December 2002, she ordered they be recommenced. In May 2003, several meetings were held in Washington between United States Ambassador-at-Large for War Crimes Issues Pierre Prosper, Carla Del Ponte, and representatives of the Rwandan Government. Prosper wanted Del Ponte to defer investigations of RPF crimes to the Rwandan Government. She refused.[9]

The only solution was to remove Carla Del Ponte from the ICTR by splitting the prosecutor's position into two, one for the ICTY and one for the ICTR. At the behest of the US and the UK, negotiations to split the prosecutor's position began in July 2003.

WikiLeaks revealed a US diplomatic cable, dated July 17, 2003, reporting a meeting on July 16, 2003 between the American Ambassador and ICTY Judge President Theodor Meron. Judge Meron was critical of Del Ponte's management and urged that she not be renewed as prosecutor. He supported the idea of a separate prosecutor for the ICTR and the ICTY.[10]

The Security Council adopted Resolution 1503 on September 28 creating a separate prosecutor's position for the ICTR, distinct from that of the ICTY. Theoretically, the new prosecutor, Gambian Hassan Jallow, appointed on September 15, 2003, would be independent. Not so! He learned from his predecessor's lessons of that the RPF could not be charged. Jallow charged no member of the RPF for its war crimes and crimes against humanity committed in 1994, which indicates that he heeded implicit—or explicit—orders from, or pressure by, the United States and Britain.

Had the leadership of Rwanda been charged as it should have been, its legitimacy to govern would have been seriously undermined. The obstruction of justice by the United States, Britain, and Rwanda, and the collaboration of ICTR authorities, further reinforced the Rwandan dictatorship.

## Referral to National Courts and Rwandan impunity

In 2012, the ICTR once again reinforced the Rwandan Patriotic Front by declaring, contrary to common knowledge, that Rwanda can hold fair trials.

The ICTR Rules were amended progressively in 2002 and 2003 to allow referral of indictments to national jurisdictions considered able and willing to hold the trials. Referral has come to mean that cases before the ICTR can be referred Rwanda. There were two referrals to France in 2007 for accused persons arrested in France. Since then, the only referrals have been to Rwanda.

Referral from the ICTR in Arusha to Rwanda is an astounding procedure. The ICTR prosecutor is bestowed with exceptional supra-national powers to arrest, detain, and transfer accused to Arusha to be tried before the august international jurisdiction. Then, almost out of the blue, the prosecutor takes procedures to send the same accused to Rwanda to be tried before local courts having little or no credibility. The logic is hard to fathom. Is there no pride or dignity at the ICTR, or just cynical subservience to the United States and Rwanda? Under this agenda, referral to Rwanda has become the rule for most recent ICTR indictees, including some six who have not been arrested.[11]

Rwanda is known for its unfair national trials, the most glaring of which is the recent conviction on appeal of Victoire Ingabire Umuhoza, former presidential candidate. Her conviction was maintained on appeal and her sentence increased to fifteen years. She has been denied a fair trial by expedient judges who accept improperly gathered evidence and disregard procedural justice.[12] Expedited justice, arbitrary sentences, and absence of the Rule of Law are well documented.[13]

Despite the manifest incapacity of the Rwandan dictatorship to render justice and its complete control over the judicial system, the ICTR has effectively rehabilitated and buttressed the regime by decreeing that Rwanda can hold fair trials. On February 23, 2012, the ICTR Appeals Chamber ordered ICTR accused Jean Uwinkindi transferred to Rwanda for trial.[14] Uwinkindi had been arrested in 2010 in Uganda. Without his arrest by the ICTR in Uganda, he could not have been legally transferred to Rwanda. The same happened to Bernard Munyagishari[15] who was arrested on May 27, 2011 in the Democratic Republic of the Congo, which was at war with Rwanda. He was transferred to the ICTR and the ICTR then referred his case to Rwanda. The ICTR unfairly permitted a transfer from the Congo to Rwanda when a direct extradition would have been impossible. The Rule of Law and the respect for norms in international relations is not important for the ICTR.

Canada and European countries have acted on the ICTR's loud—and dishonest—message that Rwanda can hold fair trials. Individuals can be transferred/expelled and extradited because the ICTR has decreed that Rwanda has "fair" trials. The most striking example is the expulsion of Dr. Léon Mugesera to Rwanda in January 2012. More such cases are expected.

## Myths and Lies

Despite ICTR failure to prove there was a planned genocide, the ICTR Registrar consciously helps the myth prevail.

The ICTR has failed abysmally in its attempt to validate the theory of the meticulously planned genocide organised either by the Hutu or the *Akazu* circle close to President Habyarimana or by General Théoneste Bagosora and the army.

It has never taken into account the major cause, namely, the Rwandan Patriotic Front's attack on the presidential plane on April 6, 1994, which was the spark that ignited the extreme political violence referred to as "the genocide."

The trial and appeal of Mr. Bagosora and three other military leaders lasted from 2001 to December 14, 2011. Mr. Bagosora was arrested in 1996. With all the financial and other resources of the United Nations, the prosecutor failed to prove that Mr. Bagosora and the military leaders conspired to commit genocide. After appeal, Théoneste Bagosora was absolved of all individual personal liability. He was only considered guilty for the crimes of soldiers considered under his responsibility, for which he would be responsible by negligence or failure to act.[16]

Similarly, Protais Zigiranyirazo was charged with conspiring to commit genocide together with his sister, Agathe Kanziga, wife of the assassinated president, and other members of the so-called *Akazu,* the alleged circle of conspirators around the president. Mr. Zigiranyirazo was acquitted of this conspiracy charge and then, on appeal, of all remaining accusations. This acquittal was based on lack of evidence to convict and not on technicalities. After nine years of detention, he was released from prison without any indemnity and without being returned to Belgium where he was arrested.[17]

In the media trial, the Appeals Chamber held there had been no conspiracy between Jean-Bosco Barayagwiza, Ferdinand Nahimana, and Hassan Ngeze.[18]

In what is called the Military II Trial, the four accused, Augustin Ndindiliyimana, Augustin Bizimungu, François-Xavier Nzuwonemeye, and Innocent Sagahutu, were acquitted of conspiring or of agreeing to commit genocide on May 17, 2011. This conspiracy ruling was maintained on appeal, with acquittals entered for two of the four and with one judgment postponed.[19]

The broadest finding of the so-called master plan was in the trial judgment of Mathieu Ngirumpatse and Édouard Karemera. That judgment found the conspiracy to be proven by the date of May 25, 1994, a far cry from the widely publicised pre-existing master plan that the "genocide" had been meticulously planned prior to April 6, 1994.[20] At paragraphs 1583 ss. the Chamber found that an agreement to destroy the Tutsi had materialised prior to May 25, 1994 and that the Accused Ngirumpatse and Karemera were therefore party to the conspiracy as leaders of the MRND party and, in the case of Mr. Karemera, also Minister of the Interior. The Appeals judgment has not yet been rendered.

The prosecutor left no stone unturned in trying to pin the responsibility on the *Akazu* and the Hutu leadership. Under Prosecutor Stephen Rapp, the prosecution formed the prosecutor's "*Akazu* team" of investigators and attorneys. Based on the gang theories prevalent in the United States, Canada, and Europe, Stephen Rapp undertook his proof by a botched use of a first so-called insider witness, Michel Bagaragaza, and then a second attempt which led to the December 2005 murder in Belgium of a former minister, Juvénal Uwilingiyimana. From September to December 2004, the former director of the national tea industry of Rwanda (OCIR-Thé), Michel Bagaragaza, was enticed to make some three months of false declarations against Protais Zigiranyirazo, one of the prime targets of the US Prosecutor Stephen Rapp. Bagaragaza, who may have had some blood on his hands in northwest Rwanda in April 1994, was promised a trial in Europe, a short prison sentence, and relocation of his complete family to the US along with financial support. The Trial Chamber refused to accept his many lies.[21]

The prosecution team led by Mr. Rapp also used Bagaragaza to recruit a second insider witness, a former minister, Juvénal Uwilingiyimana. Under the threat of the sealed genocide indictment by the ICTR, Mr. Uwilingiyimana agreed to meet prosecution staff on a regular basis between September and November 2005 in Lille, France. They tried to make him tell lies about Protais Zigiranyirazo and Mathieu Ngirumpatse. When Mr. Uwilingiyimana wanted to withdraw from the dishonest investigation and be transferred to Arusha to be tried, prosecution investigators Réjean Tremblay and André Delvaux told him that he would be lynched, crushed, that his body would be trampled on in the street, and the dogs would piss on him. I was in Brussels when Mr. Uwilingiyimana disappeared on November 28, 2005. He explained what had happened in his letter to the prosecutor and had given a copy of the letter to several friends since he was worried about his security.[22] His dismembered body was found in the Charleroi Canal several weeks later. The prosecution threats had been carried out. The prosecutor bears serious responsibility for this death, the cause of which has never been elucidated. The physical elimination of Mr. Uwilingiyimana was probably necessary for the ICTR prosecutor and Rwanda: one can only imagine how the credibility of the prosecutor's dishonest "*Akazu* team" would have been undermined if Mr. Uwilingiyimana had been tried in Arusha and had spoken up about the prosecutor's attempt to corrupt justice and fabricate evidence against Mr. Zigiranyirazo and Mr. Ngirumpatse.

Despite the acquittal of Protais Zigiranyirazo, the alleged leader of the *Akazu*, and the abject failure of the strategy to invent a pre-existing conspiracy or plan, the ICTR website still has an *Akazu* cartoon contradicting the tribunal's own judgment. The cartoon demonises the *Akazu*, saying that the president and the *Akazu* refused to share power, that it organised a hate radio station, and that it organised the Interahamwe militia group to kill Tutsi.[23] The ICTR serves as an organ of propaganda in contempt of its own judgments. If the ICTR was dignified and interested in truth, it would actively publicise the failure to find planning in the Rwandan "genocide".

## The War: An Internal or International Conflict?

Under the principle of judicial notice, the tribunal decided that the war was non-international in character and no evidence to the contrary would be admissible. This decision distorts the understanding of the war.

All evidence available indicates that the war in Rwanda beginning on October 1, 1990 was an international war. The actions of the RPF were launched from Uganda and the Rwandan Patriotic front was in fact part of the Ugandan army. Four thousand troops bearing Ugandan uniforms crossed the Rwandan border on October 1. The consequences of the international nature of the war are important. Another analysis of the conflict is readily available and arguable:

- The Rwandan Government in its fight against the RPF was acting in self-defence; the RPF/Ugandan army were invading a sovereign nation. The war was not a revolutionary war or internal uprising.
- The law of Nuremberg would apply against the RPF/Ugandan army. The RPF/Ugandan army were the aggressors who committed the crime of aggression and war crimes in the war and therefore would be liable.
- In this historical context, the many political parties who allied themselves directly or indirectly with the RPF in 1991, 1992, and 1993 would be collaborators and guilty of treason.
- Similarly, countries and individuals who help the RPF aggressors are guilty of the crimes committed in the war. This could apply to politicians in the United States, Great Britain, Uganda, Belgium, and Canada.

The ICTR Trial Chambers and Appeals Chamber held, however, that the armed conflict in Rwanda was internal in character, was not subject to reasonable dispute, and should be judicially noticed.[24] The concept of judicial notice means that no evidence contrary to the finding can be brought at trial. No evidence of the international character of the war would be admissible in any trial since all trials would be bound under the principle of *stare decisis* (to stand by things decided).

Judicial notice is a concept used in Common Law for issues that need not be proven in court, such as "the sun rises in the morning and sets at night" or that April 6, 1994 was a Wednesday. That the war was not international in nature was decreed to be absolutely true and could not even be questioned in court.

The court, ironically, is named the International Criminal Tribunal for Rwanda for a conflict that was deemed by the same court unquestionably internal. This judicial notice ruling that the war was internal in character denatures the war and rewrites African history by a judicial lie. It prevents any inquiry into the causes of the war, that is, the interests of the United States, Britain, Canada, Belgium, or Uganda in the victory of the Rwandan Patriotic Front. Wars of this magnitude cannot be reduced to simple internal conflicts.

The war on Rwanda launched on the Ugandan border can be likened to the war on Syria, which began in early 2011. At the beginning, some may have thought it was an internal conflict, the Syrian "Arab Spring," although it broke out in areas of Syria bordering on Jordan, Turkey, and Lebanon. In 2014, it has become clear that to the world and above all to the Syrians that it is an international war with massive intervention by foreign mercenaries trained and organised by armed forces of France, Britain, Saudi Arabia, Qatar, and the United States. Syria has resisted with the support of Russia, Iran, and the Lebanese Hezbollah, whereas from 1990 to 1994, Rwanda was almost fully isolated.

The ICTR did not search for truth but rather endeavoured to hide it.

## Double Standard on Review Proceedings

The abuse of the review proceedings casts the ICTR in a bad light. Review of a judgment is a narrow recourse allowing the reopening of a case when a convicted person or the prosecutor discovers a new fact unknown and unavailable at the time of trial and which could have been a decisive factor in the final judgment.[25]

Review was applied to incarcerate Jean-Bosco Barayagwiza unfairly and to avoid release of Jean-Paul Akayesu. In the former case, the prosecutor applied for review; in the latter, the defence applied.

## Jean-Bosco Barayagwiza

The landmark decision—shameful for the ICTR—is the treatment of the late Jean-Bosco Barayagwiza. The Appeals Chamber released Mr. Barayagwiza on November 3, 1999, but the prosecutor applied to review the decision for very dubious reasons.

Jean-Bosco Barayagwiza was a Rwandan diplomat who fled to Cameroun after the RPF took power in Rwanda. After temporary arrest and failed extradition to Rwanda, he was arrested in Cameroun on March 4, 1997, on the basis of an application by the ICTR prosecutor dated February 24, 1997. After transfer to Arusha failed, Mr. Barayagwiza filed a writ of *Habeas Corpus* on September 29, 1997. He was only trans-ferred to Arusha on November 19, 1997. Even after transfer, he did not appear before a judge until February 23, 1998, almost one year after his arrest in Cameroun by order of the tribunal.

On February 24, 1998, he applied to quash his arrest. Almost eight months later, on November 17, 1998, the Trial Chamber refused his urgent request. He appealed to the Appeals Chamber a few days later. On November 3, 1999, the Appeals Chamber dismissed his indictment and ordered his immediate release because of the violation of his rights as a travesty of justice. The integrity of the tribunal was considered to be at stake.[26]

This small, bright light in international justice was soon to be extinguished. A reconstituted Appeals Chamber bench heard a review of the November 3, 1999 decision. David Scheffer, United States Ambassador-at-Large for War Crimes Issues, came to the rescue and provided prior available evidence that the delay of some forty days in Cameroun was due to the electoral process. It also allowed new, pre-viously known evidence that the accused, through his counsel, had accepted delay in appearance.

The Rwandan Government threatened the tribunal that witnesses would not be allowed to come from Rwanda to Arusha to testify.

In principle, review is only allowed when unknown facts or facts not readily available would allow a different decision. Judgments are meant to be final under the principle of *res judicata* (matter already judged). This time the Appeals Chamber succumbed to pressure from Rwanda and bent the law to keep Mr. Barayagwiza in prison, citing the principle that even information readily available could reverse an appeals decision if it would change the decision.[27] Mr. Barayagwiza subsequently died in prison in Benin.

The Appeals Chamber, with the help of David Scheffer, US Ambassador-at-Large for War Crimes Issues, acted with celerity to keep Jean-Bosco Barayagwiza in detention and save the tribunal from the wrath of Rwanda which controlled the flow of witnesses to the Court.[28]

## Jean-Paul Akayesu

Jean-Paul Akayesu did not benefit from his review application as he should have. The Appeals Chamber instead twisted the facts to confirm the conviction of an innocent man.

Jean-Paul Akayesu was the first person at the ICTR convicted after a trial. He only had a show trial of limited value defended by unprepared attorneys imposed on Mr. Akayesu against his will. His attorneys grossly neglected the defence, found few witnesses, and simply went through the motions. On September 4, 1998, the ICTR found Mr. Akayesu guilty and sentenced him to life in prison for crimes allegedly committed in Taba Commune, Gitarama Prefecture.[29]

He was defended on Appeal, over the objection of the Registrar, by the lawyers of his choice, myself and Professor André Tremblay. However, Mr. Akayesu and twenty-five of his co-accused had to go on a hunger strike and then Mr. Akayesu launched long legal proceedings in order to obtain the attorneys of his choice.

Akayesu's defence at trial had been purely factual, denying the accusations against him. Nowhere at trial did his counsel raise the issue of conspiracy to fabricate evidence by Rwandan authorities since no one in defence seemed to be aware of the machinations of the Rwandan authorities to manufacture the case against Mr. Akayesu. Only later, during the appeal process in March 2001, did this conspiracy to fabricate evidence come to light. Mr. Akayesu's sister called me from Belgium to say that a Tutsi man from Taba Commune had participated in the fabrication of the case against Akayesu. He wanted to inform the court of this outright fabrication of evidence in which he had participated. Owing to witness protection requirements, this witness can only be referred to as BBB.[30]

Witness BBB described how leading citizens of Taba conspired with RPF military authorities to invent a false story and false evidence against Jean-Paul Akayesu. The leading conspirator was Mr. Ephrem Karangwa, the key witness against Akayesu and also the *bourgmestre* (mayor) who replaced him. The witness was present at a series of meetings held under the supervision of the military prefect to concoct evidence against Akayesu. He even provided the name of a witness who did not testify but whose statement was in the possession of the defence. Several of the witnesses, including Ephrem Karangwa, were not even in Taba at the time, although they testified about the actions of Mr. Akayesu in Taba. Virtually all the evidence was concocted by this group. Ephrem Karangwa also participated later in fabricating accusations of sexual assault allegedly urged on by Akayesu.

This time, the Appeals Chamber acted expeditiously to stop Mr. Akayesu from telling the truth about his false conviction. The Chamber rejected the evidence claiming it was not related to a "new fact" under the legal terms of review, but was simply a question of witness credibility.[31] If a conspiracy to fabricate evidence was not a new fact, it is hard to imagine what could be a new fact. The Appeals Chamber was not interested in verifying the existence of a criminal conspiracy to corrupt the justice system or a form of public mischief by Rwandan authorities. It was not interested in uncovering the machinations behind the judicial lynching of Mr. Akayesu. Since he was the first person convicted, Jean-Paul Akayesu's necessary acquittal and release would not bode well for the future of the ICTR.

Ironically, Mr. Barayagwiza was held in prison based on the testimony and impetus of the United States Ambassador-at-large for War Crimes Issues, David Scheffer. Jean-Paul Akayesu was prosecuted with fabricated evidence by the American attorney Pierre Prosper, who was soon to become the George W. Bush Ambassador-at-large for War Crimes Issues. The role of the United States in these flagrant injustices requires more thorough investigation.

Further information about Jean-Paul Akayesu and his role in Taba between April and July 1994 is now available. In 2011, his lawyers interviewed a Tutsi woman from Taba commune in the context of another trial. She explained the role of Mr. Akayesu in saving Tutsis in Taba and that he was considered in 1994 as a buttress against the terrible killings going on. The tragedy lies in the fact that this evidence is possibly not admissible because the trial has been over since 1998 and because her evidence may not be a "new fact" in legal terms. Badly defended by unprepared lawyers and judged by a convicting-minded bench, Jean-Paul Akayesu was locked up and any key to release was thrown away.[32]

Review and reconsideration of judgments are now almost impossible since the Appeals Chamber applies the principle of *res judicata* and a narrow conception of "new facts" on review to a situation where new evidence and new unknown facts are always emerging.[33] One can only imagine the new evidence that will become available when and if the Kagame government is swept from office, but also the difficulty convicted persons will have in obtaining redress.

## Lengthy Prejudgment Detention and Mistreatment of the Acquitted

Trials and pre-trial detention at the ICTR are extremely long, as shown by the statistics available on the ICTR website.[34]

Pauline Nyiramasuhuko was arrested in July 1997 in Nairobi and had not yet been judged on appeal when this article went to press. No judgment is likely until sometime in 2015, some eighteen years after arrest. This travesty of justice casts shame on the ICTR. Many others have been detained until final judgment up to fifteen years later.

The plight of those acquitted suggests that those who drafted the ICTR Statute had no intention of allowing for acquittals. Twelve men have been acquitted and only five have been relocated with their families in Europe. The remaining seven are living in Arusha, Tanzania, in ICTR accommodation with no apparent chance to be reunited with their families in Europe or North America. Canadian immigration legislation presumes these former officials to be guilty of human or international rights violations despite their acquittal by a tribunal that Canada supposedly supports.[35] The tribunal has no power to return acquitted persons to the countries where they were arrested even if the prosecutor exercised supra-national powers to arrest them and transfer them to Arusha. There is only a one-way road to Arusha. The Tribunal has no power to grant indemnities to persons acquitted after lengthy detention.[36]

## The Behaviour of Judge Navanethem Pillay

One of the Akayesu judges was Mrs. Navanethem Pillay, who was United Nations High Commissioner for Human Rights at the time this article was written. On November 12, 1997, this sitting judge toured Canada and gave a radio interview to Canadian CBC affirming that there were some 200,000 rapes in Rwanda during the conflict. She continued in a Colloquium at York University. This inflated language was used while she was sitting on the trial of Mr. Akayesu, who was accused of rape, an allegation that he has always rejected. A sitting judge should not be a propagandist as Mrs. Pillay was in this case.

Navanethem Pillay went on to treat Mr. Akayesu (and other convicted persons such as the late Georges Rutaganda) like trophies in her *curriculum vitae* as a candidate to become a judge at the International Criminal Court in 2003.[37] It is in extremely bad taste for this judge to boast whom she had convicted with details of the crimes committed. She acquitted no one, which, it appears, would make her more qualified to be appointed judge at the ICC. After all, she had convicted those people at the ICTR.

After her stint at the ICC, Navanethem Pillay was named United Nations High Commissioner for Human Rights in June 2008.

## Evidence and Defence

Defence lawyers at the ICTR and the ICTY have found work very frustrating. In the context of total impunity for people like Paul Kagame, RPF leader and war criminal from 1990 on, lawyers struggle and often succeed in putting up a very good defence against the syndicated witnesses programmed and organised by the Rwandan Government and its partner, the ICTR prosecutor. Many feel that we have been successful in proving the innocence of our clients. The law says we must only raise doubt as to guilt but, in reality, innocence must be proven beyond all reasonable doubt. Our clients, and we as counsel, are astounded by the shocking judgments of guilt.

Many are astonished by the quality of evidence accepted by the international courts. We are confronted with non-public testimony serving to "protect" witnesses. Secret testimony is risky since potential lies are not subject to public scrutiny even if the accused knows the witnesses' names. The ICTR prosecution cases depend considerably on non-public testimony replete with lies. If counsel releases the names, they are subject to sanctions.

Almost any evidence is admitted at trial and the judges are free to evaluate the evidence. The law is often interpreted to allow for a finding against the defence. The term "result-oriented law" is often used to characterise judicial rulings. Professor Nancy Combs wrote the seminal book *Fact-Finding Without Facts: The Uncertain Evidentiary Foundations of International Criminal Convictions*. It should be compulsory reading in International Criminal Justice.

## Conclusion

It is now well established by insider and eyewitness accounts that the RPF killed President Habyarimana and planned to take power using whatever means necessary. Paul Kagame, the man most responsible along with his international sponsors for the massive killings in Rwanda and the Congo from 1990 to the present, is scot-free and in charge of a mono-ethnic dictatorship.

The ICTR refused to consider the crime of assassination of the Rwandan and Burundian presidents. It did not want to search for truth but only to condemn the losers of the war who were also the political victims of the war. The Rwandan army under Paul Kagame invaded the Congo from 1996 to the present and continues to live with total impunity. The death toll is upwards of four million. He receives red carpet treatment in the United States where he has received honorary doctorates from prestigious universities. In the United Kingdom, Oxford University's prestigious business school invited him to speak in May 2013. The ICTR has played a role in this by creating wholesale impunity for the Rwandan Patriotic Front.

It is hard to imagine that there can be reconciliation. Victoire Ingabire was a candidate for president of Rwanda in 2010. She admitted that there was genocide in Rwanda but said that both sides of the war had committed war crimes. She called for reconciliation in Rwanda. In spite of her popularity—or because of her popularity—she was accused of working for the insurgents in the Democratic Republic of the Congo and was recently sentenced on appeal to fifteen years in prison.[38]

The ICTR has not permitted or encouraged reconciliation; it has not led to peace in the region, but rather the contrary, in its blind direct and indirect support for Paul Kagame and United States foreign policy.

## Notes

1.  Preamble to Resolution 955 of the Security Council on November 8, 1994 establishing the International Criminal Tribunal for Rwanda.
2.  DRC: Mapping human rights violations 1993-2003, http://www.ohchr.org/en/countries/africaregion/Pages/rdcProjetmapping.aspx.
3.  http://rwandadelaguerreaugenocide. univ-paris1.fr/wp-content/uploads/2010/01/Annexe_49.pdf.
4.  Michael Mandel, *How America Gets Away with Murder: Illegal Wars, Collateral Damage and Crimes against Humanity*, Pluto Press, 1994, pp. 57-114
5.  David Scheffer, *All the Missing Souls*, Princeton University Press, 2012, p. 291.
6.  Gunnar Willum and Bjorn Willum, "The Rwanda Genocide Seen in a New Light," *Actuelt*, Denmark, April 17, 2000.
7.  Carla Del Ponte, *La caccia. Io e i criminali di guerra*, Feltrinelli, October 2008.
8.  Carla Del Ponte Tells of her Attempts to Investigate RPF in her New Book, http://www.hirondellenews.com com/ictr-rwanda/collaboration-with-states/collaboration-with-states-rwanda/21710-en-en-020408-ictrrwanda-carla-del-ponte-tells-of-her-attempts-to-investigate-rpf-in-her-new-book1076110761.
9.  Florence Hartmann, *Paix et Châtiment: Les Guerres secrètes de la politique et la justice internationale*, Flammarion, 2007, pp. 266-283.
10. See document at www.johnphilpot.com.
11. See http://www.unictr.org/Cases/tabid/204/Default.aspx. Some of the transferred cases refer to accused at large.
12. See Chapter 3 above, Joseph Bukeye, "Victoire Ingabire: Chronology of a Pinochet-style Case of Repression."
13. Human Rights Watch, https://www.hrw.org/fr/node/121997, http://www.hrw.org/world-report-2011/rwanda; Secret Detentions Centers and Torture, Amnesty International, http://www.amnesty.org/en/library/info/AFR47/004/2012/en.
14. Decision on Uwinkindi's Motion for Review or Reconsideration of the Decision on Referral to Rwanda and the Related Prosecution Motion, February 23, 2012, The Prosecutor v. Jean Uwinkindi, Case No. ICTR-01-75ARIbis, http://www.unictr.org/Portals/0/Case/English/Uwinkindi/decisions/120223.pdf.
15. http://www.unictr.org/Portals/0/Case/English/Munyagishari/decisions/130503.pdf.
16. *Théoneste Bagosora, Anatole Nsengiyumva v. The Prosecutor*, Case No. ICTR-98-41-A, Judgment, December 14, 2011 (Appeal), available on the Tribunal website.
17. See the section below on the plight of acquitted persons.
18. Nahimana *et al.* Appeals Judgment, November 28, 2007, pp. 346-347 on the ICTR website.

19. See the trial judgment and the Appeal Judgment on the ICTR website.
20. *The Prosecutor v. Édouard Karemera and Mathieu Ngirumpatse*, Judgment and Sentence, February 2, 2012, Case No. ICTR-98-44-T, http://www.unictr.org/Portals/0/Case/English/Karemera/Judgement/120202%20-%20JUDGEMENT.pdf.
21. Trial judgment, *Prosecutor v. Protais Zigiranyirazo*, ICTR-01-73-T, December 18, 2008, paras. 137-140.
22. See translation of original letter and an authentic copy of the original French version at www.johnphilpot.com.
23. ICTR cartoon, 2011, pages 12, 13, 14 at http://www.unictr.org/Portals/0/English/News/Cartoon%20Book/ICTR%20Cartoon%20Book%202011.pdf.
24. *Semanza v. Prosecutor*, Case No. ICTR-97-20-A, *Judgment*, May 20, 2005, para. 198; *Prosecutor v. Karemera et al.*, Case No. ICTR-98-44-AR73(C), Decision on Prosecutor's Interlocutory Appeal of Decision on Judicial Notice, June 16, 2006, para. 29; *Prosecutor v. Kalimanzira*, Case No. ICTR-2005-88-I, Decision on Judicial Notice of Facts of Common Knowledge, February 22, 2008.
25. ICTR Statute, Article 25.
26. Barayagwiza, Appeals Chamber Decision, November 3, 1999, No. TPIR-97-19-AR72.
27. Barayagwiza, Decision (Prosecutor's Request For Review Or Reconsideration), March 31, 2000, No. TPIR-97-19-AR72.
28. Barayagwiza, Decision (Prosecutor's Request For Review Or Reconsideration), March 31, 2000, No. TPIR-97-19-AR72, para. 56, subparagraph 2.
29. Akayesu trial judgment, September 4, 1998, on the Tribunal website. The Appeal Judgment dated June 1, 2001, is also available.
30. Releasing his name could lead to a fine or imprisonment. A redacted copy of his statement will be provided on request; write to john@johnphilpot.com.
31. Jean-Paul Akayesu (Requérant) c/Le Procureur (Intimé) Affaire No. ICTR-96-4-A, *Arrêt, Requête aux fins de Renvoi de l'affaire devant la Chambre de première instance I*, May 16, 2001.
32. See above Chapter 10 by André Sirois for more details on how evidence was gathered in Rwanda.
33. See the many post-conviction decisions of the Appeals Chamber in the files of Mr. Eliézer Niyitegeka and the late Georges Rutaganda.
34. Status of Detainees, http://www.unictr.org/Cases/StatusofDetainees/tabid/202/Default.aspx.
35. Article 35 of the Immigration and Refugee Protection Act.
36. Decision on Zigiranyirazo's Motion for damages, ICTR, ICTR-2001-01-073 Trial Chamber III, June 18, 2012, http://www.unictr.org/Portals/0/Case%5CEnglish%5CZigiranyirazo%5Cdecisions%5C120618.pdf. In an unpublished decision available from the author, the Appeals Chamber rejected an application to appeal the Trial Chamber's refusal to relocate and grant damages.
37. http://www.iccnow.org/documents/CVDigest200212Eng.pdf.
38. See Chapter 3 above for details on Ms Ingabire's situation.

# 12

## "The ICTR is war by other means"— Ramsey Clark

PHIL TAYLOR

The UN tribunal in Arusha, Tanzania, declared that it would prosecute those who committed crimes against humanity in 1994 in Rwanda. Armies and civilians on both sides had violated international law and would be tried and the guilty punished. There would be no "victors' justice." The UN was out to establish a high standard, said the opening speeches and regular commentary on this first such tribunal in Africa; a demonstration, as it were, for Africa in the time of the New World Order.

A second theme came in the phrase, "we are going to end the 'culture of impunity in Africa.'" Looking back we can see that these mission statements were drafted by people steeped in imperial assumptions. The Tribunal in Arusha, Tanzania, in fact re-established the culture of colonialism. The money and the leading lights came from the US and Britain. Where else? One of the first VIP visits to Arusha was Princess Anne; the judges all had their pictures taken with her. Later Hillary Clinton arrived, which pleased the locals because potholes were filled for the occasion.

No one who followed news of the Rwandan war of April-July 1994 could doubt that the Rwandan Patriotic Front/Army was a major factor in the war and anti-civilian violence of 1994, known to the world as the Rwandan genocide. Yet no one from the RPF was ever accused let alone tried at the International Criminal Tribunal for Rwanda. So it was victors' justice after all! And this victors' justice was a political victory for the RPF. But more importantly for our understanding, it was a victory for Kagame's not-so-silent partners, the US and Britain.

Placing a presumably high-minded international court in Arusha with a mandate to prosecute perpetrators of serious crimes against humanity became, as a victors' court, a way to aid and abet the

consolidation of power by the Rwandan Patriotic Front. Had Kagame as
military victor claimed to be establishing a court to try war criminals,
he would not have gotten cooperation from neighbouring states, who
knew him too well. But in the dawning days of the New World Order,
how many countries could say no when a "UN" court asked them to
turn over Kagame's targeted enemies? To allay their conscience they
were assured it would not be victors' justice. The President of Kenya
received assurances there would be an investigation into who had
downed President Juvénal Habyarimana's plane, the seminal moment
that triggered the war/genocide.

By bowing to the US/Kagame, the ICTR wish to prosecute those of
the former government side, all Hutus, effectively demonised and criminalised all opponents of the new regime. The Arusha Peace Accord,
which had brought the opposition into the interim government and
was on its way to elections and a new government, was smashed by the
decision of the RPF to go back to war, beginning most likely with the
shooting down of the plane bearing the Hutu presidents of Rwanda and
Burundi as well as the commander of the Rwandan army. In the words
of UNAMIR commander Dallaire, on the night of April 6, 1994, the
RPF army (RPA) was in an "offensive mode" and the army of Rwanda
was in a "defensive mode."

Paul Kagame's apologists have a pet phrase: "Kagame captured power
and ended the genocide." Had ending the genocide been his intent, he
would have agreed to a ceasefire and the implementation of the Arusha
Accord, which would have meant the continuation of a multi-party
democratic process and the saving of thousands of lives. But the RPF
put aside political parties and popular leaders and made a naked power
grab. Kagame publicists claimed he was fighting a government and army
that were carrying out a well-planned genocide of Tutsis.

With the United States and Britain as Kagame's advocates, former
Rwandan army and political leaders were rounded up in various countries, delivered to Arusha, and tried on the false claims and rhetoric of
the RPF and its admirers. Now twenty years after the events we have dis-
turbing news. Those military and political leaders (from various political parties) accused by Kagame were not found guilty of conspiring to
commit genocide. Several were acquitted outright. These leaders, who

wanted a ceasefire to be maintained from the first moments of April 7, 1994, did not carry out a genocide plan.

The truth came out in the hard-fought legal battles waged by defence counsel at the ICTR. In nearly deserted courtrooms with virtually no media (except for Kagame apologists and NGOs who specialised in obscurantism), the lawyers tackled the prosecution's case. From counsel's efforts the great RPF rescue narrative was dismantled.

Defence lawyers did their jobs; they were not inoculated with seminars and legal retreats where the gurus of "international justice" have established cults. One good criminal lawyer is worth an entire college of in-bred legal human rights specialists. Study the cases and watch the sparks fly up from lawyers not in awe of robes and celebrity witnesses. This must be noted because there is steady pressure from the funded apparatchiks of the new "international courts" to deprive accused of counsel of choice, the goal being to bring into being a bar that shares the new "mission." The ICTR experience shows you're better off with a good lawyer who, to paraphrase John Floyd, has attended other rodeos.

The ICTR record shows the accused were not enemies of the Arusha process; that a democratic system, socially inclusive, was aborted/murdered by a strongman with no political loyalties. As for the "rescue" legend, UN commander Roméo Dallaire has observed that Kagame did not move his troops to rescue anyone but rather to guarantee victory in a war. In Dallaire's words, "As he conducted his time-consuming maneuvers, the killings of civilians only escalated."[1] Whatever might happen to the civilian population, especially the Tutsis, was not his main concern, if indeed it was a concern at all.

The moment the RPF seized power, the US gave them immediate recognition. They chose the strongman over the Arusha Peace Accord and arranged for the defeated government to go to the Arusha court. Now, all these years of imprisonment later, the courts have *not* found a conspiracy or orders to commit genocide. Supporters of the Arusha Peace Accord have been doing time, while a military adventurer, personally advised by former British Prime Minister Tony Blair, rules Rwanda, intervenes in Congo, assassinates opponents, and receives foreign admirers in Kigali.

President Obama has a favourite homily that "Africa doesn't need strong men, Africa needs strong institutions." If that is true, why does America support a strongman who belongs in an institution?

## A Victory for the RPF and an Incitement to Further Crimes

Far from ending impunity, the ICTR has virtually granted impunity to the RPF. While the ICTR publicists were sanctimoniously assuring the gullible that a new wind of justice and freedom was blowing through Africa, Rwanda crossed the border of Zaïre and attacked United Nations refugee camps at the cost of thousands of lives. Then, together with elements of the Ugandan army, they drove across Zaïre at the cost of many more thousands of Congolese and Rwandan lives to install Laurent-Désiré Kabila in power in Kinshasa. No one in Washington or London said, "Stop, thief!" The RPF troops may as well have been called the hordes of impunity. Meanwhile Hutu internal refugees were massacred by the RPF at Kibeho. The UN personnel who witnessed that crime marvel to this day that no leaders were charged.[2]

No ICTR charges against any RPF members meant that they had impunity. They could assume the mantle of victim and liberator and do as they pleased. If the ICTR had done its duty and prosecuted RPF members for crimes against humanity in 1994 Rwanda, the special "heroic" status would have been undermined. Loud questions would have been asked about the attacks on UN camps, and about the assassination of RPF defectors in Nairobi, former Interior Minister, Seth Sendashonga, and Colonel Theoneste Lizinde. Had the RPF members been charged with war crimes, which all acknowledge they surely committed, reconciliation would have been possible and political inclusiveness a necessity. Instead, Paul Kagame, the RPF's cult-commander and president of the country (after a fashion), was provided impunity. In order that he might attack Zaïre/Congo and occupy its mineral-rich eastern region, it was necessary that the ICTR see to it that the hem of his garments was kept clean. And they did so. You have only to read Carla Del Ponte's memoir to know the unsavoury details.[3]

We should recall that Pierre Prosper, the US ambassador who told Del Ponte that she should not open a file for RPF crimes, had served as a prosecutor at the UN Tribunal in Arusha.[4]

I suppose it helps that President Kagame has former British Prime Minister Tony Blair as a special advisor. How did the two become so intimate? And another intimate friend is former President Bill Clinton. It is said Clinton supports Kagame because he feels guilty that he did not send US troops to Rwanda in 1994. Think about the career and life of Bill Clinton and see if you believe he has problem with guilt feelings. One thing Clinton and Kagame know of each other (and the world seems not to remember) is that in 1994 Kagame never asked for the US to intervene in Rwanda and Clinton never offered![5]

It had to be victors' justice, otherwise there would be no choice but to question Kagame's grip on power. The original internationally agreed formula for Rwanda, the Arusha Peace Accord, would have to be implemented. The ICTR allowed Kagame to wear the mask of virtue; he was/ is permitted to judge the court. On many occasions the UN Court had to accommodate Paul Kagame. Word would come that the RPF leader was upset and Judge Navanethem Pillay or ICTR Prosecutor Carla Del Ponte would have to fly to Kigali to soothe the pouting president. Judge Gabriel Kirk McDonald of the UN Appeals court ruled that the accused, Jean-Bosco Barayagwiza (PhD, International Law), must be released with prejudice from prison because his rights had been egregiously violated by the ICTR prosecution but no, he was not released. A deeper victors' court intervened. Kagame and an American emissary wanted him kept in prison and made to stand trial. Guess who won. The appeal court, *sans* McDonald, overruled itself. Barayagwiza died in prison.

Dr. Barayagwiza, incidentally, had been a member of the Rwandan government delegation that went to New York and pleaded with the United Nations to intervene in Rwanda to save lives and guarantee the Arusha Peace Accord. Guess why Kagame did not want that? And another question: why did Human Rights Watch, in the person of Alison Des Forges, among others, work to undermine the delegation that called for intervention to save lives, going to such lengths as trying to serve an American court summons on Barayagwiza?[6] Ms. Des Forges, who acted against a peace delegation with such zealotry, later became a star prosecution "expert" witness. Any possibility she was biased?

On one occasion a protected witness arrived in Arusha to testify for the defence. Rwandan radio announced he was arriving on a particular flight and that a warrant had been issued for his arrest as a *génocidaire*. All the particulars of his identity were revealed and he was accused of crimes. There was a scramble to keep the Tanzanians from acting on the warrant. A protected witness! Observers of the court many times heard the judges admonish all counsels with the importance of shielding the identification of protected witnesses. Did the ICTR consider a contempt charge? Did they admonish the Kigali regime? If you ask these questions you may have been born yesterday.

Again, by not prosecuting any RPF members, the ICTR helped destroy the political instrument for solving Rwanda's political crisis, the Arusha Peace Accord. The one-side-is-guilty doctrine enables Kagame to vet and choose who can serve in public life. He can label anyone a *génocidaire* or revisionist, eliminate them from public life, jail them, or worse. Many of his former colleagues testify to this and of course there were others who said so and have been assassinated. Another ugly result of the righteous RPF narrative is that in various countries around the world, groups have been formed to stalk the Hutus or dissident Tutsis in search of extremists. These groups include Europeans who derive a vicarious pride in their search for *génocidaires*, never for a moment acknowledging they might be helping a dictator, and of course never looking for RPF henchmen. UN victors' justice opened the door for this vigilantism.

Carla Del Ponte, in her book *Madame Prosecutor*, noted the consequences of impunity: "Failure to investigate the RPF would send an unambiguous signal that the Tutsi leaders enjoyed impunity, that they were above the law... This failure would not bode well for the future of Rwanda or for the Rwandans scattered across east Africa and beyond."[7]

The arrogant notion of ending impunity in Africa should have been challenged from the beginning because it is racist. A properly organised international tribunal would not claim to be bringing light to a benighted Africa. Africa is a continent with many countries, languages, cultures, parliaments, and courts. "Culture of impunity" was said to Africans as though the ICTR was holding a cross and addressing pagans. This proposition infected the proceedings and media accounts without ever having been shown to be true, or certainly no truer than the culture of impunity enjoyed by Mr. Kissinger or various Cuban-American terrorists who enjoy cachet in Florida.

Judge Mose, a UN ICTR judge, once took leave to give an address before his highness, the King of Norway. Does he know that the King enjoys a bit of impunity? Why not look for the mote in Europe's eye before venturing to Africa to "end the culture of impunity"? And of course the eyesore of impunity central: the US has informed the world that its personnel are immune from prosecution by international courts and has a bi-lateral agreement with Rwanda and some other countries not to surrender one another's nationals to the International Criminal Court. However, that fact does not inhibit them from invoking international law and demanding the overthrow and arrest of leaders of nations, when the mood strikes them. Nor does it deter the US from providing prosecutors (often from the US military) for various *ad hoc* international tribunals. It is war by other means.

Charles Taylor, former President of Liberia who had stepped down in a political agreement, was arrested on US initiative in Nigeria, charged with crimes in Sierra Leone, had his case tried at the Hague, and is now imprisoned in Britain. It reads like a colonial gulag or penal colony story from the nineteenth century. It had to be thus, say the busybodies of Europe, because the various African courts are not "ready." This was precisely the language used in the attempt to deny independence to colonies in the mid-twentieth century. Colonialism is back like Mack the Knife.

Many "human rights" institutes, experts, and academics have established themselves in the wake of the neo-colonial program for ending "impunity" in Africa. They provide the rationale that the ICTR may be flawed, but it is a start and "we can't turn back." The have a need to speak this way as they are stakeholders. There is a lot of money in the "human rights" field, and the money comes from the so-called Great Mother Church of Western capital, which makes debate fairly unproductive. As Upton Sinclair remarked, "It is difficult to get a man to understand something when his salary depends on his not understanding it."

In Africa the UN justice system is UN special. If you are charged, they will put you in jail. If you are acquitted, they will not release you. Several acquitted are presently living in halfway houses. Other convicted Rwandans are scattered around Africa in a gulag of obscure prisons, to the satisfaction of rights advocates raised on the values of colonialism. The apparatchiks of high-flown international justice can't/won't return them to their loved ones, and Rwanda remains a state that doesn't trouble itself with justice. Mission accomplished. Thus Blair-advised Rwanda remains a state that can assassinate with impunity, thanks in large part to the enabling work of the UN ICTR.

## Notes

1.  Roméo Dallaire, *Shake Hands with the Devil*, Random House, Canada, 2003, p. 288.
2.  Terry Pickard, *Combat Medic: An Australian's Eyewitness Account of the Kibeho Masscre*, Big Sky Publishing, 2008, p. 11; also, Guy Tousignant and François Bugingo, *La Mission au Rwanda : Entretiens avec le général Guy Tousignant*, Liber, Montréal, 1997, pp. 65-85.
3.  Carla Del Ponte, *Madame Prosecutor: Confrontations with Humanity's Worst Criminals and the Culture of Impunity*, Other Press, 2009.
4.  For more on Pierre Prosper's role as a prosecutor, see 2.4 above.
5.  Theogene Rudasingwa, *Healing A Nation: Waging and Winning a Peaceful Revolution to Unite and Heal a Broken Rwanda*, Createspace, 2014, p. 156.
6.  See statement by Jérôme Bicamumpaka in *Rwanda and the New Scramble for Africa*, Appendix II, Baraka Books, Montreal, 2013, p. 265.
7.  Carla Del Ponte, *op. cit.*, p. 179.

# PART III

# Universal Jurisdiction...
# in a Single Country

# 13

## Transitional Justice in Rwanda and Democratic Republic of the Congo: From War to Peace?

JORDI PALOU-LOVERDOS

*"That since wars begin in the minds of men, it is in the minds of men that the defences of peace must be constructed."*

UNESCO's Constitution

### Introduction

The Security Council of the UN decided on November 8, 1994, within the framework of Chapter VII of the UN Charter, to create the International Criminal Tribunal for Rwanda (ICTR). Its purpose was to prosecute persons responsible for genocide and other serious violations of international humanitarian law committed in the territory of Rwanda, as well as Rwandan citizens responsible for genocide and other such violations committed in the territory of neighbouring states between January 1, 1994 and December 31, 1994.[1] The statute itself linked prosecution of the international crimes committed in Rwanda in 1994 to justice and reconciliation.[2]

Questions arose: could this tribunal fulfill its mission of reconciliation when it excluded from its temporal jurisdiction crimes committed during the military invasion from Uganda and war from October 1990 to the end of 1993? And when it also excluded the crimes committed by the Rwandan Patriotic Front (RPF) from 1995 on? And when its territorial jurisdiction excluded crimes committed by the RPF outside of Rwanda? Did it not thus provide the RPF with impunity for crimes committed in the Democratic Republic of the Congo from 1996 to now? Many Rwandans everywhere consider that the recourse to justice at the ICTR with its obvious limits, combined with the national and Gacaca courts that sent thousands of Rwandans to prison, were simply victors' justice that made no contribution to universal justice and reconciliation.

Memorials to the victims of the war were constructed, yet many victims, Hutu and Twa, consider themselves excluded.[3] Many Tutsi, formerly close collaborators of Paul Kagame, have explained the RPF government strategy: manipulation of public opinion, appropriation of the victims by the state, and creation of guilt for the international community (but only in favour of Tutsi victims). Rwanda, like Spain,[4] is confronted with the difficulty of remembering victims in an inclusive manner.

How can goals of sustainable peace and reconciliation be achieved? Several known studies imply that recourse to justice and prosecution is at odds or is even incompatible with such goals. The war gave rise to different forms of judicial prosecution. This paper focuses on the Spanish and Rwandan experiment. Other approaches to conflict resolution have been used but powerful interests have attempted to prevent the search for truth and reconciliation.

## Transitional Justice Initiatives in Central Africa

New transitional processes have brought novel means to finding remedies for the pain and suffering and promoting individual and collective harmony. Generally described as "transitional justice," this approach was developed at the end of the 1980s and early 1990s as a broadly based and all-encompassing response to the systematic violations of human rights and past abuses in violent conflicts committed by authoritarian regimes. Countries adopted varied approaches, including judicial investigation of those responsible for massive and systematic crimes, truth commissions, and analogous mechanisms using different names (sometimes incorporating concepts of justice, reparations, or reconciliation). The mechanisms served to investigate and reveal human rights violations, recommend remedies, and provide assurances that such violations would not occur again.

Governments provided reparations, either material or symbolic, to victims, both individually and collectively. They could include economic compensation, acts of atonement, memorials, policies of commemoration with the participation of victims and their families, memorial institutions, community education, dedication of spaces to remembrance, museums, public monuments, centres of interpretation and remembrance, and oral histories of the victims, all of which contribute to creating a collective conscience of past abuses and helping avoid future crimes, thereby creating a strong foundation for democracy and peace.

Different mechanisms are proposed for reforming state institutions to avoid future abuses: army, police, courts, civil servants, and the administration all serving to bring about structural change in state organs of repression in order to create a public service for the people. Other complementary proposals include traditional courts and other mechanisms for peaceful resolution of conflict such as conciliation, mediation, public discussion, participatory proceedings directed at avoiding violence and favouring peaceful co-existence, and national dialogue. The diverse mechanisms should be adapted to the particular society.

This holistic approach and the vision of complementarity have become accepted. The UN Human Rights Council agreed to create the position of a Special Rapporteur with the specific mandate for the "promotion of truth, justice reparation and guarantees of non-recurrence." The first report of the Special Rapporteur, dated August 9, 2012,[5] stressed the global focus and the requirement to relate the four distinct aspects defined in the mandate, correlating furthermore the two medium-term objectives: recognising the victims and inspiring confidence in the process, with the two long-term objectives of contributing to reconciliation and consolidating the Rule of Law.

Following is a brief analysis of Rwandan national courts, traditional courts, and universal jurisdiction from the standpoint of "transitional justice," with a particular focus on Spanish initiatives, first with respect to justice and then to efforts at reconciliation.[6]

1. Rwanda has the means to investigate and charge senior officials for crimes committed from 1990 to the present. Its national courts have convicted more than two thousand people. However, investigations in the civilian and military command structures have been inadequate and biased. Many thousands of the losers in the war are charged, convicted, and heavily sentenced,

sometimes to death. All senior officials who won the war have benefitted from total impunity.[7] Numerous international organisations have complained about the lack of impartiality and the failure of Rwandan justice to respect national and international standards. France, Great Britain, Canada, Sweden, Finland, Norway, Denmark, Italy, and Holland face or have faced about thirty extradition applications issued by Rwanda and Rwandan tribunals for crimes related to the official version of the genocide in Rwanda in 1994. Rwandan national courts have sought to extradite Rwandans investigated by the ICTR for the 1994 genocide. In some cases, extradition applications have been accepted.[8]

Nevertheless, both the ICTR at first,[9] followed by national entities, from both civil and common law traditions, have often refused extradition/transfer to Rwanda on legal grounds based on the lack of due process and legal guarantees of the Rwandan justice system (e.g., absence of judicial independence, risk of unfair trial, impossibility to exercise defence rights with minimal guarantees, systematic violation of the presumption of innocence, risk of prison sentences of life in solitary confinement, risk of cruelty, and unusual punishment). Congolese national courts have not carried out systematic investigation of crimes committed in war and other conflicts occurring on its territory from 1996 on. Different Congolese and international human rights groups in the Congo have called for the creation of national tribunals or hybrid tribunals through the United Nations to investigate the most serious crimes committed in the wars by Congolese or Rwandans. We consider that the Rwandan national courts have simply applied victors' justice.

2. The Rwandan government adopted a special law to transform traditional tribunals known as the Gacaca courts. According to official Rwandan data, this traditional justice system convicted and sent to prison more than 100,000 persons for genocide.[10] Rwanda has used traditional domestic-conflict court procedures (e.g., family, land disputes, etc.) with untrained personnel to investigate and convict people with few legal guarantees. Complicated crimes such as genocide did not exist in Rwandan

culture. Only one ethnic group was charged for crimes limited to 1994 and it was impossible to denounce and investigate crimes committed by the victors in the war—the Rwandan Patriotic Front (RPF) and the Rwandan Patriotic Army (RPA). This is another form of victors' justice.

3. Universal Jurisdiction: Belgium, Canada, Switzerland, Germany, France, and Spain are among the countries that have initiated investigations and accusations under the principle of universal jurisdiction for alleged international crimes that were not committed in their territory. In all cases but one, the accused are the presumed authors of the 1994 genocide and are Hutu. Spain is the only country where there have been judicial investigations of the victors for massive crimes committed in Rwanda and the Democratic Republic of the Congo.

Charging and convicting under the principle of victors' justice in these difference jurisdictions have exacerbated the political conflict in Rwanda and the Congo.

## Civil Societies, Justice Processes, and Peace Processes

The roles of civil society and victims have changed from that of spectators and victims to participants in legal proceedings or peace processes. Many governmental and international organisations have misgivings about these developments, perceiving them as invading turf that "does not belong" to victims or civil society, but rather to those who count and have the required knowledge and expertise. Some organisations, however, foster this development.

Spain and other countries with continental justice systems allow victims, to varying degrees, to participate formally in judicial proceedings. Examples include the decisive intervention by Argentina's *Madres y Abuelas de la Plaza de Mayo*; by Spanish, Argentine, and Chilean victims; Spanish and Guatemalan Maya victims; Catalonian, Spanish, Rwandan, and Congolese victims; Tibetan victims; Palestinian victims, etc. Victims have played varying roles in articulating, presenting, investigating, and even filing formal charges in processes of universal justice in application of current international law. On the other hand,

the Nuremberg and Tokyo Trials, or the *ad hoc* courts for the former
Yugoslavia and Rwanda, or other mixed courts largely inspired by the
Anglo-Saxon law deem intervention or legal representation of victims
unthinkable. However, the International Criminal Court has created a
new system of justice. This new system, a hybrid between the continental and Anglo-Saxon systems, marks the first time ever that an international court offers victims the real possibility of participating and having
legal representation—albeit in a more restricted way than in continental national systems of justice. It remains to be seen if the ICC will act
independently and allow all victims to influence prosecutorial policy
and lead to prosecution of powerful countries and leaders.

The increasing involvement of representatives of civil society in peace
processes, including victims and relatives of victims, has had a significant impact. Scholars have argued in empirical studies that participation of civil society in peace negotiations enables agreements to be more
feasible and sustainable.[11] Agreements are more legitimate and stronger,
and create conciliatory and integrative dynamics between the parties.[12]

## The Spanish Two-Track Approach for Rwanda and the DRC

The extended war in Rwanda and the Democratic Republic of the Congo
has killed almost seven million people, including Rwandan, Congolese,
Burundian, Spanish, Italian, Canadian, Belgian, and British victims,
and has left more civilians dead than any conflict since World War II
(not to mention the heads of state of Burundi, Rwanda, and the DRC).

The Spanish case was a joint initiative in which civil society and the
victims of this conflict came together to create a mixed approach com-
bining the path of justice and prosecution with a dialogue for peace[13] in
an attempt to transform the conflict by non-violent means.

### Criminal Charges: The Legal Approach

At the end of the nineties, the International Forum for Truth and Justice
in the African Great Lakes Region, which included a number of prominent personalities (including Nobel Peace Prize winner Adolfo Pérez
Esquival and US Congresswoman Cynthia McKinney), victims, relatives

of Spanish, Rwandan, and Congolese victims, national and international NGOs, and some public institutions, initiated an international process to investigate major international crimes perpetrated in Rwanda and the DRC between October 1990 (military invasion from Uganda) and July 2002 (International Criminal Court starting competence for DRC).

## Justice and the Struggle against Impunity in Central Africa

In 2005, after years of evidence collecting, the parties filed a lawsuit at the Spanish courts under the principle of universal justice. On February 6, 2008, after a full investigation, the Spanish courts issued a bill of indictment and international arrest warrants for forty top officials of Rwanda's incumbent political-military group that has held power in Rwanda since 1994.[14] The arrest warrants charged them with the crimes of genocide, crimes against humanity, war crimes, and terrorism. According to the decision made public by the Spanish courts,[15] the judge had obtained extensive testimonial and documentary evidence and expert testimony regarding the crimes allegedly perpetrated by the RPA/RPF in Rwanda and the DRC in the period 1990-2000. This investigation revealed that the RPA/RPF's rigid, hierarchical chain of command, headed by President Paul Kagame, was responsible for three major and closely interrelated blocks of crime.[16] The investigation showed that large-scale crimes took place in Central Africa in every stage of the war: prior to, during, and after the mass killings of the Tutsi population occurring between April and July 1994. The April-July killings were classified as genocide by the UN Security Council in its *ad hoc* resolution and in the ICTR judgments. The official version in international public opinion only recognises the killings between April and July 1994.

On the other hand, the Spanish decision sheds light on a particular array of facts. First, RPA/RPF army units with 2,400 soldiers backed by Ugandan military, logistical, and political support, invaded northern Rwanda from October 1, 1990, causing the death of countless Hutu civilians. Secondly, from 1991 to 1993, the RPA/RPF carried out many open and carefully targeted military operations against civilians through its two main forces—the RPA's regular army and the Directorate of Military Intelligence's (DMI) secret services—creating also special death squads

such as the "Network Commando." Thirdly, in 1994 the RPA buried
and hid in Uganda large amounts of weapons to be smuggled later into
Rwanda prior to planning the April 6, 1994 attack against Rwandan
President Juvénal Habyarimana, which triggered the ensuing chaos.

Then later in 1994 and in 1995, the RPA and DMI perpetrated mass
and targeted crimes against civilians, mostly Hutu, following Paul
Kagame's explicit instructions to eliminate the Hutu population. The
RPA and DMI also organised collective burials in mass graves and mass
incineration of corpses in Akagera and Nyungwe Parks. The investigation also revealed that in 1996 and 1997, the RPA/RPF systematically
attacked Hutu refugee camps in former Zaïre, killing hundreds of thousands of Rwandans and Congolese. According to the decision—and
UN reports[17]—it also organised the plundering of mineral resources
such as diamonds, coltan, and gold, thereby creating the intricate web
of corruption led by the "Congo Desk," the DMI and Rwandan companies—among them, Tristar Investment—all of whom were backed by
multinational corporations and Western powers. During the second
military invasion starting in 1998, the RPF/RPA continued in the same
vein with a trail of killing and plundering in the DRC which continues
until now.

## Impact of the 2008 Spanish Court Decision

Social scientists and jurists will study *ad hoc* tribunals such as the ICTR
and the ICTY and their contributions, if any, to reconciliation and peace.
They will also examine the Spanish court's work under universal jurisdiction for similar impacts. The Spanish case attempted to bring before
the court those primarily responsible for these international crimes to
end impunity and have an impact on individuals and communities.

The Spanish court decision has affected the ICTR, the African Union,
the European Union, the United Nations, and other countries including as follows:[18]

1.  The February 6, 2008[19] decision deals with international crimes
    allegedly committed in Rwanda and the DRC between October 1,
    1990 and July 1, 2002, most of which were not yet being officially
    investigated by any court. Some of these crimes presumably com-

mitted in the 1994 calendar year and therefore under the ICTR's temporal jurisdiction include the kidnapping and disappearance of Catalan missionary Joaquim Vallamajó on April 26, 1994 in North Rwanda (Byumba); the killing of internally displaced Rwandans on April 23, 1994 in the football Stadium of Byumba (less than one kilometre from where Vallamajó resided and was kidnapped three days before); and the killing of fifteen religious and non-religious civilians, among them three Rwandan Catholic bishops in Gakurazo on June 5, 1994—all three wanton murders committed during the "official genocide."

When the Spanish Court made its decision public, there were some significant international impacts. One very important ICTR-related consequence was the statement presented by ICTR Prosecutor Hassan Bubacar Jallow before the UN Security Council on June 4, 2008,[20] explaining that he had decided to open the first file in ICTR history against RPF/RPA officials. In it he attested that his office had evidence showing that members of the RPA were allegedly responsible for the Gakurazo crime of June 5, 1994 where the priests were murdered. He did not refer to any other crime committed by the RPF/RPA in 1994.

It is now known that the ICTR prosecutor had investigated and kept evidence about this crime since at least 2001, but it was not until 2008, just after the Spanish court decision (including explicitly the Gakurazo crime, its victims, and alleged killers) that the chief prosecutor decided to open a case. Less than one week later, on June 11, 2008, the Rwandan prosecutor general stated that Rwanda had reached an agreement with the ICTR to organise a Rwandan trial for the four suspects who had been arrested.[21] So the first and only ICTR case allegedly involving RPA officials for crimes executed during ICTR's temporal jurisdiction was quickly neutralised.

The ICTR promised to supervise this domestic trial closely. The results are public and outrageous: the two high-ranking officials were acquitted, and the two soldiers were condemned for facts considered "revenge reactions." Families of the victims have asked the ICTR prosecutor to show them the prosecutor's evidence that had not been considered or used in the domestic trial. This evidence has not yet been given to the families of the victims.[22] Human Rights Watch has exchanged several letters with the ICTR prosecutor in the same sense, noting the lack of interest of the ICTR in delivering all the pieces of evidence and the absence of real ICTR prosecutor supervision of the domestic judicial process as promised.[23] International justice at the ICTR failed and the prosecution should have brought its own proceedings if it were to respect its mandate.

2. Four Rwandan military officials deployed in UN forces were prosecuted in 2008. On September 3, 2008, the US State Department donated military equipment worth twenty million US dollars to the Rwandan defence force, led by one of the four officials. His UN appointment in Sudan was in fact ratified by the UN Secretary General a few weeks later and extended for an irrevocable six-month period until March 2009.[24]

3. International efforts were deployed to neutralise the Spanish court case. The Rwandan head of state tried to avoid the application of the international arrest warrant on the African continent and to influence the European Union to revise the criteria for applying the principle of universal jurisdiction. In parallel, it was learned in 2008 that senior US administration officials pressured the Spanish government, the office of the general prosecutor (Fiscalía General del Estado), and other bodies to suspend the proceedings. It also closely monitored the judge of the *Audiencia Nacional* (National Court) and those working on that proceeding in order to paralyse.[25]

In 2010, the UN Secretary General called a meeting of the heads of state to advance his Millennium Development Goals. He proposed a co-presidency, one from a developed country and one from a developing country. Supposedly by chance, the two candidates were Rwandan President Paul Kagame and Spanish President Zapatero. The meeting of the heads of state was to take place in the Presidential Palace, but based on pressure from the families of Rwandan and Spanish victims, President Zapatero refused to participate and the meeting was moved to a nearby hotel. These events prompted the Spanish Government to actively solicit the extradition from South Africa of Rwandan General Kayumba Nyamwasa,[26] accused of the murder of four Spanish nationals between 1994 and 1997 and thousands of Rwandans in the north of Rwanda and the DRC.

This all happened in 2010 as the UN High Commission for Human Rights was concluding an investigation initiated in the DRC. The UNHCR investigation was initiated in 2008, a few months after the Spanish court issued arrest warrants for the forty Rwandan officials.

Simultaneously, the UN Secretary General and President Kagame met in Madrid with other world leaders. A heated debate occurred in Geneva at that time to reach a consensus as to the final conclusions to the investigation by the UNHCR-mandated experts concerning crimes committed in the DRC. Military and civilian intelligence from Rwanda attempted to neutralise publication of conclusions implicating Rwanda and its army in the commission of international crimes in the DRC. A few short weeks after the meeting, investigators leaked to the press some of the conclusions implicating the Rwandan army for crimes against Rwandans and Congolese. After much difficulty, the UNHCR published the official report on October 1, 2010, known as the DRC Mapping Report, establishing the commission of serious violations of international humanitarian law including possibly genocide by the Rwandan Army and the senior authorities of Rwandan government both in Rwanda and in the DRC.[27] This report referred specifically to the resolutions of the Spanish Court (*Audiencia Nacional*), its strengths, and its approval of the universal jurisdiction of the Spanish Court.[28]

This decision had consequences and more may come. Many forces in Congolese civil society, both in the Congo and elsewhere, can provide impetus for investigating and judging crimes before Congolese Courts or for the formation of mixed or hybrid courts, shared with the UN. This is necessary since the jurisdiction of the International Criminal Court only commenced on July 1, 2002. The UN has called for investigation and prosecution of these past abuses to end impunity and avoid the repetition of similar crimes.

## Universal Jurisdiction and Changes in Spanish Law

The doctrine of universal jurisdiction allows national courts to try cases of the gravest crimes against humanity, even if these crimes are not committed in the national territory and even if they are committed by government leaders of other states. Courts apply international law. These initiatives have been both widely applauded and criticised.[29] The ICTR encouraged states to use their universal jurisdiction for international crimes committed in Rwanda.[30] As we saw above from the actions of Prosecutor Jallow, the effect on the ICTR was ephemeral.

Following the 2008 Spanish court decision, Rwandan President Kagame asked the United Nations, the African Union, and the European Union to stop the "abuse" of universal jurisdiction by refusing to execute the international arrest warrants.[31] Paul Kagame succeeded at the African Union in its Eleventh Summit in Sharm el-Sheikh on July 1, 2008.[32] This occurred prior to the well-known decision of the African Union about Sudanese President Al Bashir's International Criminal Court indictment. In 2009, at the UN General Assembly, Paul Kagame congratulated himself that this initiative about universal jurisdiction was taking place at the UN.[33]

In Spain, after many years of the application of the principle of universal jurisdiction, following the Eichmann trial in Israel (but with respect of international law), the government and the parliament have taken initiatives to neutralise or paralyse the application of universal jurisdiction. Pressure, either open or veiled, has been applied on the Spanish government, the prosecutor, members of the court, deputies, and senators, with a view to amending the law on universal jurisdiction. It was similar to US pressure on Belgium with the threat to move Nato headquarters from Brussels. Pressure was applied through state organisations or multinational companies. In Spain, it came from Rwanda and the US. These are examples of how economic and geo-political interests can influence legislators and state administrators to establish effective impunity for Rwandan criminals. In Spain, there were several stages:

1. On June 25, 2009, the Spanish Congress passed a bill amending existing universal jurisdiction legislation in Spain and the Senate approved it.[34] The bill follows an agreement between

Spain's two main political parties on amending Article 23.4 of the Spanish Organic Law of the Judiciary Power. The purpose of this amendment is to limit the capacity of Spanish courts to exercise jurisdiction over international crimes committed abroad by non-Spanish nationals. This legislation is a setback to our common humanity.[35] Spanish courts have been exercising universal jurisdiction for over a decade now. They have made an extraordinary contribution to the development of international criminal law and the fight against impunity. Article 23.4 of the law established that the *Audiencia Nacional* has a jurisdiction over acts perpetrated by Spanish nationals and by foreigners outside of Spain if such acts are alleged to constitute: genocide, terrorism, war crimes, and any other crime which should be prosecuted by Spain in accordance with international treaties.

2. On March 14, 2014, an additional step was taken with the voting of a new amendment to Article 23.4 of the law, which for all intents and purposes eliminates the universal jurisdiction in Spain by making pre-conditions which cannot be met. It provides that a proceeding for genocide or crimes against humanity can only charge a Spanish national or a foreigner residing habitually in Spain or a foreigner who is present in Spain and whose extradition would have been refused by Spanish authorities.[36] It is not clear if this would be applicable considering international treaty obligations which require Spain to investigate and prosecute, all of which form part of Spanish Law after formal ratification as is required by the Spanish Constitution.

3. One additional risk to the Rule of Law (national and international) is contained in a proposal to abandon the Spanish and continental approach to criminal investigation. Since the nineteenth century, criminal investigation is carried out under the supervision of an impartial judge with the intervention of the prosecutor and attorneys for the victims. The new proposal, under guise of being progressive and modern, assigns investigation to the prosecutor, who will investigate and prosecute crimes including international crimes under the supervision of a judge to guarantee the proceedings (*juez de garantias*).

It must be stressed that the prosecutor (*Ministerio Fiscal*), unlike in Anglo-Saxon countries, is organically part of the government, since the prosecutor general is named by the executive branch. This is a very serious change since it violates the principle of the separation of powers with respect to crimes in general and with respect to international crimes and the principle of extra-territoriality (and the compromise between investigating and rendering judgment according to the principle *aut dedere aut judicare* (Latin for "extradite or prosecute"). It would violate the principles of universal justice since it would be based on limits imposed by the government over such initiatives and lead to a serious risk that Spain's international obligations would not be respected.

The Spanish courts first exercised universal jurisdiction in 1998 when the *Audiencia Nacional* indicted several Argentinean and Chilean officials for their alleged roles in abuses committed as part of Plan Condor.[37] Spanish courts have continued to address serious violations around the globe for which no alternate forum has been found.

States have not only a right but also a duty to guarantee that the most severe crimes—those which are considered to be committed not only against the victims, but against the international community as a whole—do not remain unpunished. The amendments introduced to Spanish law constitute an important step backwards in the effort to develop coherent global processes of accountability for human rights atrocities. International law has developed since the Nuremberg and Tokyo trials to provide norms and venues for the exercise of universal justice, as seen in the *ad hoc* Criminal Tribunals for the Former Yugoslavia and Rwanda, the Special Courts for Sierra Leone, East Timor, and Cambodia, and the International Criminal Court. Each mechanism, acting in tandem with domestic courts, serves as an instrument for the enforcement of human rights and international humanitarian law. Universal jurisdiction is only one of the tools available in the fight against impunity for severe human rights violations. Until now, the Spanish universal jurisdiction law had managed to withstand political pressure rising to the level of that which ultimately compelled Belgium to revise its own universal jurisdiction legislation. It is in the interest of the international community as a whole to preserve this instrument as another avenue of justice, complementary to the ICC and potential hybrid courts.

In spite of Rwandan President Kagame's statement that universal jurisdiction does not apply to "local laws," it is essential for it to apply to the most serious crimes recognised in most countries of the world

## Dialogue among Rwandans

Since the legal prosecutorial approach represented an important but insufficient step towards transforming the Rwandan conflict, preventing further violent incidents, and overcoming the tragedy of the last two decades, a group of prominent members of Rwandan civil society living abroad set out to start a dialogue from exile. Two people initiated the dialogue: the Hutu president of a victims' association who lived in Brussels and the Tutsi former plenipotentiary ambassador of the current Rwandan government to the United Nations who lived in New York.

In 2004, ten Rwandan men and women from the diaspora met for the first time at a meeting organised by international facilitators in Mallorca, Spain. The Rwandans, both Tutsi and Hutu, were able to ascertain the different ways in which they each understood Rwandan history and the past according to their own personal, family, and community experiences. At the same time, they also discovered the extent to which they agreed on constructive proposals for the future. In 2006, after two years in the works, a second encounter referred to as the Intra-Rwandan Dialogue took place in Barcelona, Spain, giving rise to the International Network for Truth and Reconciliation in Central Africa. Twenty Rwandan nationals, both Hutu and Tutsi from the diaspora and the Rwandan heartlands, took part in this event. The meeting was organised with the sponsorship of Nobel Peace Prize nominee/candidate Juan Carrero and the support of both Nobel Peace Laureate Adolfo Pérez Esquivel, present at the meeting, and of the president of Senegal Abdoulaye Wade. The protocol of findings of the 2006 event, which called for a more inclusive Inter-Rwandan Dialogue, served as the foundation for the talks held at five subsequent meetings, entitled Dialogue Platforms, in 2007 and 2008.[38]

These five events took place in Washington, D.C. for twenty participants from the US and Canada; in Amsterdam for twenty participants
from Holland, Belgium, and Germany; in Orléans, France, for twenty
participants from France and Italy; in Barcelona, where the Platform for
Rwandan Women was held; and finally in Kinshasa, DRC, where a special *ad hoc* platform was organised for Congolese participants coming
from the eastern region of the country bordering with Rwanda.

In 2007 the Spanish parliament extended its support for this initiative and passed a resolution where all political parties unanimously
agreed to offer technical, legal, diplomatic, and political support and
urged to take it to an international level.[39] Later in 2009, the State of
Vermont Senate voted a resolution approving this international initiative for dialogue, affirming as follows:

> Whereas, all of these individuals and organizations have focused on the
> future and continuing this larger Inter-Rwandan Dialogue as the legitimate
> foundation upon which to build a new Rwanda that all political, ethnic,
> social, and economic groups in the country, as well as the international
> community, can widely accept... Whereas, the Inter-Rwandan Dialogue
> is an exemplary and realistic model for the bringing together of opposing
> ethnic groups involved in major national and international conflicts, and
> this unusual and praiseworthy international dialogue should be universally
> applauded and encouraged, and if possible, this dialogue model should
> be extended to other countries in conflict, now therefore be it... the State
> of Vermont supports the implementation of the Inter-Rwandan Dialogue
> in its development and continuing implementation of the Inter-Rwandan
> Dialogue.[40]

In early 2009, the eighth Dialogue held in Mallorca, Spain, featured the participation of thirty Rwandan men and women from
all Rwandan ethnic groups—Hutu, Tutsi and Twa—as well as two
Congolese. Participants came from Africa, Europe, and North America.
Celebrating five years of dialogue, they agreed to formally ask a Central
African government to hold a Highly Inclusive Inter-Rwandan Dialogue,
and request institutional and financial support from the international
community.[41] This process has continued until now to consider various
initiatives at the international level. In all, more than 150 Rwandan leaders have participated in the process, including two former prime min-

isters, various former cabinet ministers, former ambassadors, political leaders, representatives from civil society, victims, as well as human rights organisations, and institutions devoted to peace and economic research. All have set their eyes on the future and on carrying on this inter-Rwandan dialogue as the legitimate foundation upon which to build a new Rwanda that can be widely accepted by all political, ethnic, social, and economic groups as well as by the international community.

## Notes

1.  It is important to mention that the 1993 Arusha Peace Agreement, facilitated by UN officials, tried to put an end to a war that, according to the signed document, started October 1, 1990. Unlike the Statute of the International Criminal Tribunal for the Former Yugoslavia (ICTY), the Security Council decided in November 1994 to limit the temporal jurisdiction of the Tribunal to the 1994 calendar year, although the year was not over; crimes committed prior to 1994 or after 1994 were not investigated.

2.  Considering that the ICTR Statute states, among other provisions: "Expressing once again its grave concern at the reports indicating that genocide and other systematic, widespread and flagrant violations of international humanitarian law have been committed in Rwanda; Determined to put an end to such crimes and to take effective measures to bring to justice the persons who are responsible for them; Convinced that in the particular circumstances of Rwanda, the prosecution of persons responsible for serious violations of international humanitarian law would enable this aim to be achieved and would contribute to the process of national reconciliation and to the restoration and maintenance of peace," in Article 1, ICTR Statute, http://www.un.org/ictr/statute.html.

3.  See the official statement about the conflict delivered by the Rwandan goverment (that many Rwandans would not assume): "For centuries, Rwanda existed as a centralized monarchy under a succession of Tutsi kings from one clan, who ruled through cattle chiefs, land chiefs and military chiefs. The king was supreme but the rest of the population, Bahutu, Batutsi and Batwa, lived in symbiotic harmony... On 1 October 1990, the RPF launched an armed liberation struggle that ultimately ousted the dictatorship in 1994 and ended the genocide of more than one million Batutsi and massacres of moderate Bahutu who opposed the genocide. After Kigali fell to RPA (RPF's armed wing) on 4 July 1994, RPF formed a Government of National Unity headed by President Pasteur Bizimungu, bringing parties that did not participate in the genocide together.", "History," *Republic of Rwanda*, http://www.gov.rw/History?lang=en.

4.  In Spain, thirty-five years after the end of the military dictatorship, there has been no success in re-orienting Franco's memorial in the Valle de los Caídos (Valley of the Fallen), which continues to honour "those who died for God and Spain" and forgetting the dead among the defeated. Although thousands—considered

enemies of the nation—were executed or put in prison after military and civil trials, no democratic government has declared illegal, null, or void such processes (including the 1940 military trial and execution of the democratic elected president of Catalonia, delivered to Franco by Gestapo from France). While victims of the victors were officially recognised and honoured, more than 100,000 forced disappeared continue to be in mass graves without identification and the real right to truth, mourning, and reparation.

5.  See Pablo de Greiff, *Report of the Special Rapporteur on the promotion of truth, justice, reparation and guarantees of non-recurrence* (first annual report submitted to the Human Rights Council), August 9, 2012, http://www.ohchr.org/Documents/HRBodies/HRCouncil/RegularSession/Session21/A-HRC-21-46_en.pdf,.

6.  A full analysis of the different judicial processes (ICTR, ICC, Universal jurisdiction; and initiatives for peaceful resolution of the conflicts in Rwanda and the Democratic Republic of the Congo can be found in Jordi Palou-Loverdos, "Justice et paix inéquitables: des risques? Compétence juridictionnelle, réalités judiciaires, vérité et résolution pacifique des conflits en Afrique Centrale," in the frame of international seminar lessons for the defence at the *ad hoc* UN tribunals and prospects for International Justice at the ICC, Brussels, 2010, http://www.tpirheritagedefense.org/Conference2/Papers/Jordi_Palou_Loverdos_Justice_et_paix_inequitables_aussi_des_risques.pdf.

7.  Spain does not set an example for crimes committed in the civil war between 1936 and 1939. See: http://ep00.epimg.net/descargables/2012/02/27/c38da9aeed-611d25e02b591d615891a5.pdf.

8.  ICTR sources indicate that ten people have been transferred from the ICTR to the national jurisdictions of France and Rwanda. See http://www.unictr.org/Cases/tabid/204/Default.aspx.

9.  In at least three difference cases, the ICTR has refused to transfer cases to Rwanda on the basis of sub-rule 11*bis* of the Rules. See *The Prosecutor v. Yussuf Munyakazi*, Case No. ICTR- 97-36-R11*bis*, May 28, 2008; *The Prosecutor v. Ildephonse Hategekimana*, Case No. ICTR-00-55B-11*bis*, June 19, 2008; *The Prosecutor v. Gaspard Kanyarukiga*, Case No. ICTR-2002-78-R11*bis*, June 6, 2008. The ICTR has recently allowed transfers of Jean-Bosco Uwinkindi and Bernard Munyagishari, as can be viewed on the ICTR website.

10. See Gacaca Courts and other official Rwandan information on justice and reconciliation, http://www.gov.rw/Justice-Reconciliation?lang=en.

11. Thania Pfaffenholz, Darren Kew and Anthony Wanis-St. John, "Civil Society and Peace Negotiations: Why, Whether and how they could be involved," *Centre for Humanitarian Dialogue*, June 26, 2006, http://www.hdcentre.org/en/resources/publications/filter/thania-pfaffenholz-darren-kew-and-anthony-wanis-st-john/.

12. Priscilla Hayner, "Negotiating justice: Guidance for mediators," *Centre for Humanitarian Dialogue*, February 2009, pp. 12-13, http://www.peacemaker.un.org/sites/peacemaker.un.org/files/NegotiatingJustice_Hayner2009.pdf.

13. Colombia is another example. See Felipe Gómez Isa, "Paramilitary Demobilization in Colombia: Between Peace and Justice," *Fundación para las Relaciones Internacionales y el Diálogo Exterior*, Working Paper Nr. 57, Madrid, April 2008, http://www.fride.org/download/WP57_Colombia_Desmili_ENG_abr08.pdf.

14. At least nine of them were away from Rwanda when the decision was made public; they held prominent positions, even within the UN: four of them worked for the hybrid peacekeeping forces in Sudan (UNAMID), including a Rwandan army general who was the second commander of such forces. A fifth served at the demobilisation arm of the UN Development Program (UNDP) in Nepal. Several public institutions had formally requested that the UN remove them and turn them over to justice (see: http://www.veritasrwandaforum.org/dosier/resol_Ban_Ki_Moon_es.pdf.).

15. See judicial resolution: http://www.veritasrwandaforum.org/dosier/resol_auto_esp_06022008.pdf; See also Martin Vidal, "Mistrust of Rwanda and African Union related to universal and international justice initiatives," 2008, pp. 3-6. A lot of international media and international experts reported about that universal jurisdiction preliminary decision. See a selection of it in different languages at http://www.veritasrwandaforum.org/dossier_40ordres.htm. See also expert reports such as "The Spanish Indictment of High-ranking Rwandan Officials," *Journal of International Criminal Justice*, Vol. 6, No. 5, pp. 1003-1011, http://jicj.oxfordjournals.org/cgi/content/abstract/6/5/1003.

16. Specifically, a) crimes perpetrated against nine Spanish victims—missionaries and aid workers—whose first priority was helping the local population and by so doing, were all inconvenient observers of the killings of Hutu inhabitants in both countries; (The cases of two Canadian victims, Fathers Claude Simard killed on Oct. 18, 1994, and Father Guy Pinard killed on Feb. 2, 1997, were also examined in this context.) b) crimes against Rwandans and Congolese, either perpetrated pointedly against various specific leaders, or systematically carried out as mass murders of hundreds of thousands of civilians; and c) crimes of war pillage: the systematic, large-scale plundering of natural resources, especially strategically valuable minerals.

17. See various UN Group of Experts Reports on Illegal Exploitation in the DRC, e.g., S/2001/357, April 12, 2001; S/2002/1146, October 16, 2002; and S/2008/773, December 12, 2008, among others.

18. See also video statement: "La tragedie rwandaise (1990-2000) à partir de l'instruction espagnole; du passé vers l'avenir: le dialogue intrarwandais" by Jordi Palou-Loverdos in the colloquium "Le drame rwandais: la verité des acteurs", held before the French Senate, April 1, 2014, https://www.youtube.com/watch?v=mzSGKIF2rYs.

19. See official Spanish version: http://www.veritasrwandaforum.org/dosier/resol_auto_esp_06022008.pdf.

20. Statement made at the occasion of the presentation of the Report by the ICTR President before the UN Security Council, 5904th Meeting.

21. The statement written by RDF spokesman, Major Jill Rutaremara is quoted as saying, "The Military Prosecution authorities have today (11 June 2008) ordered and effected arrest of four suspects: Brig Gen Wilson Gumisiriza, Major Wilson Ukwishaka, Captain John Butera and Captain (Rtd) Dieudonné Rukeba." See *Ibid.*: http://politics.nationmedia.com/inner.asp?sid=1981.

22. In a letter to a victim's relative dated September 1, 2009 by Mr. William Egbe, Senior Trial Attorney, the Office of the Prosecutor states: "Whilst the Prosecutor sympathises with you for the tragic loss of your relative he is unable to institute a

new proceedings in respect of his murder as the incident in which he was killed has already been the subject of a final determination. The Prosecutor is aware of allegations relating to the involvement of various persons but the evidence available to him cannot form the basis for the indictment of any persons other than Brigadier General Wilson Gumisiriza, Major Wilson Ukwishaka, Captain Dieudonné Rukeba and Captain John Butera who have been already been prosecuted for this offence. The Prosecutor is also satisfied that the trial in Rwanda was carried out with due process and in accordance with international standards of fair trial. He has accordingly closed the case file."

23. See exchange between Human Rights Watch (HRW) and ICTR Prosecutor, letter dated May 26, 2009 by Kenneth Roth, Executive Director of HRW; letter dated June 22, 2009 of ICTR Chief Prosecutor; letter dated August 14, 2009 by Kenneth Roth, http://www.hrw.org/en/news/2009/08/14/letter-ictr-chief-prosecutor-has-san-jallow-response-his-letter-prosecution-rpf-crime.

24. See official information from the US Embassy in Rwanda: http://rwanda.usembassy.gov/u.s._embassy_donates_equipment_to_the_rwanda_defense_forces.

25. See cables from US Embassy in Madrid to US State Department: February 2, 2008, http://www.veritasrwandaforum.org/dosier/03.03.11_cable1.pdf; March 13, 2008, http://www.veritasrwandaforum.org/dosier/03.03.11_cable2.pdf; May 9, 20018, http://www.veritasrwandaforum.org/dosier/03.03.11_cable3.pdf; and May 23, 2008, http://www.veritasrwandaforum.org/dosier/03.03.11_cable4.pdf.

26. See English version of the Spanish Government Press release about the request of extradition, September 17, 2010, http://www.veritasrwandaforum.org/dosier/sol_extrad/100917_consejo_ministros_en.pdf.

27. "Statement by the High Commissioner for Human Rights Navi Pillay," October 1, 2010, United Nations Human Rights Office of the High Commissioner, http://www.ohchr.org/Documents/Countries/CD/HC_Statement_on_Release_EN.pdf.

28. See "Final Report on most serious violations of human rights and international humanitarian law between 1993 and 2003 in the Democratic Republic of Congo (DRC)," http://www.ohchr.org/Documents/Countries/CD/DRC_MAPPING_REPORT_FINAL_EN.pdf, United Nations Human Rights Office of the High Commissioner, particularly p. 461, para. 1029. The UN High Commissioner stated: "The Mapping Report provides the most extensive account to date of the most serious violations of human rights and international humanitarian law committed in the DRC between 1993 and 2003. In listing these incidents, province by province, and in chronological order, it reveals the suffering that years of instability and conflict have inflicted on the country. In doing so, the Mapping report seeks to honour the memory of victims of the conflict, and helps reiterate the importance of ensuring accountability for past human rights abuses. We hope the report serves as an important step on the difficult path towards coming to terms with this period of intense human suffering... civil society, both international and national, contributed to this project by sharing information and discussing their views on transitional justice... In conflict situations, the biggest challenges include ensuring that civilians remain protected, that the laws of war are respected, and that the harm done to victims of violence is repaired. While we cannot undo human rights violations, we can try to ensure that they do not re-occur, by holding to account

those responsible for past abuses," http://www.ohchr.org/Documents/Countries/
CD/HC_Statement_on_Release_EN.pdf.

29. See only three examples: Henry Kissinger (US former Secretary of State and
National Security Advisor), "The Pitfalls of Universal Jurisdiction" for one side,
Global Policy, July-August 2001, http://www.globalpolicy.org/component/con-
tent/article/163/28174.html; and Kenneth Roth (Executive Director of Human
Rights Watch), "The Case for Universal Jurisdiction" for the other, Global Policy,
September-October 2001, http://www.globalpolicy.org/component/content/arti-
cle/163/28202.html. Years ago, giving their opinion about Universal Jurisdiction,
former members of US Presidents Reagan and Bush Sr.'s administrations stated:
"The most recent example involved a Rwandan general, Emmanuel Karake
Karenzi, and whether he should be reappointed by the United Nations to serve
as deputy commander of the joint United/Nations/African Union implementation force in Darfur. Karenzi commanded military forces accused of war crimes
in the 1990s... For its part, Rwanda stood behind its general—so much so that it
threatened to withdraw its (crucial) troops from the Darfur mission if Karenzi
were forced out... But the situation became more complicated early this year,
when a Spanish judge indicted Karenzi for offenses in Rwanda. Although Spanish
nationals also were allegedly killed by the general's forces, the indictment mostly
involved Rwandan victims and was based on a theory of universal jurisdiction...
What we are seeing is not the birth of a global rule of law but a type of judicial
anarchy. Spain's Judges should not be driving foreign policy at the United Nations,
but they are;" see David B. Rivkin Jr. and Lee A. Casey, "Judgment without borders," Los Angeles Times, October 6, 2008, http://www.latimes.com/news/opinion/
commentary/la-oe-rivkin6-2008oct06,0,2219226.story.

30. See The Prosecutor v. Bernard Ntuyahaga, Case No. ICTR-98-40-T, Decision, March
18, 1999, p. 4.

31. James Karuhanga, "Rwanda: Abusing Universal Jurisdiction Dangerous -
Kagame Tells UN," AllAfrica.com, September 25, 2008, http://allafrica.com/sto-
ries/200809250330.html.

32. Sam Ruburika, "Rwanda: African Union Refuses Arrest Warrants Against Rwandans," AllAfrica.com, July 7, 2008, http://allafrica.com/stories/200807071845.html.

33. See: "President of Rwanda Paul Kagame Addresses UN General Assembly,"
MaximsNewsNetwork, http://www.maximsnews.com/news20091005Rwandapres-
identUNGA1091000106.htm; see also: Legal Committee Delegates See Principle
of Universal Law as Safeguard against Impunity for Major Crimes: Some Caution
on Risk of Abuse," UN General Assembly, http://www.un.org:80/News/Press/
docs//2009/gal3371.doc.htm.

34. See: Non-Legislative Motion 161/000433, http://www.veritasrwandaforum.org/
dosier/D_126-14_eng.pdf.

35. See Jordi Palou-Loverdos and Olga Martin Ortega, "Preserving Spain's Universal
Jurisdiction Law in the Common Interest," in Jurist, University of Pittsburgh
School of Law http://jurist.law.pitt.edu/forumy/2009/06/protecting-spains-uni-
versal.php.

36. See: "Ley Orgánica 1/2014, de 13 de marzo, de modificación de la Ley Orgánica
6/1985, de 1 de julio, del Poder Judicial, relativa a la justicia universal," Agencia

*Estatal Boletín Oficial del Estado*, http://www.boe.es/diario_boe/txt.php?id=
BOE-A-2014-2709.

37. The fate of the proceedings against General Augusto Pinochet is well known.
While most of the 99 indicted Argentines were not extradited by Argentina,
Mexico extradited former Argentinean military official Ricardo Miguel Cavallo
in 2000. In 2001, Adolfo Scilingo was also detained, tried, and sentenced to a long
prison term by the *Audiencia Nacional* for crimes against humanity committed
in Argentina.

38. Supporters included Federico Mayor-Zaragoza, former UNESCO Secretary
General (1987-1999), president of *Cultura de Paz*, and co-chairman of a top-level
UN group, Alliance of Civilizations, and United States Congresswoman Cynthia
McKinney.

39. See *Non-Legislative Motion in support of the Inter-Rwandan Dialogue Process*, April
25, 2007, http://www.veritasrwandaforum.org/dosier/congreso_diputados_eng.
pdf.

40. See *Senate Resolution*, http://www.leg.state.vt.us/docs/2010/resolutn/SR0024.pdf.

41. See *Veritas Rwanda Forum*, http://www.veritasrwandaforum.org/dialogo.htm.

# 14

## The Kuala Lumpur War Crimes Tribunal: Interview with Professor Michel Chossudovsky

*What is the Kuala Lumpur War Crimes Tribunal?*[*]

Michel Chossudovsky: First, I would like to provide a bit of a background. The Global Peace Organization was led by the former Prime Minister of Malaysia, Mr. Mahathir Mohamad, in 2005. A major initiative was launched called "The Kuala Lumpur Initiative to Criminalise War." It includes a number of very important statements that subsequently led to the formation of the Tribunal and the War Crimes Commission. The Tribunal was involved in several important judgments, including that directed against Bush, *et al*.

*You refer to some principles. What is the essential nature of these principles?*

MC: Well, The Kuala Lumpur Initiative to Criminalise War essentially criminalises any activity that supports war and wars of aggression. One might say that it adopts the basic premises of the supreme crime, which is crime against the peace, but it formulates them in a somewhat different way. This document was drafted by a number of people—I was on the drafting committee of the main document—and for instance it looks at the role of nuclear weapons, but it also looks at economic processes which underlie the war economy and it states explicitly that all commercial, financial, industrial, and scientific activities that aid and abet war should be criminalised. Essentially, this document constitutes the founding principles of subsequent legal procedures.

---

[*] Interview conducted by John Philpot on February 27, 2013. Professor Michel Chossudovsky is founder and director of the Centre for Research on Globalization that hosts one of the world's most important alternative media websites, *GlobalResearch.ca*, as well as *Mondialisation.ca* (in French). The Site of the Kuala Lumpur War Crimes Commission is at http://criminalisewar.org.

*Who did the prosecutors of this Tribunal charge?*
MC: We had several procedures. One was a procedure directed against George Walker Bush *et al.* ...
*Meaning... Tony Blair?*
MC: ...and it also included a number of politicians including Donald Henry Rumsfeld, Richard Cheney, Albert Gonzalez. There was no mention, in that procedure, of Tony Blair. It was essentially directed against the Bush administration.

*These were criminal charges. Were the defendants served with these proceedings?*
MC: Well, the way the Tribunal functioned is that they formed an *amicus curiae*...

*But did they receive the charges?*
MC: Absolutely. The accusations were submitted by the legal team, I believe through the US embassy, and the United States was invited to defend George Bush *et al.* The same procedures were adopted in relation to the State of Israel on the charge of genocide, and those were transmitted, I believe through the embassy of Singapore. They were served and they declined to send any legal representatives. Then the Court created an *amicus curiae*, to defend their interests.

*Were witnesses called in these different trials?*
MC: Witnesses were called and there is a large archive of witnesses. I should mention, in relation to Iraq, we had testimony from Abu Ghraib, Fallujah, and we also had testimony from people who had been in prison in Guantanamo. Among the key witnesses—and I mention this because everybody worldwide knows about it—there was the testimony of Ali Shalal. He was arrested and sent to Abu Ghraib. He was a professor of theology at the university, he was tortured in Abu Ghraib, and he is known as "the man behind the hood." It is not he as such but the images of him being tortured went all over the world. Ali Shalal managed to survive and he was released but he also provided a very detailed testimony of the torture. He also said that many of his inmates, who were tortured and released, were assassinated upon their release at the

moment they left the building, and he was aware of that. Ali Shalal is a very composed and intelligent man, and I had the opportunity of meeting him personally.

*His testimony is generally available on the Internet, on the site of the Tribunal?*
MC: These testimonies are available on the site of the Tribunal. The Centre for Research on Globalization has published many of these testimonies over the last few years.

*And you are the director of the Centre for Research on Globalization?*
MC: Yes, and I was a member of the Kuala Lumpur War Crimes Commission which, ultimately, served these charges against George W. Bush *et al.* and the State of Israel in subsequent cases.

*So you mentioned charges... How many judgments have been rendered with respect to the government in the US, for Britain, and the State of Israel?*
MC: There were only two main judgments: one in May 2012, which was *Chief Prosecutor of the Kuala Lumpur War Crimes Commission v. George Walker Bush*, and another one, a related one, in the previous year, which was *the Kuala Lumpur War Crimes Commission v. George W. Bush and Anthony L. Blair*, in November 2011. Subsequently, we had a judgment against the State of Israel. In all, there were four judgments. There also was an advisor opinion in October 2009.

*Who were the judges on this Tribunal? Were they experienced people?*
MC: The way the Tribunal was built was that we had a number of Malaysian judges, and then there was the participation of one or more foreign judges throughout. All of these judges are permanent jurists, either involved in prosecution, but several of them had been judges and there was a judge from the Supreme Court of Malaysia, so that, essentially, all the legal procedures were followed, even though the Tribunal itself did not have any status to enforce these judgments in Malaysia. It was a tribunal of conscience. The defence was made up of a team of *amicus curiae*.

*You mentioned the judgment against the State of Israel that was rendered, I believe, on November 25, 2013. What was its nature; what did that trial hear?*
MC: The evidence was based on crimes committed by the Israeli armed forces, militia...

*Where did the evidence come from?*
MC: Well, essentially, there were three areas that were envisaged: one was Sabra and Shatila, going back of course to the 1980s; then there was Gaza and the West Bank. We had testimony from all three regions. They did not pertain to any particular, specific time span, there were various time spans involved, and it was on the basis of this testimony that the judgment was rendered. Some of the testimonies had been collected at an earlier period, and other testimonies were submitted on the final days of the judgment.

*Was there expert testimony?*
MC: There was also expert testimony in all of these procedures. We had people involved who were experts in the use of particular types of weapon systems; there was an examination of the impacts of depleted uranium by prominent scientists. I should mention that in one of the first procedures in 2009, we also had the testimony of people who had been in prison and tortured in Guantanamo, at the concentration camp of the United States. The narrative of these testimonies was quite dramatic because most of the people, if not all of them, were not enemy combatants—they were civilians. In one particular case, the case of Sami al-Hajj, who was actually a journalist working for Al Jazeera, he was picked up by US forces, interrogated, and tortured, and then, after some time, they said to him: "Mr. Al-Hajj, I think we made a mistake, you are not the person we are looking for." And then they asked him, "What are you going to do when you get out of here?" He responded, "Well, you know, I am a journalist."

*What happened to him for that?*
MC: What happened to him for that? He was sent to Guantanamo for seven years. As a journalist, he said what he was going to report on what

he saw, and then he was arrested. One issue that I raised as a member of the Commission is who was being arrested, because, in effect, we know that in November 2001, the United States and the Pakistani air force actually airlifted enemy combatants to Waziristan, in Northern Pakistan. So the enemy combatants were rescued in a sense, they were not sent to Guantanamo and this is confirmed in an article by Seymour M. Hersh entitled, "The Getaway."[1]

*Could you identify yourself, so that we know who you are?*
MC: OK. I am Michel Chossudovsky, I am professor *emeritus* of Economics at the University of Ottawa, founder and director of the Centre for Research on Globalization, which hosts the *Globalresearch. ca* website.

*Could you give us references to this on your website please?*
MC: Certainly. There is a lot of material that we published, including the testimonies of Ali Shalal, of Moazzam Begg, a British citizen who was arrested in Afghanistan and who then sued the British government, and he is a human rights activist and has recently been arrested by the British government on alleged charges of terrorism.

## Notes

1.  Seymour M. Hersh, "The Getaway: Questions Surround a Secret Pakistani Airlift," *The New Yorker*, January 28, 2002.

# PART IV

# Justice for All?

# 15

# And Justice for All? International Criminal Justice in the Time of High Expectations

FANNIE LAFONTAINE AND ÉRICK SULLIVAN

## Introduction

The theme of the Third International Conference of Defence Counsels on International Criminal Law that led to this collection of essays was "International Justice, Justice for Whom?" That theme underlies some of the direst challenges of the global justice system put in place to deal with genocide, crimes against humanity, and war crimes, prominent among which are the issues of selectivity and politicisation. In the face of an International Criminal Tribunal for Rwanda that failed to look at both sides of the conflict, or of an International Criminal Court where investigations are exclusively focused on situations in Africa, observers and participants have begun questioning whether justice for international crimes is indeed true justice according to the rule of law or rather (in)justice for an unlucky few who fell out of favour of the superpowers. These are legitimate concerns that must be discussed and confronted if the idea of justice for the worst crimes known to mankind is to survive its own renaissance in the mid-nineties after the long paralysis of the Cold War that followed the Second World War and the military tribunals put in place to judge the Nazis and members of the Axis.

Just as some of the most problematic aspects of anti-terrorism laws adopted post-9/11 are symbols of the dangers of abuse of the law when the objective of fighting criminality is pursued too aggressively, so must one be careful of similar overreach in the domains of genocide, crimes against humanity, and war crimes. No one is against virtue, and no one is consequently against the objective of fighting international crimes. But we must be guarded against the temptation to cast the net of repression too wide and sacrifice, in our noble endeavour, not only principles that should remain indisputable, like the right to make full answer and ·

defence and the right to an impartial and fair trial, but also actual persons, physical individuals who might become 'collateral damage' of laws that are either outright unfair (like most of the early antiterrorism laws) or overly broad—some would say the interpretation given to certain modes of participation to offenses by the *ad hoc* tribunals. The international criminal justice system, like all justice systems, is vulnerable to abusive or unjust interpretations and applications of the law.

Defence lawyers are particularly well placed to witness these defects. In a sense, the sensible evolution of any justice system, including the international criminal justice system, relies on their capacity of indignation. It is this indignation and those thoughtful attacks on the law that prevent the international justice system from turning into a cheerful circus of do-gooders patting each other's backs in satisfaction every time one more 'war criminal' goes to prison. Having said that, we should also guard against adopting un-nuanced or extreme position about the system: we should be careful of those idealists who see international criminal justice as a panacea and as the grander achievement of mankind, just as we should be careful with those hopeless cynics who see it as a completely worthless and corrupt enterprise.

In this short essay, we wish to discuss some aspects of the background that mark the coming into life of the permanent international criminal jurisdiction—the International Criminal Court. Namely, these include the expectations that were placed on international criminal justice institutions in the nineties and beyond, and the partial failure of these institutions to live up to these unrealistic anticipations (Part 1 below).

We will then address some elements of consideration for the future of the international criminal justice system. We will mention some of the foundations upon which it is built, serving as a basis for our argument that despite a mixed legacy and various shortcomings, there will be no turning back to a legal void in international law as regards accountability for international crimes. We will also discuss the gradual and promising shift of responsibility from international bodies towards states in the investigation and prosecution of international crimes.

## The Background: (Not) Living Up to Unrealistic Expectations

*High Expectations for International Criminal Justice*

The creation of the *ad hoc* tribunals in the mid-1990s and the adoption of the Rome Statute of the International Criminal Court in 1998 spurred a wave of excitement and tremendous hope in the human rights community and among victims of atrocities. The individuals responsible for committing the gravest violations of international human rights law and of international humanitarian law would be brought to justice. If the international community could not or would not prevent crimes, it would at least ensure that they would not go unpunished. However, aside from the punishment of those who bear the greatest responsibility for the commission of mass crimes, international criminal justice institutions were expected to play a great role in the restoration and or maintenance of peace and security.

In 1993, the UN Security Council stated that, "the establishment [...] of an international tribunal and the prosecution of persons responsible for serious violations of international humanitarian law would [...] contribute to the restoration and maintenance of peace."[1] It was the first time that the belief that criminal accountability might be essential for the restoration and maintenance of peace and security was explicitly expressed. Massive human rights violations, including those occurring within a state's borders, were considered threats to international peace and security, and individual accountability for such violations was considered a measure to restore or maintain them. This objective became a trend, as all international and internationalised tribunals created since then pursued it to more or less explicit degrees.[2]

However, this was not the only objective international criminal tribunals were expected to reach. Indeed, international criminal justice was seen as a way not only to deter the individual perpetrator, but also to act as a general deterrent for the commission of international crimes worldwide and to prevent the escalation of war, or at the very least diminish the capacity of a group to commit violations. Moreover, international criminal tribunals were also supposed to tell the truth and shed light on events, providing a sense of justice for victims. They further had an 'educational' role aimed at "conveying the message that rules of international humanitarian law have to be obeyed under all circumstances."[3] It was also thought that they would allow victims and perpetrators to reconcile and reinstate the torn societies in a country where the rule of law would have been re-established.[4]

Even with such a rapid and non-exhaustive overview, it can easily be observed that very high expectations were put on international criminal justice, consequently setting a high threshold for success. In the background of the work of international criminal institutions nowadays, therefore, lies a very difficult endeavour, that of managing expectations: expectations of states, of civil society, of "public opinion" and, above all, those of victims. As put dramatically by Rob Crilly:

> [T]he crowd of children, their eyes wide with hope as they held their handwritten signs calling for the UN and ICC to save the people of Darfur… was one of the most depressing sights I had ever seen. In some ways it is easier to deal with misery, with mothers holding skeletal children as they tell how their village was burned and their menfolk killed… *What is infinitely more difficult to deal with is hope:* the belief that the outside world can solve the problems of Darfur; that the soldiers of the UN will one day ride to the rescue; or that the ICC will end Sudan's culture of impunity.[5]

### An Unsurprising Mixed Legacy

In the face of such high anticipation, it was to be expected that international criminal institutions would be vulnerable to critiques. For one thing, the interaction between and compatibility of peace and security on the one hand, and justice on the other, is at the heart of a raging debate that plays out in most if not all post-conflict settings, as well as in situations of ongoing violence and human rights abuses. The idea that international criminal justice mechanisms can (contribute to) restore peace and security is one of the most hotly debated issue in the literature and in international fora. There is certainly no definite answer to this debate.

Clearly, the adoption of some criminal law measures to deal with international crimes cannot be ignored in peace-building processes (though they may, arguably, be delayed). For one thing, it should be recalled that criminal prosecutions are mandated by international treaty law for some international crimes[6] and arguably by international customary law for others.[7] Without romanticising the transformative potential of such trials, we are of the view that criminal justice for international crimes has a role to play in post-conflict recovery and indeed perhaps in ongoing conflict situations.

Having said that, the focus on international criminal justice may have shadowed the fact, at least in the beginning, that criminal trials can only be one element of a complex web of measures that need to be implemented for the transition from war to peace to succeed. Only holistic strategies devised on a case-by-case basis after consultation with national constituencies, including the groups most affected by conflict, can hope to balance "a variety of goals, including the pursuit of accountability, truth and reparation, the preservation of peace and the building of democracy and the rule of law."[8] Insistence on criminal trials without due regard to complementary and alternative (legal and non-legal) mechanisms can indeed jeopardise the quest for truth, justice, and reconciliation. Complementarity is necessary not only with other—non-criminal—transitional justice mechanisms, but also, for instance, with judicial and political measures aimed at recognising state responsibility for the crimes committed.[9] The various transitional justice approaches in turn need to be implemented in coordination with overlapping initiatives such as security sector and rule of law reforms as well as human rights-based development programming.[10]

Now, even if one recognises that criminal justice has a role to play for the maintenance or restoration of peace and security, it must be acknowledged that international criminal courts have at times taken roads that are not easy to reconcile with the idea of peace. As a striking example, the failure of the ICTR to look at both sides of the conflict has most probably led to tensions in Rwanda.[11] Criminal trials can contribute to peace and reconciliation among other ways by presenting "an accurate collective memory... based on the model of closure. It is said that war crimes trials can permit entire societies to 'draw a clear line between past and future, allowing the beginning of a healing process.'"[12] Beyond closure, which is said to be too ambitious an agenda for criminal trials, it remains that they can promote debates about the history of a conflict or about specific cases through the lens of the law, lessening the chances of blank assertions of guilt from both sides.[13] However, post-conflict criminal trials can hope to fulfill this promise only if they look at both sides of a conflict. The ICTR, for reasons of political expediency, blatantly failed in this regard.

As another example, the decision of the then International Criminal Court prosecutor to indict the sitting president of Sudan, Omar Al-Bashir, for crimes against humanity and genocide in Darfur was a surprising move at the time, for legal and strategic reasons, and it proved to be devastating for the legitimacy and credibility of the ICC. Legally speaking, it was rather bold to go directly to the top of the political hierarchy without having previously built the chain of power and command through other, less high-profile cases, in a highly complex situation like that of Darfur. It was also quite intrepid to indict the president for the crime of genocide, a very difficult crime to prove, in a case where even the International Commission of Inquiry that investigated the issue, and whose report led to the Security Council referral of the Darfur situation to the ICC, had not found sufficient evidence to conclude that genocide had occurred.[14] Strategically speaking, going after a sitting president when the state was already hardly cooperating with the court was a guarantee of rebuttal and a promise that no alleged Darfur war criminal would make his or her way to The Hague. This decision has alienated the African Union and has triggered a series of very aggressive stances against the ICC, leading the court to the edge in its precious relations with African states. What the Bashir case demonstrates, too, is that one should be cautious about excess of confidence in international criminal justice as an instrument of peace, absent strong political sponsorship, namely the backing of an organ such as the Security Council. Even when the Council has found that criminal prosecutions are a desirable measure for the restoration of peace and security in a given situation, its lack of effective support with the enforcement of subsequent measures adopted within the criminal justice system seriously undermines the credibility of the international legal order: "Impunity through non-enforcement of international arrest warrants that have been backed with Chapter VII authority cannot be permitted without fundamentally undermining the credibility of the notion of an international rule of law."[15] This lack of consequent follow-up in the situation of Darfur gravely undermines the credibility of both the ICC and the Security Council and weakens the international legal order.

As for other unfulfilled expectations, the *ad hoc* tribunals quickly disappointed victims who initially hoped to have a voice in the international criminal processes. Reparations for victims were not given a prominent status in the *ad hoc* international criminal tribunals' statutes, which were heavily based on the common-law model. The ICTY and ICTR Statutes provide for restitution of property acquired through criminal conduct once a finding of guilt has been made, but the victims have no direct standing in claiming restitution.[16] The individual victim can also claim compensation through the national courts or other competent bodies, once the accused has been convicted and the judgment has been transmitted to the national authorities.[17] These provisions have had little if no impact for victims related to proceedings before the tribunals.[18]

Moreover, the idea that international criminal justice mechanisms could develop an accurate and detailed narrative of history is fairly controversial.[19] Criminal proceedings have as their principal objective determination of individual liability. When they are particularly founded on an adversarial model, they cannot realistically be hoped to build a complete factual record of an entire conflict or years of abuse. The *ad hoc* tribunals have been criticised for attempting to do so.[20]

Finally, while it is generally understood that "long-term and sustainable solutions to impunity should aim mostly at building domestic capacity to try [international] crimes,"[21] international criminal justice mechanisms produced mixed results. Internationalised (hybrid) tribunals often have a deep impact on national law, but the *ad hoc* tribunals had a low-profile and inefficient capacity-building strategy, at least in the early stages, and it took some time before they stimulated legal reforms at the domestic level. In fact, the ICTY and ICTR never really saw national capacity building as being a central part of their mandate until their completion strategy had to be crafted.[22] Their impact could be summarised as 'too little too late.'[23]

The ICC has learned from these arguable failures and has crafted an innovative mechanism for victims' participation and reparations. Victims have indeed increasingly been given a more prominent role in international criminal proceedings. The ICC has various provisions regarding victims' participation. Its strategy is based on the principles contained in international instruments regarding victims' rights.[24] It is based on the fact that "positive engagement with victims can have a significant effect on how victims experience and perceive justice and, as such, contribute to their healing process"[25] and on the understanding that the "ICC has not only a punitive but also a restorative function. It reflects growing international consensus that participation and reparations play an important role in achieving justice for victims."[26] Participation in criminal proceedings is not without difficulties, however, particularly where it clashes with the rights of the accused.[27] The Extraordinary Chambers in the Court of Cambodia and the Special Tribunal for Lebanon also allow for victims' participation in court proceedings.[28] This confirms the trend of recognising victims not only as potential witnesses and sources of information, but as active actors of the criminal process who are granted specific rights.[29] As for national capacity building, as we shall see, the founding principle of the ICC—complementarity—is probably the most promising impact the ICC is likely to have on the global enterprise to fight impunity for the worst international crimes.

## The Way Forward: Pragmatic Justice as a Shared Responsibility

*No Turning Back: An International Criminal*
*Justice System Based on Unquestionable Foundations*

It is trite to say that the *ad hoc* tribunals and the ICC were created on the foundations of Nuremberg and, particularly for the ICC, were aimed at providing a permanent home to the noble idea that "crimes against international law are committed by men, not by abstract entities, and only by punishing individuals who commit such crimes can the provisions of international law be enforced."[30] This principle is that of individual criminal liability, the idea that behind the curtains of statehood are persons actually committing, ordering, planning, and so forth, international crimes. This principle is now firmly embedded in both treaty and customary international law, as hinted above, and cannot be ignored, both in law and in practice. International criminal tribunals have had an indisputable role in promoting and building the rule of law at the international level and in building an international normative public order.

It is undeniable that international criminal statutes and courts have brought greater clarity to the definitions of international crimes and to the modes of participation to such crimes. The impressive amount of jurisprudence emanating from these courts and the vibrant academic literature that accompanied it certainly made an immense contribution to the international legal framework. Suffice it to mention, for instance, the tremendous impact on the definition of the crime of genocide by the two first genocide judgments in *Akayesu*[31] and *Kambanda*,[32] which gave unprecedented "vitality and relevance" to the 1948 Convention,[33] notably declaring that genocide is "undeniably considered part of customary international law."[34] The *Akayesu* judgment is also ground-breaking for its affirmation of rape as constitutive of international crimes.[35] As with other crimes of sexual violence, it is now considered an underlying crime of all core crimes by international courts and can also be constitutive of torture or persecution.[36] The Rome Statute codified this statement of international customary law and lists numerous acts of sexual violence within its definitions of crimes against humanity and war crimes.[37]

One of the most significant developments in international criminal law has occurred with respect to crimes against humanity. These crimes have grown out of their link with armed conflicts and their definition has been progressively refined (regarding the attack requirement, for instance) and expanded (a broad list of sexual crimes and enforced disappearance, for instance). They cover a wide range of conduct committed in both peace and war times that would not necessarily qualify as genocide or war crimes. Despite the current absence of a specific treaty concerning crimes against humanity, they now form a central part of the international criminal legal order. As regards war crimes, the *ad hoc* tribunals and the ICC Statute have made numerous important contributions, the most significant and well-known being the extension of the legal regime applicable to war crimes to internal armed conflicts.[38] This development has been codified generally in the ICC Statute, which sets forth the most detailed listing thus far of underlying offences constitutive of war crimes committed in internal armed conflicts.[39]

Apart from the definitions of crimes, international criminal institutions have defined modes of individual criminal liability, trying to find a way to deal with individual criminal responsibility in a context where there is a plurality of perpetrators, some of whom may not have physically committed the crime.[40] The doctrines of superior responsibility and joint criminal enterprise were developed to cope with what has been labelled "system criminality."[41] Though they have been criticised,[42] the doctrines have been the basis for a vast number of convictions before all international criminal tribunals[43] and have contributed, along with the vibrant literature they have stimulated, to building a better understanding of how criminal law may capture collective and massive criminality. Finally, it is worth noting that the building of international criminal justice has also contributed to weakening the legal basis for amnesties for gross human rights violations, it has opened a breach in the long-standing legal regime concerning immunities, and it has severely limited the application or statutes of limitations, all of which welcome developments where applied within the bounds of law, which includes the preservation of state sovereignty.

Individual criminal liability for genocide, crimes against humanity, and war crimes is here to stay. There will be no turning back to a legal vacuum allowing alleged perpetrators of genocide, crimes against humanity, and war crimes to retire to a quiet holiday on a beach somewhere—if not in practice in all cases, at least in terms of states' rhetoric and, above all, in international law. To fix any current weaknesses of the current international criminal justice system, it is necessary to work from within it instead of pushing pointlessly for its breakdown.

That said, the way of the future will not necessarily be that of the past. With the *ad hoc* tribunals, the international community chose to favour a distant and disincarnated form of justice, putting the emphasis on international courts. At the heart of the system put in place by the ICC to ensure accountability for the core crimes instead lies the principle of complementarity. States bear the primary responsibility to prosecute those responsible for international crimes. The ICC will exercise its jurisdiction only if the competent state is inactive, "unable" or "unwilling" to do so.[44] National legislations such as Canada's *Crimes Against Humanity and War Crimes Act*, S.C. 2000, c. 24, are therefore called to play an increasingly important role in the global system put in place to fight impunity. By acting locally, states like Canada can indeed make a significant contribution for the "sustainable development" of international criminal justice.[45] International criminal justice mechanisms will not disappear, but the international criminal justice system will rely more than ever on states to implement international criminal law.

## A Shift Towards States

The Rome Statute, in its preamble[46] and by implication of the complementarity principle, provides for states parties' duty to prosecute the international crimes contemplated therein. The Appeals Chamber of the ICC has recognised that states "have a duty to exercise their criminal jurisdiction over international crimes."[47] However, there is no explicit obligation in the Rome Statute on the part of states parties to establish jurisdiction over the crimes and certainly no obligation to assert it on the basis of universality.[48] Regardless of the absence of a clear obligation in this regard in the Statute, many states have taken the opportunity presented by the need to modify their domestic law to implement their obligations under the Rome Statute and give their domestic courts jurisdiction to try these crimes, including on the basis of universality. The "ICC train" is creating an irrevocable momentum toward the criminalisation of the ICC offences in national laws and toward providing national courts with jurisdiction to try these crimes. Many observers argue that the impact of the complementarity principle on domestic legal systems—particularly if promoted 'proactively' by the Courts' organs— is the ICC's most promising contribution to the fight against impunity and to lasting peace and security.[49]

This renewed (or new) emphasis on domestic systems has at least two consequences in addition to the one just mentioned, namely, the need to change national laws to comply with international criminal law obligations and responsibilities. The first consequence is that states where the crimes occurred or whose nationality the alleged perpetrator possesses have a particular responsibility in ensuring that the crimes do not go unpunished. Two remarks can be made regarding this commonplace assertion. First, territorial or national states do not exactly have an immaculate pedigree in this regard. In fact, the need to internationalise accountability initiatives to address past human rights violations is often due to a lack of institutional capacity or political will at the local level. Second, having the primary responsibility to investigate and prosecute international crimes is perhaps a privilege respectful of state sovereignty, but it is also a very onerous duty. It is easy to see the inherent difficulties states coming out of conflict can face in living up to this challenge, particularly with respect to ensuring a fair trial to the suspects, in a political environment not always favourable to such noble aims. For instance, Côte d'Ivoire has asked the ICC to inquire into the crimes committed in the electoral period for fear of creating political instability in the country.[50] It is also going into some challenges in attempting to hold to account sympathisers of the incumbent president who are alleged to have committed graves violations of international law.[51] Similarly, for decades, numerous states and the ICTR have had great difficulties with extraditing or transferring suspects to Rwanda, despite clear political will there to take charge of the cases, essentially because of concerns for the suspects' security or, more often, for fears that they could not get a fair trial. This long-standing debate has led to an important decision by a Chamber of the European Court of Human Rights (ECHR) on October 27, 2011, which dismissed the application by a Rwandan genocide suspect who was fighting extradition to Rwanda by Sweden because, according to the Court, "he would not risk a flagrant denial of justice."[52] The Appeals Chamber of the ICTR in December 2011 also confirmed the transfer of Jean-Bosco Uwinkindi to Rwandan courts, a first such transfer from the ICTR,[53] and some states have also subsequently allowed such transfers, not without concerns expressed by defendants that a fair trial would be illusory on the current political context.[54] As a last example, one can only mention the struggle of Libya to convince the ICC and world opinion that it can and will offer a fair trial to Saif Al-Islam Gaddafi.[55] The responsibility to ensure accountability for international crimes thus brings about highly delicate challenges for the states involved.

A second consequence of this shift towards states in the global fight against impunity for international crimes is that where territorial or national states do not or cannot investigate and prosecute, not only the ICC can act as a last bulwark against impunity, but also third states, notably through the principle of universal jurisdiction. Universal jurisdiction is the assertion of jurisdiction by a state for crimes which, at the time of commission, had no territorial or national link with the state in question. Clearly, the ICC cannot be expected to be able to ensure justice for all perpetrators of international crimes. "As Cesare Beccaria stated as long ago as 1764, 'the conviction of finding nowhere a span of earth where real crimes were pardoned might be the most efficacious way of preventing their occurrence' and the rule of law."[56]

The exercise of universal jurisdiction can in our view contribute to close the 'impunity gap' by ensuring that those responsible for international crimes do not escape justice. This extraordinary head of jurisdiction does not come without its own challenges, however, be it for both prosecution and defence to gather evidence, to obtain the territorial state's cooperation, to apply international law to an unknown foreign context, to finance the investigations and the trials, to manage political tensions that might inevitably ensue, and so on. However, the collective undertaking to fight impunity depends largely on the serious commitment of all nations. This commitment must be directed at the proper functioning of the international institutions that have been established for that purpose, like the ICC, but it must also include the will and capacity to use national institutions towards realisation of the same fundamental objective.[57]

## Conclusion

A lot was expected from the tribunals created by the United Nations Security Council in the midst of the deadly events of Rwanda and the Former Yugoslavia: restoration and maintenance of peace and security, deterrence, reconciliation, education, truth-telling, retribution, denunciation, reparation, etc. The ICC was created in 1998 in this environment of great hopes and tremendous expectations, which no criminal law institution, be it national or international, could ever meet. After nearly twenty years since the revival of international criminal justice, a common understanding emerges: criminal justice is only one measure that can be used in ongoing and post-conflict situations and we must not expect from it more than it can deliver.

The *raison d'être* of international criminal justice, the idea of individual criminal accountability for the most serious international crimes, is here to stay. There will be no turning back to a legal vacuum where no law and no institution could implement this principle. The ICC is not just an international institution; it has created a global system to fight against the impunity of those responsible for the commission of genocide, crimes against humanity and war crimes, a system which relies primarily on states. The seminar that led to this collection of essays asked the question Justice for Whom? To answer it requires looking beyond the *ad hoc* tribunals and beyond the ICC. The future of the global system of accountability for international crimes relies on states. The strengthening of national laws and judicial institutions is the priority challenge of the next decades. The political will to let justice follow its course, its main threat. The recent successes or attempts of national courts in states like Guatemala, Argentina, and Haïti, and the use of universal jurisdiction not only in Western states like Canada, Spain, Belgium, and the like, but also by Senegal, South Africa, and Argentina, perhaps points to what might be the most profound impact of the system created by the ICC: justice must be a matter for all, if the aim is that it not be directed against only a few.

## Notes

1. *Resolution 827*, SC Resolution 827, UNSCOR, 48th Session, UN Doc S/RES/827, 1993, Preamble, para. 6.

2. *Ibid., Resolution 955*, SC Resolution 955, UNSCOR, 49th Session, UN Doc S/RES/955, 1994, Preamble. As regards the Special Court of Sierra Leone (SCSL), see *Resolution 1315*, SC Resolution 1315, UNSCOR, 55th Session, UN Doc S/RES/1315, 2000, Preamble, para. 7. For the International Criminal Court (ICC), see *Rome Statute of the International Criminal Court*, July 17, 1998, 2187 UNTS 3, Preamble, paras. 3 and 5, Art. 13(b) ["*Rome Statute*"]. Similar links between peace and justice can be found regarding the establishment of the Panels in Timor-Leste: *Resolution 1272*, SC Resolution 1272, UNSCOR, 54th Session, UN Doc S/RES/1272, 1999, Preamble, para. 1; the Khmer Rouge Trials in Cambodia: *Khmer Rouge Trials*, GA Res 57/228B, 57th Session, Supp. No. 49, UN Doc A/RES/57/228B, 2003, Preamble; and the Special Tribunal for Lebanon: *Resolution 1757*, SC Resolution 1757, UNSCOR, 61st Session, UN Doc S/RES/1757, 2007, Preamble.

3. *Prosecutor v. Kordić and Čerkez*, IT-95-14/2-A, Judgment, December 17, 2004, para. 1080 (International Criminal Tribunal for the Former Yugoslavia, Appeals Chamber ["ICTY App. Ch."]).

4. *The Rule of Law and Transitional Justice in Conflict and Post-Conflict Societies: Report of the Secretary-General*, UNSCOR, 59th Session, UN Doc S/2004/616, 2004, para. 38 [*"Secretary-General Report on the rule of law and transitional justice"*].

5. Rob Crilly, *Saving Darfur: Everyone's Favourite African War*, Reportage Press, 2010, pp. 39-40 [emphasis added].

6. *Convention on the Prevention and Punishment of the Crime of Genocide*, December 9, 1948, 78 UNTS 277 at Arts. IV-VI; *Geneva Convention (I) for the Amelioration of the Condition of the Wounded and Sick in Armed Forces in the Field*, August 12, 1949, 75 UNTS 31 at Art. 49; *Geneva Convention (II) for the Amelioration of the Condition of Wounded, Sick and Shipwrecked Members of Armed Forces at Sea*, August 12, 1949, 75 UNTS 85, Art. 50; *Geneva Convention (III) relative to the Treatment of Prisoners of War*, August 12, 1949, 75 UNTS 135, Art. 129; *Geneva Convention (IV) relative to the Protection of Civilian Persons in Time of War*, August 12, 1949, 75 UNTS 287, Art. 146; *Protocol Additional to the Geneva Conventions of August 12, 1949, and relating to the Protection of Victims of International Armed Conflicts (Protocol I)*, June 8, 1977, 1125 UNTS 3, Arts. 85-87; *International Convention on the Suppression and Punishment of the Crime of Apartheid*, November 30, 1973, 1015 UNTS 243, Art. IV (note that, as an exception, at Art. V, the exercise of jurisdiction is phrased in permissive terms ('may')); *International Convention for the Protection of All Persons from Enforced Disappearance*, December 20, 2006 (not yet into force: see *International Convention for the Protection of All Persons from Enforced Disappearance*, GA Res 61/277, UNGAOR, 61st Session, Supp. No. 49, UN Doc A/61/49 (2006) 408 at Arts. 4-11; Third Committee, *Report of the Human Rights Council: Report of the 3rd Committee*, UN Doc A/61/448 (2006) at para. 28, Arts. 4-11); *Convention against Torture and Other Cruel, Inhuman or Degrading Treatment or Punishment*, December 10, 1984, 1465 UNTS 85, Art. 4-7. Jurisprudence interpreting various regional and international human rights treaties has also increasingly recognised the duty to prosecute those responsible for human rights violations: see e.g. review in Anja Seibert-Fohr, "Reconstruction through Accountability," 2005, Max Planck Yearbook of United Nations Law, Vol. 9, p. 555.

7. See review of argument in e.g., Robert Cryer *et al.*, *An Introduction to International Criminal Law and Procedure*, Cambridge, Cambridge University Press, 2007, pp. 31-33, 58-61.

8. *Secretary-General Report on the rule of law and transitional justice, supra* note 4 at para. 25. On national consultations, see Office of the High Commissioner for Human Rights (OHCHR), *Rule-of-law Tools for Post-conflict States: National Consultations on Transitional Justice*, UN Doc HR/PUB/09/2, 2009.

9. See Saira Mohamed, "A Neglected Option: The Contributions of State Responsibility for Genocide to Transitional Justice," 2009, University of Colorado Law Review, Vol. 80, p. 327.

10. Jane E. Stromseth, "Pursuing Accountability for Atrocities After Conflict: What Impact on Building the Rule of Law?" 2006-2007, Georgetown Journal of International Law, Vol. 28, p. 256; OHCHR, *Frequently asked questions on a human rights-based approach to development cooperation*, UN Doc HR/PUB/06/8, 2006. See also the interesting proposal of an emergency post-conflict justice that would

work alongside other justice initiatives such as international criminal proceedings: Louise Otis and Eric H. Reiter, "Front-Line Justice," 2006, *Virginia Journal of International Law,* Vol. 46, p. 677.

11.  Human Rights Watch, "Rwanda: End Attacks on Opposition Parties," February 10, 2010, http://www.hrw.org/news/2010/02/10/rwanda-end-attacks-opposition-parties. An opposition figure "has been widely condemned in official and quasi-official media and described as a 'negationist' of the genocide for stating publicly that crimes committed against Hutu citizens by the RPF and the Rwandan army should be investigated and those responsible brought to justice."

12.  Jose Alvarez, "Rush to Closure: Lessons from the Tadić Judgment," 1998, 96 *Michigan Law Review* 2031 at 2034, citing Naomi Roth-Arriaza, "Introduction" in Naomi Roth-Arriaza, ed., *Impunity and Human Rights in International Law and Practice,* New York, Oxford University Press, 1995, p. 7.

13.  *Ibid.,* pp. 2084-2085.

14.  *Report of the International Commission of Inquiry on Darfur to the United Nations Secretary-General,* UN Doc S/2005/60, 2005, paras. 640-642.

15.  C. Reiger, "Fulfilling the Justice Promise: Guiding Principles for Resolving the Ongoing Responsibilities of International Tribunals," October 8, 2009, p. 2, http://www.ictj.org/static/Prosecutions/Arria_Presentation091008.pdf (unretrievable as of June 13, 2014).

16.  *Statute of the International Tribunal for the Prosecution of Persons Responsible for Serious Violations of International Humanitarian Law in the Territory of the Former Yugoslavia since 1991,* Art. 24(3); *Statute of the International Criminal Tribunal for the Prosecution of Persons Responsible for Genocide and Other Serious Violations of International Humanitarian Law Committed in the Territory of Rwanda and Rwanda Citizens Responsible for Genocide and Other Such Violations Committed in the Territory of Neighbouring States, between 1 January and 31 December 1994,* Art 23(3); ICTY, *Rules of Procedure and Evidence,* rules 98*ter*(B), 105 ["ICTY RPE"]; ICTR, *Rules of Procedure and Evidence,* rules 88(b), 105 ["ICTR RPE"].

17.  ICTY RPE, rule 106; ICTR RPE, rule 106.

18.  See e.g. Anne-Marie De Brouwer, *Supranational Criminal Prosecution of Sexual Violence: The ICC and the Practice of the ICTY and the ICTR,* Antwerpen, Intersentia, 2005, p. 394 and following; William A. Schabas, *The UN International Criminal Tribunals: The Former Yugoslavia, Rwanda and Sierra Leone,* Cambridge, Cambridge University Press, 2006, p. 149 and following; Susanne Malström, "Restitution of Property and Compensation to Victims" in Richard May *et al.,* eds, *Essays on ICTY Procedure and Evidence in Honour of Gabrielle Kirk McDonald,* The Hague, Kluwer Law International, 2001, 373 at 376. In Rwanda, the compensation orders have not been implemented: International Crisis Group, *International Criminal Tribunal for Rwanda: Justice Delayed,* June 7, 2001, Africa Report No. 30, http://www.crisisgroup.org/en/regions/africa/central-africa/rwanda/030-international-criminal-tribunal-for-rwanda-justice-delayed.aspx.

19.  Jose Alvarez, "Rush to Closure: Lessons from the Tadić Judgment", *supra* note 12; Mark J. Osiel, *Mass Atrocity, Collective Memory and the Law,* New Brunswick,

Transaction Publishers, 1997; Martha Minow, *Between Vengeance and Forgiveness: Facing History after Genocide and Mass Violence*, Boston, Beacon Press, 1998.

20. See e.g. *Prosecutor v. Tadić*, IT-94-1-T, Opinion and Judgement, May 7, 1997, ICTY Trial Chamber ["ICTY T. Ch."]; *Prosecutor v. Akayesu*, ICTR-96-4-T, Judgment, September 2, 1998, ICTR Trial Chamber; for critiques, see e.g. José Alvarez, "Lessons from the Akayesu Judgment," 1998-1999, ILSA Journal of International and Comparative Law, Vol. 5, p. 359; Jose Alvarez, "Rush to Closure: Lessons from the Tadić Judgment", *supra* note 12.

21. OHCHR, *Rule of Law Tools for Post-Conflict States: Prosecution Initiatives*, UN Doc HR/PUB/06/4, 2006, p. 1; also, *Secretary-General Report on the Rule of Law and Transitional Justice, supra* note 4. para. 34; Kerstin McCourt, "Judicial Defenders: Their Role in Postgenocide Justice and Sustained Legal Development," 2009, *The International Journal of Transitional Justice*, Vol 3:2, pp. 272-273.

22. *Resolution 1503*, SC Resolution 1503, UNSCOR, 58th Session, UN Doc. S/RES/1503, 2003, (*inter alia*, "recalls that the strengthening of national judicial systems is crucially important to the rule of law in general and to the implementation of the ICTY and ICTR Completion Strategies in particular"; see also *Statute by the President of the Security Council*, 57th Session, UN Doc S/PRST/2002/21, 2002.

23. See generally Jane E. Stromseth, *supra* note 10, p. 279.

24. International Criminal Court ["ICC"], *Report of the Court on the strategy in relation to victims*, ICC-ASP/8/45, November 10, 2009, para. 6. The Office of the Prosecutor has also prepared a *Policy Paper on Victims' Participation*, RC/ST/V/M.1, April 12, 2010, http://www.icc-cpi.int/iccdocs/asp_docs/RC2010/RC-ST-V-M.1-ENG.pdf.

25. ICC, *Report of the Court on the strategy in relation to victims, supra* note 24, para. 2.

26. *Ibid.*, para. 3.

27. See Salvatore Zappalà, "The Rights of Victims v. the Rights of the Accused," 2010, Journal of International Criminal Justice, Vol. 8:1, p. 137.

28. See e.g. Extraordinary Chambers in the Court of Cambodia, *Internal Rules*, rules 23-23 *quinquies*; Special Tribunal for Lebanon ["STL"], *Rules of Procedure and Evidence*, rules 86-87 ["STL RPE"]; STL, *RPE Explanatory Memorandum by the Tribunal's President*, June 10, 2009, para. 14; for a comment, see Jérôme de Hemptinne, "Challenges Raised by Victims' Participation in the Proceedings of the Special Tribunal for Lebanon," 2010, Journal of International Criminal Justice, Vol. 8:1, p. 165.

29. There are a growing number of jurisprudential interpretations of the criteria necessary to qualify as a victim under Art. 68(3) of the ICC Statute, including on the notion of harm suffered by the victim and the link with the alleged crime. See e.g. *The Prosecutor v. Thomas Lubanga Dyilo*, Judgment on the appeals of The Prosecutor and The Defence against Trial Chamber I's Decision on Victims' Participation of 18 January 2008, ICC-01/04-01/06-1432, July 11, 2008.

30. International Military Tribunal, *Trial of the Major War Criminals before the International Military Tribunal*, Nürnberg, November 14, 1945 - October 1, 1946, published at Nürnberg, Germany, 1947, p 223.

31. *Prosecutor v. Akayesu, supra* note 20.

32. *Prosecutor v. Kambanda,* ICTR-97-23-S, Judgment and sentence, September 4, 1998, ICTR Trial Chamber.

33. *Convention on the Prevention and Punishment of the Crime of Genocide, supra* note 6; Payam Akhavan, "The Crime of Genocide in the ICTR Jurisprudence," 2005, Journal of International Criminal Justice, Vol. 3, p. 990.

34. *Prosecutor v. Akayesu, supra* note 20, p. 495.

35. Kelly Dawn Askin, "Gender Crimes Jurisprudence in the ICTR: Positive Developments," 2005, Journal of International Criminal Justice, Vol. 3, p. 1011.

36. *Ibid.* p. 1014; see *Prosecutor v. Semanza,* ICTR-97-20-T, Judgment and Sentence, May 15, 2003, ICTR Trial Chamber); *Prosecutor v. Gacumbitsi,* ICTR-01-64-T, Judgment, June 17, 2004, para. 215, ICTR Trial Chamber; *Prosecutor v. Nahimana et al.,* ICTR-99-52-T, Judgment and Sentence, December 3, 2003, ICTR Trial Chamber. The test of equal gravity has helped to enlarge the scope of acts falling under the crime of persecution: *Prosecutor v. Karadzic,* IT-95-5/18-PT, Decision on Six Preliminary Motions Challenging Jurisdiction, April 28, 2009, para. 43, ICTY Trial Chamber.

37. *Rome Statute, supra* note 4, Arts. 7(1)(g), 8(b)(xxii), 8(e)(vi). *The Elements of Crimes of the International Criminal Court,* ICC-ASP OR, ICC-ASP/1/3, 2002, p. 108, also confirm that it can be constitutive of genocide at Art 6(b), note 3.

38. *Report of the Secretary General Pursuant to Paragraph 5 of Security Council Resolution 955,* 50th Sess, UN Doc S/1995/134, 1995, para. 12; see *Prosecutor v. Tadić, supra* note 22, para. 134; *Prosecutor v. Delalić et al.,* IT-96-21, Judgment. November 16, 1998, para. 308, ICTY Trial Chamber; Lindsay Moir, "Grave Breaches and Internal Armed Conflicts," 2009, Journal of International Criminal Justice, Vol. 7, p. 764; Denise Plattner, "The Penal Repression of Violations of International Humanitarian Law Applicable in Non-international Armed Conflicts," 1990, International Review of the Red Cross, Vol. 30:278, p. 414.

39. *Rome Statute, supra* note 2, Arts. 8(2)(c), 8(2)(e).

40. Harmen G. van der Wilt, "The Continuous Quest for Proper Modes of Criminal Responsibility," 2009, Journal of International Criminal Justice, Vol. 7, pp. 307-8.

41. *Ibid.*

42. See among many others Jens David Ohlin, "Three Conceptual Problems with the Doctrine of Joint Criminal Enterprise," 2007, Journal of International Criminal Justice, Vol. 2, pp. 69-90.

43. Gideon Boas, James L. Bischoff & Natalie L. Reid, *Forms of Responsibility in International Criminal Law,* vol 1 (Cambridge: Cambridge University Press, 2007) at 9.

44. *Rome Statute, supra* note 2, Preamble, para. 6, Arts, 1, 17.

45. See Fannie Lafontaine, "'Think Globally, Act Locally': Using Canada's Crimes against Humanity and War Crimes Act for the 'Sustainable Development' of International Criminal Law", Proceedings of the 36th Annual Conference of the Canadian Council of International Law which focused on "Canada's Contribution to International Law", Ottawa, October 2007; Fannie Lafontaine & Edith-Farah Elassal, "La prison à vie pour Désiré Munyaneza—Vers un « développement durable » de la justice pénale internationale", *Le Devoir,* November 2, 2009, http://www.ledevoir.com/2009/11/02/274892.html.

46. *Rome Statute, supra* note 2, Preamble, paras. 4 and 6.

47. *Prosecutor v. Germain Katanga and Mathieu Ngudjolo Chui,* ICC-01/04-01/07, Judgement on the Appeal of Mr. Germain Katanga against the Oral Decision of Trial Chamber II of 12 June 2009 on the Admissibility of the Case, September 25, 2009, para. 85, ICC, Appeals Chamber.

48. See e.g. Payam Akhavan, "Whiter National Courts? The Rome Statute's Missing Half," 2010, Journal of International Criminal Justice, Vol. 8, p. 1248.

49. See e.g. William W. Burke-White, "Proactive Complementarity: The International Criminal Court and National Courts in the Rome System of Justice," 2008, Harvard International Law Journal, Vol. 49, p. 53; Mark S. Ellis, "International Justice and the Rule of Law: Strengthening the ICC through Domestic Prosecutions," 2009, Hague Journal on the Rule of Law, Vol. 1, p. 79.

50. Mark Kersten, "Outsourcing Justice to the ICC—What Should Be Done?" *Justice in Conflict,* October 31, 2012, http://justiceinconflict.org/2012/10/31/outsourcing-justice-to-the-icc-what-should-be-done/; Pia Navazo, "Closer to Justice? Côte d'Ivoire and the ICC One Year On", *The Laws of Rule,* April 11, 2012, http://www.lawsofrule. net/2012/04/11/closer-to-justice-cote-divoire-and-the-icc-one-year-on/; The Office of the Prosecutor, *Report on Preliminary Examination Activities,* December 13, 2011, para. 120.

51. "Supporting National Prosecutions in Côte d'Ivoire", *International Center for Transitional Justice,* June 6, 2013, http://ictj.org/news/supporting-national-prosecutions-cote-divoire.

52. *Case of Ahorugeze v. Sweden,* No 37375/09, 2011, ECHR.

53. *Jean Uwinkindi v. The Prosecutor,* ICTR-01-75-AR11bis, Decision of Uwinkindi's Appeal against the Referral of his Case to Rwanda and Related Motions. December 16, 2011, ICTR Appeals Chamber.

54. See e.g. the expulsion of Léon Mugesera from Canada: *Motifs d'une décision en application de l'alinéa 115(2)b) de la Loi sur l'immigration et la protection des réfugiés (LIPR),* numéro de dossier HQ7-65767, on file with author, p. 53, and the discussion on fair trial guarantees generally at pp. 57-63. See discussion in Fannie Lafontaine, "Mugesera: Canada's First Faltering Steps in the Debate Over Transferring Genocide Suspects to Rwanda," *International & Transnational Criminal Law,* January 5, 2012, http://rjcurrie.typepad.com/international-and-transna/2012/01/mugesera-canadas-first-faltering-steps-in-the-debate-over-transferring-genocide-suspects-to-rwanda.html.

55. See e.g. *The Prosecutor v. Saif Al-Islam Gaddafi and Abdullah Al-Senussi,* ICC-01/11-01/11, Libyan Government's consolidated reply to the responses of the Prosecution, OPCD, and OPCV to its further submissions on issues related to the admissibility of the case against Saif Al-Islam Gaddafi, March 4, 2013, http://www.icc-cpi.int/iccdocs/doc/doc1562659.pdf. The Appeals Chamber has now decided on admissibility, finding the case admissible: *The Prosecutor v. Saif Al-Islam Gaddafi and Abdullah Al-Senussi,* ICC-01/11-01/11, Judgment on the appeal of Libya against the decision of Pre-Trial Chamber I of 31 May 2013 entitled "Decision on the admissibility of the case against Saif Al-Islam Gaddafi," May 21, 2014, http://www.icc-cpi.int/iccdocs/doc/doc1779877.pdf.

56. Antonio Cassese, "On the Current Trends towards Criminal Prosecution and Punishment of Breaches of International Humanitarian Law," 1998, European Journal of International Law, Vol. 9, p. 17, citing Cesare Beccaria, 'Dei delitti e delle pene,' translated in J. Farrar, *Crimes & Punishment,* 1880, pp. 193-194.

57. Fannie Lafontaine, "Universal Jurisdiction: The Realistic Utopia," 2012, Journal of International Criminal Justice, Vol. 10, p. 1277; Fannie Lafontaine, "The Unbearable Lightness of International Obligations: When and How to Exercise Jurisdiction under Canada's *Crimes against Humanity and War Crimes Act,*" 2011, 23:2, *Revue québécoise de droit international 1.*

# 16

## How the International Criminal Law Movement Undermined International Law— Michael Mandel's Groundbreaking Analyses

DAVID JACOBS

On October 27, 2013, the world lost Professor Michael Mandel, a pioneering scholar in the field of international criminal law, among other things, and I lost a dear friend and colleague. He was irreplaceable. It is an immeasurable loss.

Michael did not merely set about applying his prodigious scholarship to interpreting the world in various ways; he set out to change it. Michael's passion for peace and social justice was reflected in his fearless commitment to political engagement as part of his legal scholarship. His devotion to truth and logic marked his work. He was an expert in the law and translated this expertise into activism—including activism against war. Although Michael was a rigorous international law scholar, he was an opponent of what he described, without approval, as the "international criminal law movement."[1]

What follows is a brief appreciation of Michael's contribution to the critique of the international criminal law movement. It is not intended to be comprehensive and I am certain that it does not begin to do justice (and justice was the ideal Michael passionately believed in and courageously fought for) to the breadth and incisiveness of his scholarship. I am hopeful that these few words will inspire readers to study his work.

The phrase "international criminal law movement" bears a sense that one is dealing with a political phenomenon—a movement in search of legitimacy. The addition of the term "movement" connotes a campaign. Michael concluded that although its campaigners may have believed that they were contributing to the struggle against war and its atrocities, the international criminal law movement made a bigger contribution to the promotion of war and war crimes than to their prevention.[2]

The trick of imagining international criminal law (as practiced by current international criminal law tribunals) as an antidote to war and war crimes while failing to consider the pro-war political dimensions of such praxis exemplifies one of Michael's favoured aphorisms: "They used to say that if you were able to think of something that was related to another thing without thinking about that other thing, then you had the legal mind."[3] The unimagined "other thing," which is in fact the condition precedent to the practice of international criminal tribunals, is the waging of the aggressive war in the first place. As Michael put it, it is "the quite massive and unspeakable criminality of the world's richest countries and particularly that of the United States of America."[4]

> The only rational assumptions are that international criminal law will be firmly subordinated to power, that impunity will be a perk of economic and military hegemony, and that the usual suspects will continue to be rounded up while America gets away with murder.[5]

Michael surgically eviscerated the foundational pretensions of the international criminal law movement in works such as his 2004 publication, *How America Gets Away With Murder: Illegal Wars, Collateral Damage And Crimes Against Humanity.* Michael's view was that the old, anti-war order of international law, which recognised the sovereign equality of nations and anathematised unilateral aggressive war, had to be overthrown to legitimise the "new world order" crystallising after the end of the Cold War. The new order was characterised by the desire of the United States to violently and unilaterally impose "regime change" on governments it held in contempt. This new order needed legal sanction, and the international criminal law movement obliged by fatally undermining the old order governed by the UN Charter and the Nuremberg Principles.

Michael's argument, made with unassailable logic, is that given the context of NATO's illegal attack on Yugoslavia in 1999, the International Criminal Tribunal for the Former Yugoslavia (the "flagship"[6] post-Nuremberg tribunal first promoted by the international criminal law movement), in turning a blind eye to the illegality of the attack, had no option but to become implicated in "the overthrow of international law and the UN Charter's fundamental principles."[7] Thus the ICTY (and by extension the International Criminal Court and the ad hoc tribunals such as the

International Criminal Tribunal for Rwanda) had to fashion a "substitute legality"[8] in the form of the current face of international criminal law promoted by the international criminal law movement.

Michael's starting points include the Charter of the United Nations: the "fundamental document of the old world order,"[9] the "world's constitution,"[10] and the Nuremberg Principles.[11] The central tenets of the UN Charter are:

> [T]he equality of states and the prohibition of the use of force in international relations. Violence is only permissible when authorized by the Security Council... The only permissible unilateral use of military force is the strictly limited right of self-defence, temporarily available until the Security Council can deal with the situation.[12]

The Preamble to the UN Charter expressly sets out as its goal "to save succeeding generations from the scourge of war." Principle IV of the Nuremberg Principles sets out that crimes against peace, war crimes, and crimes against humanity are punishable as crimes under international law. Principle IV defines crimes against peace, in part, as "planning, preparation, initiation or waging of a war of aggression or a war in violation of international treaties, agreements or assurances." In a statement often cited by Michael in his writings and speeches, the judgment of the Nuremberg Tribunal famously declared:

> War is essentially an evil thing. Its consequences are not confined to the belligerent states alone, but affect the whole world. To initiate a war of aggression, therefore, is not only an international crime; it is the supreme international crime differing only from other war crimes in that it contains within itself the accumulated evil of the whole.[13]

Michael pointed out that collateral to the establishment of the various new international criminal tribunals to try war crimes and crimes against humanity was the 1999 war over Kosovo "fought under the legally preposterous claim of unilateral 'humanitarian intervention,'" and the "mortal blow" to the UN Charter of the 2001 war against Afghanistan, "under the equally preposterous claim of self-defence."[14]

It is in the furnace of the NATO attack on Yugoslavia that the ICTY and the "substitute legality," which the international criminal law movement is enamoured of, were forged. Under the "old world order," the forcible violation of national sovereignty was a violation of the "sound and precious anti-war principles of the"[15] UN Charter and the supreme international crime. While NATO spokespersons tried to justify the attack on the pretext of "humanitarian intervention" (now renamed with the more soothing soubriquet, "responsibility to protect"[16]) such pretext was itself an admission of criminality:

> 'Humanitarian intervention' by military force finds no place in the Charter of the United Nations, because for the generation who wrote the Charter the 'scourge' was war between states, the violation of national sovereignty that was Nuremberg's 'supreme crime'... The notion of a 'humanitarian war' would have rang in the ears of the drafters of the UN Charter as nothing short of Hitlerian, because it was precisely the justification used by Hitler himself for the invasion of Poland six years earlier.

Michael showed beyond doubt that the NATO attack was a violation of the UN Charter and a crime against peace—a crime punishable under international law. It was a war of aggression, a war in violation of international treaties, agreements or assurances, not least in breach of the UN Charter and the NATO Treaty. The latter Treaty including the Preamble and Articles 1 and 7 thereto attests to the primary responsibility of the UN Security Council and the subordination of NATO to the UN Charter. As he explained:

> Neither Security Council authorization nor self-defence was even claimed by NATO as justification for the use of force... The preamble of the NATO Treaty (1949) states that the signers of this document are attesting to their commitment to the premises of the United Nations Charter as well as their resolve to live amicably with all human beings.[17]

Michael did not stand alone in concluding that the NATO aggression was illegal. The majority of legal scholars, including the ICTY's first President, Antonio Cassese, concluded that the war was illegal.[18] Michael wrote that the NATO attack was an attempt to overthrow the UN Charter and so create a precedent, the "Kosovo precedent": "It was not an authentic legal precedent, but the beginning of an open abandonment of legality itself as a fundamental point of reference in international relations."[19] For the ICTY to emerge from this conundrum without indicting NATO leaders posed a problem.

For one thing, astonishingly, the war crime which "contains within itself the accumulated evil of the whole," a crime against peace, is not justiciable under the Statute of the ICTY. It was excluded from the Statute at the primary insistence of the United States: "[I]t was no accident that this crime had been excluded from the Statute... America's desire to keep it off the law books, which it also pursued successfully against the International Criminal Court is, well, understandable."[20] At his ICTY trial, Serbian President Slobodan Milošević was not even permitted to cross-examine about the war NATO waged against Yugoslavia.[21] So the ICTY was left with only the subordinate crimes within its remit: war crimes and crimes against humanity demarcate its jurisdiction.

One would have thought that there was ample evidence for charges to proceed at the ICTY against the NATO instigators of war, even if one could think about war crimes and crimes against humanity without thinking of the "other thing": the crime against peace. There was persuasive evidence that NATO bombed civilian targets, failed to take the precautions required under the Geneva Conventions to protect civilian life, limb, and property, etc., even if one were able to edit out the fact that this criminality was undertaken in pursuit of a war of aggression, a war contrary to international treaties.

As I wrote at the outset, Michael went far beyond merely trying to (legally) interpret the world. He put the same passion, courage, and enthusiasm into trying to change it. He relished this good fight and spared no effort in persuading others to join in, myself included. In 1999, Michael worked with other lawyers around the world to found Lawyers Against the War to oppose the attack on Yugoslavia. I am grateful that he recruited me to the organisation. We engaged in extensive and well-attended lecture tours, and members, led by Michael, proposed to test the ICTY: would it pursue charges against NATO?

In May 1999, Michael drafted a "Request that the Prosecutor Investigate Named Individuals for Violations of International Humanitarian Law and Prepare Indictments against them pursuant to Articles 18.1 and 18.4 of the Tribunal Statute." I signed the final version, as did other Canadian lawyers and law professors jointly with the American Association of Jurists. Michael went to The Hague twice in 1999 to meet with the ICTY Chief Prosecutor to make the case for indictment of NATO, and I had the privilege of accompanying him on his second visit. In November 1999, we met with Carla Del Ponte, then Chief Prosecutor of the ICTY and ICTR. She was flanked by two legal advisors, both from NATO countries. We were armed with an extensive legal brief, again written in the main by Michael, and buttressed by devastatingly persuasive documentation of NATO's breaches of law. It was not as if we alone came to the conclusion that violations of the laws of war, even aside from the supreme international crime, had occurred: Amnesty International, among others, reached similar conclusions.

Even if NATO's crime against peace—the war itself—may not have been the formal subject of charges, the actions of NATO could not be excused by turning a blind eye to the illegality of the exercise. Michael quoted the American Chief Prosecutor at Nuremberg, United States Supreme Court Justice Robert H. Jackson, on precisely this point: "inherently criminal acts cannot be defended by showing that those who committed them were engaged in a war, when war itself is illegal."[22] However, the ICTY, through the Office of the Prosecutor (OTP), did just that and stopped short of even opening an investigation of NATO. The committee of expert investigators reporting to the OTP astoundingly wrote that they "tended to assume that the NATO and NATO countries' press statements are generally reliable and that explanations have been honestly given."[23] As Michael commented, "Can you imagine what kind of law enforcement a country would have if the police took their suspects' explanations at face value?"[24]

So, in Michael's submission, having chosen to overlook NATO crimes, the ICTY necessarily became implicated in them. It created a substitute legality; overthrowing the old world order anchored by the UN Charter. The ICTY failed to prosecute the instigators of the war, and lent legitimacy to the illegal "humanitarian intervention" rationale concocted by NATO. In the course of the war, the ICTY prosecutor made dramatic announcements against Serb leaders targeted by NATO, often at press conferences with NATO leaders; unveiled a secret indictment of President Milošević at a time when enthusiasm for the war was flagging in the West; and even assigned NATO the task of pursuing ICTY indictees. The ICTY served to sanction NATO aggression:

It's easy to see how all this could legitimate the use of force by NATO. If NATO was pursuing criminals indicted by the Tribunal, it could present its law-breaking as law-enforcement. And every aggressor wants to demonize its enemy. The ICTY would officially brand them international criminals— and not just any criminals, but Nazi war criminals.[25]

Michael drew the appropriate conclusion. As the subsequent events in Afghanistan, Iraq, and Libya inform us, the ICTY has changed the paradigm of international law. The tribunals nominally created to prosecute war crimes instead abet such crimes, and far from ending the scourge of war instead provide novel legal justifications for aggression. In an echo of the public unveiling of the secret indictment of President Milošević "to justify the scuttling of peace efforts" in the NATO war against Yugoslavia, so the International Criminal Court prosecutor announced the indictment of Libyan President Gaddafi and his sons in the midst of the NATO war on Libya, thereby "providing a pseudo-legal justification for... war."[26] It was noteworthy, as Michael wrote, that after the war against Libya and "the indictments had served their purpose in justifying it," the ICC handed the prosecution of President Gaddafi's son, Saif as-Islam, who had been indicted by the ICC, to the new Libyan authorities.[27]

None of the international criminal tribunals formed in the wake of the ICTY have the authority to prosecute crimes against peace. They are left with narrow windows into the actions of the warring parties, without the context that Nuremberg demanded. More tragically, while devising new means of prosecuting the losing sides for conduct during war, they undermine the obvious goal, namely, that "you need to stop the wars in the first place."[28]

All of the international criminal tribunals now extant grant extensive immunity, *de facto* and/or *de jure*, to the perpetrators of the "supreme international crime." In the case of the ICC, not only is its legitimacy hobbled by the exclusion to date of crimes against peace, but the United States is beyond the reach of the ICC; it refuses to ratify the ICC's Rome Statute, even though it had decisive input into its contents.[29] So, the "supreme crimes and crimes of the supreme powers"[30] lie outside the jurisdiction of the ICC, and to the date of this writing, the only persons indicted before the ICC are Africans.[31]

Similarly, the ICTR has never prosecuted any member of the Rwandan Patriotic Front, which emerged as the victor in the 1990-1994 war against the Rwandan Government. The victorious RPF regime was described by Michael as "a Washington client."[32] The ICTR Prosecutor "confessed that she had to ignore RPF crimes, or the RPF government would shut her down."[33] In her words, "[h]ow could we investigate and prosecute the RPF while we were based in that country. It was never going to happen. They would shut us down."[34] Michael makes the telling point that the ICTR was "an initiative of the ultimately victorious Tutsi RPF and their Ugandan sponsors, who started calling for a war crimes tribunal for their enemies on May 1994, before the killing had even stopped—in other words, as part of *their* wartime propaganda."[35]

When Chief Prosecutor Carla Del Ponte intimated that she might prosecute the RPF, "the statute was amended so that separate prosecutors would now be assigned to each [of the ICTY and the ICTR]."[36] Del Ponte was taken off the ICTR. No RPF member will ever be prosecuted by the ICTR. Notwithstanding the existence of the ICTR and the promised end of impunity, the Rwandan regime in 1998 "had embroiled itself in a war in the Congo that would take millions of lives."[37] The ICTR will not lay charges. As with the ICTY and the instigators of the attack on Yugoslavia, the RPF instigators of the war, which led to so many dead in Rwanda[38] and Congo, are beyond the reach of the ICTR.

In the end, the international criminal law tribunals perpetrate selective justice. As Michael wrote, "So the idea that international criminal law serves justice by punishing some of the lesser criminals, even if it grants impunity to supreme criminals for their supreme crimes, is already dubious."[39] By criminalising the losing side in criminal wars, the international criminal tribunals justify aggression.

Michael's view was that at the conclusion of the Cold War, the US was an unchallengeable military power. However, its ambitions were hampered by the international law regime enshrined in the UN Charter. The sovereign equality of nations and strict prohibitions of the use of force were impediments to its desire to violently effect regime change where it wished. In order for the US to bring about revolutionary change in international law, the fundamentals had to be destroyed. The UN Charter's insistence on peaceful resolution of conflict and the sovereign equality of nations had become outmoded "traditions" which should not be permitted to derail progress.

The international criminal law movement led the revolution in law. Supranational courts, with broad powers, served to "fashion a higher legality" and rehabilitate unilateral military action without UN sanction and "where no mere nation's law could possibly stand in its way."[40] The international criminal law movement has delegitimised and marginalised the UN.

In Michael's words:

> If the ICC is to survive—and it wants badly to survive—it will continue to ignore the crimes of the US and to round up the usual suspects, to regulate... but not prohibit—indeed to legitimate—the use of violence in international affairs.[41]

Michael's contribution to justice cannot be overstated. His clear, direct, fearless, and truthful indictment of the international criminal law movement stands as a beacon to us. He was an outstanding teacher and leader in a movement of jurists of conscience and he is sorely missed.

## Notes

1. Michael Mandel, *How America Gets Away With Murder: Illegal Wars, Collateral Damage And Crimes Against Humanity*, Pluto Press, London, 2004, p. 249, *et seq.*
2. Speakers' notes, Michael Mandel, unpublished, 2001.
3. Michael Mandel, "Aggressors' Rights: The Doctrine of Equality between Belligerents and the Legacy of Nuremberg" (2011), 24 *Leiden Journal of International Law* 627. 628, see also Harry Glasbeek, "Capitalist Law for Capitalists: A lawyer's notes on the eviction from St. James Park," unpublished, January 13, 2012.
4. Speakers' notes, *op cit.*
5. Michael Mandel, *How America Gets Away With Murder, supra, fn. 1, p. 233.*
6. Michael Mandel, "The Legal Institutions of the New World Order: 'Might Makes Right' and the International Criminal Tribunal for the Former Yugoslavia," in Gordana Yovanovich, ed., *The New World Order: Corporate Agenda and Parallel Reality*, McGill-Queen's University Press, Montréal, 2003, p. 72.
7. *Ibid. pp. 113-114.*
8. *Ibid., p113-114.*
9. *Ibid.*, p. 72.
10. Michael Mandel, *R2P & ICC v. UNC: The Responsibility to Protect and the International Criminal Court versus the Charter of the United Nations* in *Costituzione Economia Globalizzazione*, Edizioni Scientifiche Italiane, Napoli, 2013, p. 1379.

11. Principles of International Law Recognized in the Charter of the Nuremberg Tribunal and in the Judgment of the Tribunal. Adopted by the International Law Commission of the United Nations, 1950.

12. Michael Mandel, "The Legal Institutions of the New World Order," *supra*, fn. 6.

13. Michael Mandel, *How America Gets Away With Murder, supra, fn. 1, p. 6.*

14. Michael Mandel, "The Legal Institutions of the New World Order," *supra*, fn. 6.

15. Michael Mandel, *How America Gets Away With Murder, supra, fn. 1, p. 113.*

16. See Michael Mandel, *R2P & ICC v. UNC: The Responsibility to Protect and the International Criminal Court versus the Charter of the United Nations*, pp. 1379-1391.

17. Michael Mandel, "The Legal Institutions of the New World Order," *supra*, fn. 6, p. 75.

18. Michael Mandel, *How America Gets Away With Murder, supra, fn. 1, p. 89, et seq. Michael Mandel, UN Cannot Foster Peace When US Sidesteps It for War: On the illegitimate 'Kosovo Model' for military intervention, August 28, 2013, http://www.commondreams.org/views/2013/08/28/un-cannot-foster-peace-when-us-sidesteps-it-war.*

19. *Ibid.*, p. 112

20. *Ibid.*, pp. 177, 178.

21. Michael Mandel, *How America Gets Away With Murder, supra, fn. 1, p. 174.*

22. *Ibid., p. 6.*

23. *Ibid., p. 90.*

24. *Ibid., p.90.*

25. *Ibid.*, p. 118

26. *R2P & ICC v. UNC: The Responsibility to Protect and the International Criminal Court versus the Charter of the United Nations, supra*, fn. 10, pp. 1387-1388.

27. *Ibid.*, p. 1388.

28. Michael Mandel, Speakers' notes, unpublished, 2001.

29. *Ibid.*, pp. 207 *et seq.*

30. *Ibid.*, p. 234.

31. Michael Mandel, Interview, *What was Slobodan Milosevic accused of?* March 26, 2012, transcript, http://voiceofrussia.com/2012_03_26/69601596/.

32. *Ibid.*, p. 242.

33. *Ibid.*, p. 235.

34. *Ibid.*, p. 129

35. *Ibid.*, On Rwanda see also *R2P & ICC v. UNC: The Responsibility to Protect and the International Criminal Court versus the Charter of the United Nations*, , supra fn. 10 p. 1391, where Michael made the following observation on the "absurd" use of the Rwandan tragedy to justify the "responsibility to protect" doctrine: "The terrible Rwandan bloodshed of 1994 is often mentioned, but, as an excuse for granting the big powers that run NATO the power to make war, it is patently absurd. It is not a question of whether it was properly termed a "genocide" or who was mainly responsible, the Hutu government or the invading Tutsi RPF. Everybody agrees that intervention was intentionally prevented by the Unites States itself. It is sometimes implausibly said that this was due to a mere image problem: the United States did not want to involve its own soldiers, so it did not want to allow others to make it look bad. A far more plausible explanation is that the United States was just following the wishes of their allies in the Rwandan Patriotic Front,

the army of the Tutsi victims, who wanted the UN to stay out, despite the massacres, because they wanted their invasion from Uganda to succeed in taking over
the country, which it ultimately did. And, in fact, this shows why Rwanda is such
a bad example, because the Rwandan government was, quite naturally, begging
for intervention. It's enough to read the transcript of the Security Council meeting of 21 April 1994 where the representative of the 'genocidal' government makes
what he terms 'an anguished appeal of the people of Rwanda' to the international
community not to be 'abandoned to its sad fate' and, while the Security Council,
at the insistence of the United States, voted to reduce UNAMIR, the government
of Rwanda asked 'that UNAMIR's numbers should be increased to enable it to
contribute to the re-establishment of the ceasefire and to the establishment of
security conditions that could bring an end to the violence.' The significance of
this is that there was no need for any doctrine of R2P to 'trump' state sovereignty,
because, in the full, old-fashioned, exercise of that sovereignty, the government
was inviting intervention."

36. *Ibid.*, p. 1391.
37. *Ibid.*, p. 242.
38. *Ibid.*, p. 104.
39. *Ibid.*, p. 236.
40. *Ibid.*, p. 252.
41. *Ibid.*, pp. 252-253.

# 17

## International Criminal Law:
## An Instrument of United States Foreign Policy

JOHN PHILPOT

### Introduction

International criminal law, often promoted as a new, courageous form
of justice, is an instrument of neo-colonialism for the United States and
Western powers harkening back to the nineteenth century. It works
hand-in-hand with military actions and imperial economic and strategic interests. The overriding selectivity of international criminal law
deprives it of legitimacy.

Courts in international criminal law, as they have developed since
1990, are a far cry from the universal international criminal court many
dreamed of after the Second World War: a court whose independent
prosecutor can charge leaders from any country and punish them for
the crime of aggression, other war crimes, and crimes against humanity
committed in wars or political conflict. The new international criminal
courts have many things in common. Largely creations of the United
States, they have narrow mandates directed away from the United States
and other Western powers. The one major exception, the International
Criminal Court (ICC), confirms the rule as we shall see; the United
States has done everything in its power to prevent the ICC from having
any jurisdiction over the United States and American citizens while at
the same time trying to influence the course of affairs at the ICC.

The ICC prosecutor has only charged Africans; discriminatory justice is not justice. International criminal law and international criminal
courts have nothing to do with change, correcting fundamental inequal-
ity between the rich and the poor nations, and the unequal division of
power in the world. The many jurists, journalists, politicians, and political scientists in the West have taken a wrong turn by promoting the

use of international criminal law rather than criticising its fundamental premise and practises.

## Selective Prosecution: The Influence of the United States and Reconciliation

Prosecution in international criminal law is selective. Prosecutors are not neutral or independent. Generally, enemies of the West are prosecuted and their friends are protected. It has been argued that bringing criminals to justice encourages reconciliation in war-torn countries. This cannot be done if justice is not even handed. There has been no reconciliation resulting from the two *ad hoc* courts, the International Criminal Tribunal for Rwanda and the International Tribunal for the Former Yugoslavia.

## International Criminal Tribunal for Rwanda

The case of the ICTR is striking. When ICTR/ICTY Prosecutor Carla Del Ponte stated she was going to prosecute the Rwandan Patriotic Front leadership, she was quickly removed under pressure from the United States and Britain under the guise of having separate prosecutors for the ICTR and the ICTY.[1] Yet the issue of RPF crimes is recognised internationally.[2] The RPF was not charged, in spite of the organised and planned nature of its road to power. It is still in power, and the Hutu majority is silenced without any justice being rendered for these victims of RPF crimes. Rwandan Hutu in Rwanda and in exile know and hate the RPF and Paul Kagame, and Rwanda is once again a potential tinderbox. There is no suggestion that there has been reconciliation in Rwanda.

## The International Criminal Tribunal for the Former Yugoslavia

The prosecutor of the International Criminal Tribunal for the Former Yugoslavia has formally charged the many different parties in the Yugoslavian conflict. Many observers, however, have accused the ICTY of being fundamentally an anti-Serbian court, with its prize accused being the former president, Mr. Slobodan Milošević.

Former President Milošević had wanted to defend himself. The court-imposed counsel, British lawyers Steven Kay and Gillian Higgins, were not allowed to withdraw from the case. Mr. Milošević's trial was severely criticised for unfairness and bias.[3] Mr. Milošević died during his trial. The ICTY is now trying Mr. Radovan Karadžić, Bosnian Serb leader, and former General Ratko Mladić, Bosnian Serb former military leader.

The recent acquittals[4] of the Croatian military leaders for the crimes committed by the Croatian armed forces with the support of Nato in Operation Storm have proved the critics right. In August 1995, 2,650 Serbs (mainly civilians) were killed and some 250,000 were "ethnically cleansed" from their ancestral homes. Several thousand have disappeared, and their fate is not known to this day. This was the largest refugee crisis since World War II.[5] These criminal Croatian *bliztkreig* army generals returned to Croatia as national heroes.

This judgment was followed by the November 29, 2012 acquittal of Kosovar terrorist and leader of the UCK (Kosovo Liberation Army), Ramush Haradinaj, who returned to political life in Kosovo.[6] Following the court's judgment, former ICTY spokesperson Florence Hartmann said that the court suffered a defeat because it turned away from the truth, and that is a total collapse of the system of international justice.[7]

The overwhelming influence of the United States has been raised within the ICTY. In June 2013, sitting ICTY judge Frederik Harhoff circulated a private letter to fifty-six colleagues where he accused the American presiding judge, Theodor Meron, of relaxing criteria for liability for senior military officers, under pressure from American and Israeli sources. According to Judge Harhoff, President Meron was concerned that the jurisprudence for strict criminal responsibility for high-ranking officers was creating a dangerous precedent. It is striking that a sitting judge is willing to make such allegations.[8] The letter was leaked to the media. Many people working in international criminal justice criticised Judge Harhoff. He was subsequently disqualified from the Šešelj case for bias.[9]

These recent judgments confirm that the ICTY cannot promote reconciliation. Instead the rulings show that the court fosters division in the former Yugoslavia and also reveal the selective nature of the court.

## Special Court for Sierra Leone

Another unfair, biased court was created under the pressure of the
United States, the Special Court for Sierra Leone (SCSL).

Civil war in Sierra Leone began in 1991. The Revolutionary United
Front (RUF) was pitted against the government for control of the territory. Under international impetus, negotiations in 1999 led to the Lomé
Accords signed March 27, 1999. The agreement provided for power sharing, under which Mr. Foday Sankoh of the RUF would be vice president
while a United Nations peacekeeping force would monitor disarma-
ment. Mr. Sankoh had good relations with Libya and President Charles
Taylor of Liberia.

As the UN peacekeeping effort faulted, the British intervened militarily in its former colony in May 2000 with Operation Palliser. Its support for the government tipped the balance against the Revolutionary
United Front, whose leader, Foday Sankoh, was arrested one week later
on May 17.[10]

The United States initiated diplomatic efforts to create a war crimes
tribunal for Sierra Leone. UN Security Council Resolution 1315, adopted
on August 14, 2000, paved the way for the formation of the Special Court
for Sierra Leone by agreement between the United Nations and the victor
in the war, the government of Sierra Leone.[11] This court indicted a total
of twenty-two people. Foday Sankoh died in prison in 2003.

President Charles Taylor was the most important person indicted. In
2003, he resigned as president of Liberia and obtained asylum in Nigeria.

In 2006, Liberian President Ellen Johnson Sirleaf requested the
extradition of Taylor from Nigeria. Almost unheard of in African politics, Nigeria violated asylum and agreed to hand Taylor over to Liberia.
Nigerian President Obasanjo was scheduled to meet US President
George Bush. Just hours prior to the meeting, on March 29, 2006, Taylor
was arrested on the border with Cameroun. Desmond De Silva, a British
lawyer, was the prosecutor who indicted Charles Taylor, while both
prosecutors in his trial were Americans who had previously worked as
prosecutors for the *ad hoc* tribunals for Rwanda and Yugoslavia, namely,
Stephen Rapp from 2006 to 2009 and Brenda Hollis after 2009.

Sometimes it is argued that holding a war crimes trial close to the
scene of the crimes is a good idea since the trial is instructive for the

local populations. The Special Court for Sierra Leone was based in Sierra Leone. This was not the case for Charles Taylor. He was so popular in the area that his successor, President Sirleaf of Liberia, requested his trial be held in The Hague. Under the impetus of the United States and Prosecutor Stephen Rapp and according to Security Council Resolution 1688, Taylor was transferred to The Hague to be tried in the International Criminal Court (ICC) under the auspices of the Special Court. He was convicted on May 26, 2012, but only of aiding and abetting the crimes committed in the Sierra Leone war. As he had been charged with being the mastermind of the war, this verdict was by no means a stunning victory for the US prosecutor.

A court judgment is intimidating. To the outsider, a judgment of an international criminal court states the truth since supposedly neutral judges have ruled on the basis of evidence introduced in an allegedly fair trial. The trial verdict has been roundly criticised.[12]

The most important professional and informed participant, sitting Alternate Judge Malick Sow of Senegal, described the fatal flaws in the judgment. An alternate judge participates in the entire case along with the three judges in the event that one judge falls ill or dies. Alternate Judge *Sow* stated in court after the judgment was rendered on April 26, 2012:

> The only moment where a Judge can express his opinion is during the deliberations or in the courtroom, and pursuant to the Rules. When there is no serious deliberations, the only place left for me is in the courtroom. I won't get—because I think we have been sitting for too long but for me I have my dissenting opinion and I disagree with the findings and conclusions of the other Judges, because for me under any mode of liability, under any accepted standard of proof the guilt of the accused from the evidence provided in this trial is not proved beyond reasonable doubt by the prosecution. And my only worry is that the whole system is not consistent with all the principles we know and love, and the system is not consistent with all the values of international criminal justice, and I'm afraid the whole system is under grave danger of just losing all credibility, and I'm afraid this whole thing is headed for failure. Thank you for your attention.[13]

As he spoke, the metal grate for the public gallery and the media was lowered, muzzling Judge Sow.

The Appeals judgment rendered on September 26, 2013 has also been severely criticised. Critics point out its failure to follow the recent law on aiding and abetting, which requires specific direction to find guilt for aiding and abetting.[14] Instead, the judgment allowed guilt to be based on recklessness as to the consequences of an act.[15]

## No Appearance of Justice in the Charles Taylor Case

The judgment has other weaknesses. Charles Taylor was not found guilty of being the mastermind of the war in Sierra Leone as argued by United States Prosecutor Brenda Hollis. He was probably the main target of US diplomacy aimed at securing the entire region under United States and British influence. Ironically, the crimes of aiding and abetting for which he was found guilty are crimes being committed on a daily basis by the United States, Britain, France, Turkey, and Saudi Arabia in Syria; all actively support military intervention in Syria by bands of foreign "rebels." The International Criminal Court has a provision for similar criminal responsibility in the Rome Statute at Article 25 (3) (c). We do not see ICC Prosecutor Fatou Bensouda initiating investigations of the United States, Britain, France, Turkey, and Saudi Arabia. France and Britain have signed and ratified the Rome Statute whereas the United States, Turkey, and Saudi Arabia do not accept the ICC jurisdiction but can be charged. The double standard in international criminal law and the impunity for the powerful is flagrant once again.

## Extraordinary Chambers in the Courts of Cambodia

The United States' illegal wars on Vietnam and Cambodia and the ensuing conflicts almost forty years ago gave rise to another limited and selective court created at the instigation of the United States. On April 29, 2005, an agreement between the United Nations and Cambodia[16] came into force, setting up the Extraordinary Chambers in the Courts of Cambodia (ECCC). This court, made up of international and national judges and a national prosecutor along with an international prosecutor, had the limited mandate to bring to trial senior leaders of Democratic Kampuchea for crimes and serious violations of Cambodian penal law, international humanitarian law, and customary law committed between April 17, 1975 and January 6, 1979.

The United States initiated long negotiations in 1997 leading to the appointment of judges in March 2006. David Scheffer, US Ambassador-at-Large for War Crimes Issues, details the negotiations, which he led in his book, *All the Missing Souls: A Personal History of the War Crimes Tribunals*.[17] He even presided the meeting of experts that established the court rules.

The genesis of this court is a story in itself. The US State Department zealously sought international support. Latin America was generally opposed to a new *ad hoc* tribunal. Mexico considered that the tribunals for Rwanda and the former Yugoslavia lacked legitimacy.[18] Initially Cambodian Prime Minister Hen Sen thought that nobody should escape justice: those charged could include the Americans responsible for the carpet bombing and one million dead from 1971-1975, those who killed in the Khmer Rouge period, and anyone else who killed from 1970 to 1998.[19]

The Americans were insistent in their efforts to judge their former allies, the Khmer Rouge. By bullying and badgering, the Americans won and this special, extraordinary international court was created with a narrow mandate to judge the Khmer Rouge. Unsurprisingly, the court has no mandate to judge America for its war on Cambodia.

## Special Tribunal for Lebanon (STL)

The latest International Criminal Court is the Special Tribunal for Lebanon. Following the assassination of former Prime Minister Rafik Hariri on February 14, 2005, an international tribunal was set up to charge those responsible for the killings. On May 30, 2007, the UN Security Council, acting under Chapter VII of the UN Charter, endorsed the March 29, 2006 agreement between Lebanon and the United States to set up the Special Tribunal for Lebanon (STL).[20] The court has primacy over Lebanese courts although it is a hybrid court with a mixture of international law and Lebanese law.

The court has a special feature hitherto unknown in international criminal law. The accused may be judged *in absentia* even without receiving notification of the charges against them. Lawyers named by the

defence section must defend the interests of their clients without knowing them or taking instructions from them. No one has been arrested
under the indictments.

The accusations were first directed against Syria, then against some
Lebanese generals, and subsequently against members of the resistance
movement Hezbollah. Hezbollah, on the other hand, considers Israel
responsible for the murder of Hariri.

After the first indictments were submitted on January 17, 2011 to the
pre-trial judge, the STL issued four arrest warrants against four alleged
members of Hezbollah on June 30, 2011.

Defence council, named by the court administration, challenged the
indictments on several bases: that the Tribunal violated Lebanese sovereignty; that the Security Council had no authority to create the court
under Chapter VII of the UN Charter since there was not sufficient
threat to international peace and security; that the Resolution 1757 violated the rights of the accused; and that the Tribunal violated the will of
the Lebanese people. The accused, in the context of a trial *in absentia*,
are not informed of their rights and of the evidence against them thus
violating the Statute and the International Pact for Civil and Political
Rights. On July 27, 2012, the Tribunal rejected defence challenges,[21] pav-
ing the way for the show trial to begin.

It is an anomaly to say the least that a Tribunal was created for
an ex-Prime Minister whereas no court was created after the April 6,
1994 assassination of Rwandan President Juvénal Habyarimana and
Burundian President Cyprien Ntaryamira. Similarly, no court was created for Israeli crimes in Operation Cast Lead, the war on Gaza that
lasted three weeks from December 27, 2008.

It is more than ironic that Hezbollah, the primary resistance force
in Lebanon against Israel and declared a terrorist organisation by the
United States, is the main target of this court.

The trial began on January 16, 2014 and has been severely criticised
in Lebanon by many, including the widely read newspaper *Al-Akhbar*.

Commenting the presence of a March 14 Alliance[22] political leader
at the opening trial, Saad Hariri, son of Rafik Hariri, *Al-Akhbar* stated
that he was acting as if he were in Beirut or Saudi Arabia and as if judgment had already been rendered. *Al-Akhbar* noted also:

Saad Hariri is aware, like everyone else, that the evidence of the STL prosecutor has been prepared by the Information Branch of the Internal Security
Forces (ISF) in Beirut. It was prepared in close coordination with Hariri
personally... Final words... This court does not represent a fair consciousness. It only represents the interests of those who robbed the people of the
world, pillaged their lands, and oppressed them. It is not a viable framework to announce the undisputed truth. It is only a tool serving the enemies of resistance. Therefore it is a tribunal not for Lebanon. [23]

In a trial that will probably last for years, defence counsel faces a
daunting task. They are taken aback, for example, by the limited evidence in which the phone call records are used to link the calls to the
accused without proving the identity of the user of the alleged phones.

At the end of April 2014, the STL charged *Al-Akhbar*'s editor-in-chief
Ibrahim al-Amin and *Al-Jadeed* Television's deputy director Karma
Khayat with obstruction of justice and contempt of court for publishing
a list of the prosecution's witnesses. These media outlets have sworn not
to be silenced in their criticism of an illegitimate tribunal.

The history of this region will be written by the people of the Middle
East and their historians and not by the Special Tribunal for Lebanon.

## US War Crimes Ambassadors

With the establishment of these special international war crimes tribunals, the United States created a new type of roving ambassador to
represent its interests. All except one have been prosecutors in different tribunals, confirming the important American influence in the
International Criminal Courts.

David Scheffer was the first United States Ambassador-at-Large for
War Crimes Issues during the second Clinton mandate. He considered
himself a central figure in the creation and operation of the different *ad
hoc* war crimes tribunals, playing an important diplomatic role. While
in that position, he took part in establishing the International Criminal
Tribunal for Former Yugoslavia, the International Criminal Tribunal for
Rwanda, the Extraordinary Chambers in the Courts of Cambodia, and
the Special Court for Sierra Leone, and was involved in negotiations for
the Rome Treaty for the ICC. Speaking of the International Criminal

Tribunal for the Former Yugoslavia, he wrote unabashedly, "the tribunal was an important judicial tool, and I had enough support from President Clinton, Secretary of State Madeleine Albright, Secretary of Defence William Cohen, and other top officials in Washington to wield it like a battering ram in the execution of US and NATO policy."[24]

He was also involved in the ICTR, not as an attorney but as a key witness. He provided testimony resulting in the incarceration of ICTR accused Jean-Bosco Barayagwiza, who had been released by the Appeals Chamber because of important abuse of his rights by the ICTR prosecutor.[25]

All subsequent Ambassadors-at-Large for War Crimes Issues were former prosecutors at the ICTY and the ICTR or the Special Court for Sierra Leone.

Pierre Richard Prosper filled this ambassadorial role for the Bush administration from July 13, 2001 to October 12, 2005. He had prosecuted Jean-Paul Akayesu, the first person convicted after trial at the International Criminal Tribunal for Rwanda. The witnesses in that trial were recruited by local authorities under the supervision of Rwandan military personnel. Mr. Prosper was responsible for laying sexual assault charges against Mr. Akayesu very late in the trial, just following a visit by Hillary Clinton to the Tribunal in March 1997. His role led to the shameful conviction of Mr. Akayesu for genocide and rape as a war crime. Prosper was centrally involved in the removal of Carla Del Ponte as prosecutor of the ICTR at a time when she intended to charge leading members of the RPF for war crimes.[26] In April 2002, he led the threats by the United States to impose sanctions if Yugoslavia did not extradite suspects to the ICTY. On April 12, 2002, Yugoslavia buckled under and accepted this extradition. The same day former federal official Vlajko Stojiljković shot himself in the head in front of the federal parliament. Shortly after, Prosper, the George W. Bush ambassador, opposed any jurisdiction of the International Criminal Court over the United States since the US, according to him, was in a unique position internationally because it has the distinct responsibility to preserve international peace and security.[27]

The second Bush Ambassador-at-Large for War Crimes Issues was John Clint Williamson, who held the position from July 10, 2006 to September 8, 2009. As a prosecutor at the ICTY from 1994 to 2001, he prosecuted many, including Mr. Slobodan Milošević. In 2003, he was involved in the US occupation of Iraq as the first Senior Adviser to the Iraqi Ministry of Justice. WikiLeaks has documented that he was interfering in the internal affairs of Spain to influence the charges Spain had made against members of the Rwandan Patriotic Front for the murder of Spanish nationals.[28]

From 2009 to 2014, the US Ambassador-at-Large for War Crimes Issues was Stephen Rapp. Attorney Rapp was prosecutor at the ICTR, involved in prosecuting those considered important targets among the Hutu living in Rwanda before 1994. Mr. Rapp prosecuted the so-called Media Case at the ICTR in a trial that has been severely criticised in the legal literature.[29] He failed abysmally to convict the brother-in-law of the assassinated President Juvénal Habyarimana, Mr. Protais Zigiranyirazo, of the *Akazu* conspiracy to commit genocide. To this day, the alleged Rwandan leadership conspiracy to commit genocide remains unproven. Mr. Zigiranyirazo spent more than eight years in prison due to this malicious and politically driven prosecution steered by Stephen Rapp. Present ICC Chief Prosecutor Fatou Bensouda worked at the ICTR under the supervision of Stephen Rapp.

Mr. Rapp then became prosecutor of the Special Court for Sierra Leone, charging the former President of Liberia Charles Taylor. He failed to prove the charge that Mr. Taylor was in control of the rebellion in Sierra Leone. The fragile and limited nature of the judgments in the Taylor case is described above and in Chapter 1.4.

According to WikiLeaks, Mr. Rapp argued in 2010 for special favours for the United States of America at the ICC: if the ICC adopted Crime of Aggression, charges for aggression should only be instituted if referred to the ICC by the United Nations Security Council where, incidentally, the US has a veto. He also confirmed that the US would not ratify the Rome Statute. In other words, the United States, who rejects the jurisdiction of the ICC, would like to be a party to the laying of any charges of aggression with the right to veto any such resolution.[30]

## International Criminal Court and Western Military Intervention

The ICC, by helping demonise enemies, is closely linked to military intervention by the United States, Britain, and France. It has only charged Africans despite the many crimes committed by NATO countries in the wars on Iraq, Côte d'Ivoire, or Libya.

Libya is a primary example of how militarisation is coupled with the use of International Criminal Law. United Nations resolution 1973 of March 17, 2011 allowed a no-fly zone and military intervention to protect civilians, since Muammar Gaddafi was allegedly flying in black African mercenaries and bombing his own people. Under the resolution, NATO aircraft made 20,000 sorties in a long and protracted war. The resolution served to protect and encourage the insurgents. It allowed them to conduct massive anti-African pogroms and overthrow the Gaddafi government, one of the most powerful forces for African unity. The NATO bombing of Libya and murder of Muammar Gaddafi was accompanied by an ICC investigation of Mr. Gaddafi. It is important to remember the demagogy of Louis Moreno Ocampo, ICC prosecutor, who in June 2011 alleged that Mr. Gaddafi had ordered mass rape and distributed Viagra to urge his men on, which was pure fabrication. In fact, it was the insurgents who committed the abuse on black Libyans.[31] The ICC issued arrest warrants against Mr. Gaddafi and his son, Saif Al-Islam Gaddafi, on June 27, 2011. NATO war planes disabled the Gaddafi convoy on October 20, 2011, and the National Transitional Council militia killed Mr. Gaddafi shortly after.

It was the old one-two punch leading to knockout. Killing Mr. Gaddafi, a head of state, is a war crime that was aided and abetted by the United States and NATO and by the ICC prosecutor. Selectivity and political prosecution in international criminal law triumphed. The NATO victors and local insurgents remain untouched for their massive crimes whereas Saif al-Islam Gaddafi faces criminal charges at the ICC and in Libya. Since NATO's victory and the overthrow of the Gaddafi government, the ICC has allowed Saif al-Islam Gaddafi to be tried in Libya as the ICC was no longer needed to demonise the Gaddafi family.

The French military intervention in Côte d'Ivoire was similar; the invasion was accompanied by ICC charges. Laurent Gbagbo had won the election under the law of Côte d'Ivoire. The loser, Alassane Ouattara, did not accept the result and incited a vicious war. In April, Ouattara's war against the constitutional government was at a stalemate. France invaded Côte d'Ivoire on April 6, 2011 to maintain its influence there and to help Alassane Ouattara win the war and become president. On November 23, 2011, the ICC prosecutor issued a warrant for former President Laurent Gbagbo and placed him under arrest. On June 13, 2013, the Pre-Trial Chamber ruled it had insufficient evidence to send Mr. Gbagbo to trial, yet he was still detained since the court allowed the prosecutor to search for additional evidence. Laurent Gbagbo won the election and was evicted militarily by the French. His wife was also charged before the ICC, while Ouattara is in power and is not troubled in the slightest.

The United States, which does not accept the jurisdiction of the ICC, has sent soldiers to Uganda ostensibly to help arrest Joseph Kony of the Lord's Resistance Army who is sought by the ICC. Kony is certainly responsible for significantly fewer killings than Ugandan President Yoweri Museveni. President Museveni shares responsibility for the millions of Congolese killed since 1996. No social media campaigns are calling for his arrest as they were in the hysterical Kony 2012 campaign, and no ICC charges have been drawn up against Museveni, close ally of the United States. This type of intervention will likely be a pretext for increased US military presence in Africa. According to *US Army Times*, more than three thousand American soldiers were to be deployed in Africa in 2013. In 2012, US military activity and exercises were carried out near Somalia, Senegal, Cameroun, and Botswana, as well as Uganda. [32]

### Kenya, the ICC, and the United States

The Kenya case at the ICC is a perfect example of misguided policy. Kenya, a developed country with tremendous potential, has been conducting a foreign and economic policy without dependence on the US and Britain for some twenty years.

The election violence in the first months of 2008 has served as a pretext for the ICC prosecutor to lay charges, ostensibly against both sides in the conflict. The prosecutor conveniently failed to summons the closest ally of the West, Orange Democratic Movement (ODM) leader Raila Odinga. Yet Raila Odinga bears responsibility for the violence that rocked Kenya after December 30, 2007, with massive attacks initiated by the ODM on perceived Party of National Unity supporters. The ICC's selectivity has a direct effect on Kenyan democracy and sovereignty since Raila Odinga was a candidate for the presidential elections, while the ICC charged other potential candidates such as Uhuru Kenyatta, son of Jomo Kenyatta.

The Kenyatta trial reminds one of Kenya's independence struggles. Uhuru Kenyatta's father, Jomo Kenyatta, was convicted in 1953 of managing and being a member of the Mau Mau insurgent group. During his imprisonment, the British killed tens if not hundreds of thousands of Kikuyu in an attempt to put an end to the Mau Mau insurgency. In 1958, the primary witness against Kenyatta, Rawson Macharia, admitted by affidavit that he had lied at the Kenyatta trial. Will history repeat itself?

Reports on these trials and my personal experience as counsel for one person accused show that the accusations are based on lies by witnesses paid to perjure themselves.

In March 2011, the Kenyan Government requested in writing that the Security Council defer the case to Kenyan courts.[33] No resolution was presented, since the United States promised to veto any such attempt. Once again, the United States is involving itself in the ICC while refusing its jurisdiction. Michael Ranneberger, the US ambassador to Kenya, has also been severely criticised for intervention in the internal affairs of Kenya.

In March 2013, two of the leading accused at the ICC, Uhuru Kenyatta and William Ruto, were elected president and vice-president respectively. It was plebiscite on the ICC's role. As this paper was being written, Kenya was considering withdrawing from the ICC due to its interference in the internal affairs of a sovereign country. The trial of Mr. Ruto had begun and Mr. Kenyatta's was failing since all the witnesses have retracted. Most of the witnesses against Mr. Ruto were also refusing to testify.[34]

## Impunity at the ICC

The Achilles heel of international criminal law's is the impunity granted to major powers.

The wars on Iraq and Afghanistan are the most glaring examples. In spite of more than 100,000 civilian dead in Iraq, no efforts have been made to charge members of the US or British military. Similarly, the occupation of Afghanistan resulted in tens of thousands of civilian deaths, not including the military resistance. The ICC has turned a blind eye to the systematic torture in Iraq by American forces.

The statute of the ICC provides for impunity directly or indirectly for the major western powers. Professor Hans Köchler argues that the International Criminal Court is in fact an *ad hoc* court for the Security Council.[35] The International Criminal Court was created by a treaty—the Rome Statute—in contrast with the ICTY and the ICTR, which were creations of the Security Council itself.

The Rome Statute, notwithstanding its creation by treaty, grants exceptional powers to the Security Council. Article 13(b) of the Statute provides that the Security Council can exercise its powers under Chapter VII of the UN Charter and refer cases to the ICC for countries that are not state parties to the Rome Statute. The decision-making is in the hands of the five permanent members of the Security Council, three of which—China, Russia, and the United States—are not ICC member states. Under Article 16 of the Statute, the Security Council can also unilaterally defer an investigation for a period of one year.

The United States, a Security Council member, has some 102 bilateral agreements under Article 98 of the ICC Statute guaranteeing that US citizens would not be turned over to the ICC. They consider that Article 98 of the Rome Statute allows countries to commit themselves in advance not to turn over their citizens to the ICC. These agreements go a long way to guarantee total impunity for US citizens. This same country bombs Pakistan and Yemen with drones in total violation of international law. The lawlessness of the major powers and their immunity is in glaring contradiction with the zeal to charge African leaders who stand in the way.

In September 2012, Nobel Peace prize winner Desmond Tutu, speaking of the war on Iraq, accused the former British and US leaders of lying about weapons of mass destruction and said the invasion had left the world more destabilised and divided "than any other conflict in history." Claiming that more than 110,000 people died in the Iraq war, he added, "In a consistent world, those responsible for this suffering and loss of life should be treading the same path as some of their African and Asian peers who have been made to answer for their actions in The Hague."[36] He refused to attend a conference on leadership in Johannesburg because Tony Blair was attending (incidentally, as a paid participant).

## Does World History Begin in 1990?

International criminal law has a fundamental flaw based on the premise that beginning approximately in 1990 at the end of the Cold War, a new world was born where human rights triumph. This view holds that impunity can be terminated and that international criminal law can guarantee the end of impunity for massive violations of human rights.

Nothing could be further from the truth. The world has changed and it has taken a turn for the worse. No international prosecutions have been initiated for the many US crimes in Vietnam, Chile, Panama, or the Dominican Republic, to mention a few. The criminal economic blockade of Cuba is still in force. Israel continues its crimes in Palestine. The massive British crimes committed in Kenya and India are unpunished and almost forgotten. In Kashmir in 1949, with the British policy of divide and rule, there were about one million dead and eleven million displaced. French crimes in Algeria go unpunished. Crimes committed in Iraq in the first Gulf War 1990-1991 are virtually forgotten. No international proceedings are under way for crimes committed in Iraq or Afghanistan, for chemical warfare against Iraqis in Fallujah, or for the use of depleted uranium all over Iraq. No one is being charged for the aggression against Syria supported by the United States, Britain, and France.

We have shown that the new courts do not criminalise aggressive war and crimes against peace. Contrary to common belief, the new international criminal law courts do not follow the heritage of the Nuremberg Court for which the crimes of aggression and crimes against peace were considered the primary war crimes from which all other crimes ensued. The Nuremberg Tribunal, accompanied by the birth of the United Nations, proclaimed that the respect for national sovereignty was the foundation of a just world. The new international criminal law is the opposite, since it is based on the right of the powerful to intervene in the internal affairs of countries to protect alleged victims. The crime of aggression is not yet punishable and probably will never be without a revolution in international relations.[37]

Attorneys who raise fundamental criticisms are attacked as genocide apologists or politically motivated activists. Some ask, "How can you defend 'those people'?" The so-called informed public assumes that an accusation necessarily implies guilt. Defenders are demonised as having extremist ideas when they criticise the ICTR or the International Criminal Court.

An important debate in international criminal law sometimes pits those who wish to improve it against others who reject it outright. Alexander Zahar and Goran Sluiter have written very rigorous and convincing criticisms in their book, *International Criminal Law: A Critical Introduction*.[38] Almost any evidence is admitted at trial and the judges are free to evaluate the evidence. The law is often interpreted to allow for a finding against the defence. The term "result-oriented law" is often used to characterise judicial rulings. Professor Nancy Combs wrote the seminal and aptly titled book *Fact-Finding Without Facts: The Uncertain Evidentiary Foundations of International Criminal Convictions*.[39]

In the present context, national legal systems and political systems can often provide better instruments of justice, including trials or diverse transitional measures for reconciliation.[40] It is wrong for supposedly progressive forces to press either for charges at the International Criminal Court or for the creation of new international criminal courts. Political solutions either through the United Nations or diplomacy are preferable recourse to international criminal law.

The ideal of the United Nations charter remains important: sovereign equality of all nations, big or small, powerful or weak. No country has the right to intervene in the internal affairs of another. The principle of Nuremburg, under which the crime of aggression is the supreme war crime from which all other crimes flow, must triumph.

International criminal law may die slowly owing to the lack of respect it engenders. In my opinion, it is an error to claim that it can be salvaged and that we should not throw out the baby with the bath water, so to speak. In the name of justice and equality, the only reasonable course should be to shut them down and release all convicted persons. Lawyers have the duty to criticise these courts in public since few other people have the required knowledge to do so.

The decline of US hegemony and the realignment of the world are likely the death knell of international criminal law. Will the Security Council or the General Assembly ever show the unity required to create another court? Doubtful. The recent experience with Syria offers another path. What has happened in Syria since 2011 is similar to the Rwandan experience. Far from being a popular revolt, terrorists and jihadists financed by Western capital created havoc and killed many. The Syrian army reacted with resolve and received solid international support from some quarters, including Russia, Iran, and Hezbollah. The US plan to break up a viable modern state in the interests of its global hegemony was thus stymied... for the time being.

## Notes

1. A July 17, 2003 WikiLeaks cable explains that Judge Theodor Meron met a US ambassador in July 2003 to urge the replacement of Carla Del Ponte as prosecutor. A copy of this is available at www.johnphilpot.com.
2. Report of the Mapping Exercise documenting the most serious violations of human rights and international humanitarian law committed within the territory of the Democratic Republic of the Congo between March 1993 and June 2003, August 2010. See also Pierre-Claver Ndacyayisenga, *Dying to Live: A Rwandan Family's Five-Year Flight Across the Congo*, Baraka Books, Montreal, 2013.
3. John Laughlin, *Travesty: The Trial of Slobodan Milošević and the Corruption of International Justice*, Pluto Press, London, 2007.
4. Gotovina *et al.* (Operation Storm), Ante Gotovina and Mladen Markač acquitted on November 16, 2012, Ivan Čermak acquitted on April 15, 2011, http://www.icty.org/case/gotovina/4.
5. See http://www.icty.org/sid/11145 and related judgments on the ICTY website.
6. See http://en.wikipedia.org/wiki/Ramush_Haradinaj.
7. See his biography: http://fr.wikipedia.org/wiki/Florence_Hartmann; see also the important book by the late Professor Michael Mandel, *How America Gets Away with Murder: Illegal Wars, Collateral Damage and Crimes*, Pluto Press, London, 2004.
8. See Harhoff letter at www.johnphilpot.com.

9.  UN ICTY, Press Release, "Judge Harhoff disqualified from Šešelj case," August 29, 2013, http://www.icty.org/sid/11357.

10. David Scheffer, *All the Missing Souls: A Personal History of the War Crimes Tribunals,* Princeton University Press, Princeton, 2012, p. 321.

11. Agreement of January 16, 2002.

12. See Chapter 5 in this volume, Chief Charles Taku, "Charles Taylor: The Special Court of Sierra Leone and Questionable Verdicts"; see Kai Ambos and Ousman Njikam, "Charles Taylor's Criminal Responsibility," Journal of *International Criminal Justice,* Vol. 11, 2013, doi: 10.1093/jicj/mqt042, abstract at http://jicj.oxford-journals.org/content/11/4/789.

13. http://www.africalegalaid.com/news/justice-malick-sow-charles-taylor-trial-speaks

14. *Prosecutor v. Momčilo Perišić,* Case No. It-04-81-A, Judgment, February 28, 2013, para. 36.

15. Kevin Jon Heller, "The SCSL's Incoherent — and Selective — Analysis of Custom," *Opinio Juris,* http://opiniojuris.org/2013/09/27/scsls-incoherent-selective-analysis-custom/.

16. Agreement between the United Nations and the Royal Government of Cambodia Concerning the Prosecution under Cambodian Law of Crimes Committed during the Period of Democratic Kampuchea.

17. David Scheffer, *All the Missing Souls: A Personal History of the War Crimes Tribunals,* Princeton University Press, Princeton, 2012, pp. 341-405.

18. *Ibid. p. 368*

19. *Ibid. p. 374*

20. Security Council Resolution 1757, 2007.

21. Special Tribunal for Lebanon, Case No. STL-11-01, "Decision on the Defence Challenges to the Jurisdiction and Legality of the Tribunal", July 27, 2012, http://www.stl-tsl.org/en/the-cases/stl-11-01/main/filings/orders-and-decisions/trial-chamber/f0352.

22. The March 14 Alliance is an anti-Syrian, pro-Western alliance of political parties opposed to the March 8 Alliance, which is pro-Syrian and anti-Zionist.

23. Ibrahim al-Amin, "The Rash Verdict," *Al-Akhbar,* January 17, 2014, http://english.al-akhbar.com/content/rash-verdict.

24. David Scheffer, *op. cit.,* p. 252.

25. See Chapter 11 above.

26. Florence Hartmann, *Paix et châtiment : Les guerres secrètes de la politique et de la justice internationales,* Flammarion, 2007, pp. 247-278.

27. Interview September 12, 2002, http://www.pbs.org/wnet/wideangle/episodes/media-by-milosevic/interview-ambassador-pierre-richard-prosper/985/.

28. H. Vincent Harris, "WikiLeaks Confirm US Interference In Spanish Genocide Case Against Kagame," *Colored Opinions,* May 25, 2011, http://coloredopinions.blogspot.ca/2011/05/wikileaks-confirm-us-interference-in.html.

29. See Alexander Zahar and Goran Sluiter, *International Criminal Law: A Critical Introduction,* Oxford University Press, Oxford, 2008, pp.185-195

30. Le Soir, « Câble 10BRUSSELS23 : la Belgique et la CPI », December 19, 2010, http://blog.lesoir.be/wikileaks/2010/12/19/cable-10brussels23/.

31. Maximilian Forte, *Slouching Towards Sirte: NATO's War on Libya and Africa*, Baraka Books, Montreal, 2012, pp. 110-117.

32. Quoted in http://blackagendareport.com/content/bad-news-africa-3000-more-us-soldiers-are-way.

33. Letter Dated March 23, 2011 from the Permanent Representative of Kenya to the United Nations addressed to the President of the Security Council. Request of Kenya for deferral under Article 16 of the Rome Statute of the International Criminal Court, S/2011/201.

34. For a full description of the Kenya case, see Chapter 7 above.

35. Hans Köchler , "World Court without a World State Criminal Justice under the Dictates of Realpolitik?" July 1, 2012; I.P.O. Online Publications, International Progress Organization, Vienna.

36. Louis Peitzman, "Desmond Tutu: George W. Bush and Tony Blair Should Face Prosecution for Iraq War," *Gawker*, September 2, 2012, http://gawker.com/5939945/desmond-tutu-george-w-bush-and-tony-blair-should-face-prosecution-for-iraq-war. Additional similar reports are in *The Guardian* at http://www.theguardian.com/politics/2012/sep/02/tony-blair-iraq-war-desmond-tutu and in *The Independent* at http://www.independent.co.uk/news/world/politics/blair-should-face-war-crimes-trial-over-iraq-says-desmond-tutu-8100798.html.

37. The Rome Statute, sub-article 5(2), states that the crime of aggression can only be prosecuted once the proper definitions have been adopted. The Definition adopted in Kampala in 2010 cannot be implemented before January 1, 2017, and only if the state parties agree.

38. Oxford University Press, 2008.

39. Cambridge University Press, 2010.

40. See Chapter 13 above, Jordi Palou-Loverdos, "Transitional Justice in Rwanda and Democratic Republic of Congo: From War to Peace?"

# Conclusion

This book explores not only the injustices or the lack of fairness that have characterised the last twenty years of international criminal law but also the powerful political forces that have shaped it. These injustices can and hopefully will be a source of learning so as to influence the course of history for the better. Many short-term and long-term measures are necessary.

## The International Criminal Tribunal for Rwanda and Trials

The violations of due process and disclosure obligations, particularly in the case of the ICTR, require remedies. In many instances, considering the extent of these violations and their implications on the totality of the evidence presented, cases of convicted persons should be re-opened notwithstanding the principle of *res judicata* or the idea that judgments are final. This principle prevents a litigant from requesting a second look at the evidence when there was due process. However, when prosecutions are biased, when evidence is hidden and witnesses are unheard, and when the Rwandan government controls much of the evidence, *res judicata* becomes a bar to justice. Sooner or later, when the Kagame government falls, a flood of new information and evidence is to be expected. In this light, the ICTR or the United Nations through the residual Mechanism for International Criminal Tribunals (MICT) should provide for legal counselling for all convicted persons to assess the impact on their respective cases, with unrestricted access to the prosecutor files, to allow for appropriate remedies.

The Security Council must also vote on the appropriate resolutions to allow all acquitted persons to be reunited with their families. Seven acquitted persons are alone in Arusha, unable to return to their families, mostly in Europe or Canada.

The unfair trial of Rwandan presidential candidate Victoire Ingabire Umuhoza, as described in this book, should be sufficient evidence to convince courts and governments to refuse to transfer, extradite or deport accused persons to Rwanda. Rwanda simply cannot hold fair trials. This concerns principally Canada, the United States, and some European countries, where their respective foreign policies lead them to comply with Rwanda's wishes. The unfair—and unending—trial of Léon Mugesera, deported to Rwanda from Canada in January 2012, should be the object of a full study. Professor Fannie Lafontaine has described Canada's position in his case as "wilful blindness."[1] Indeed, Canada transferred him to Rwanda since he could supposedly have a "fair trial" and apparently has since washed its hands of this case. A change of policy toward Rwanda is required to avoid further injustice.

## The International Criminal Court

The ICC's unique focus on Africa and the impunity accorded principally to the United States, Great Britain, Israel, and their allies has colonialist overtones. This greatly undermines its credibility and profound changes are needed in its prosecutorial policies. Moreover, as Dr. David Hoile has written in a seminal work on the ICC called *Justice Denied: The Reality of the International Criminal Court*, "[t]he court has destroyed peace processes across Africa and exacerbated conflict, and that it has failed mankind's hopes for justice."[2] It also appears that many of the unfair practices regarding evidence at the ICTR have been continued at the ICC.

In all national and international jurisdictions, aiding and abetting crimes, in particular mass murder, genocide, crimes against humanity, and other war crimes, creates personal criminal responsibility. In particular, Article 25(3)(c) of the Rome Statute criminalises aiding and abetting war crimes and Article 25(3)(d) of the Rome Statute is even broader, providing a very extensive definition of personal responsibility for war crimes as contribution to crimes personally committed by others.

Two examples of "aiding and abetting" come to mind. The crimes of the foreign insurgents in Syria and the crimes of Israel in Gaza and the West Bank can be directly linked to American, French, and British politicians. Even academic institutions in Canada, the United States, and Britain as well as arms manufacturers in those countries have arguably direct responsibility for Israeli crimes. If the ICC was impartial, these foreign sponsors could be indicted for the crimes committed against the people of Gaza by Israel or the people of Syria and the insurgents respectively, in much the same way that Charles Taylor of Liberia was convicted for crimes committed in Sierra Leone, as explained in this book. If the ICC was unbiased, these foreign sponsors might be more hesitant to support wars and invasions of sovereign countries. However, given the partiality of the ICC, this type of indictment is not immediately forthcoming.

This raises questions about the usefulness of calling for charges at the International Criminal Court. Nevertheless, two obvious potential targets are undoubtedly on the tips of many tongues, Paul Kagame and Benjamin Netanyahu.

For some, the United States' friend, Paul Kagame, one of the most vicious warmongers in Africa, is the perfect candidate for charges at the ICC and many people hope that Kagame will be charged at the ICC for the crimes committed in the Congo since 2002. However, as the African Union, among others, has criticised the ICC for targeting only Africans, it raises the question about the legitimacy of further prosecution under these conditions.

The second obvious set of charges relates to Benjamin Netanyahu and other Israeli leaders for the wars on Gaza in 2008-2009, 2012, and 2014. The prosecutor claims that the ICC has no jurisdiction since Palestine has not signed the Rome Statute. However, it should also be recalled that Palestine, including the Palestinian Authority and Hamas, intended to apply to sign and ratify the Rome Statute, but the prosecutor refused the Palestinian Authority as a signatory in 2009 since Palestine was not a state. We understand that the Palestinian Authority is of two minds about the ICC but that it has maintained its recent 2014 complaint at the ICC.[3] Unfortunately, it should not be expected for the prosecutor to cooperate in this new application given the political ramifications of such a decision.

## War and Peace: Lessons

In our opposition to war and in the search for peace, we should take a closer look at the role of major NGOs. It is useful to recall the words

of Ms. Alison Des Forges of Human Rights Watch in her testimony in
the trial of Protais Zigiranyirazo. In many ways Ms. Des Forges was
instrumental in shaping the ICTR's proceedings as she influenced its
development and testified as a so-called expert witness in the trials of
some twenty ICTR accused. Under cross-examination, she admitted
that Human Rights Watch did not call for a ceasefire during the period
April-July 1994 although, in the past, Human Rights Watch had called
for ceasefires. Rather, in mid-May 1994, she explained that when Rwanda
sent Messrs Jérôme Bicamumpaka and Jean-Bosco Barayagwiza to the
United Nations where they called for a UN Chapter VII intervention
to stop the massacres, she opposed their obtaining American visas and
called for their non-recognition as representatives of the Government of
Rwanda. Along with Human Rights Watch, she had a multimillion-dol-
lar lawsuit served on Mr. Barayagwiza in New York.[4] Rather than trying
to extinguish the fire in Rwanda, Des Forges and Human Rights Watch
fanned the flames by trying to chase Rwandan representatives from the
United States, and discredit them. In short, they effectively helped prevent peace in Rwanda in 1994 thereby contributing to the death of many
thousands of Rwandans.

There is an additional lesson: a Tribunal is neither an instrument
of war, nor of peace. A major flaw in the ICTR and the ICTY is that
the two tribunals were created by the Security Council, under Chapter
VII of the United Nations Charter. Chapter VII deals with coercion
by the Security Council when immediate action is required to prevent
aggression, or maintain peace. A Tribunal created under article 29 of
the United Nations Charter is therefore an organism subsidiary to the
Security Council pursuant to the exercise of its policing functions under
Chapter VII of the Charter.[5] From this active international policing role,
an international criminal court cannot meet the requirement of neutrality and independence which must be the hallmark of any tribunal,
and all the more so of an international tribunal requiring the respect
and support of all nations. An International Criminal Courts should
necessarily be created by treaty.

## Only a Beginning

This first independent, defence-oriented book on International Criminal Law is only a beginning. Jordi Palou Loverdos has described the problems with universal jurisdiction in Spain. Trials of Rwandans under universal jurisdiction in Europe, Canada, and the United States are fraught with problems; universal jurisdiction will require further analysis. In immigration matters, Canada routinely raises unfounded war crimes allegations to exclude refugees, declare inadmissible permanent residents, deprive citizens of their status, and refuse visas to enter Canada. Important work is needed to induce change in government policy.

International criminal trials are clouded in secrecy. Under the guise of protecting witnesses, the secret testimony is removed from public scrutiny, thus threatening the fairness of the process. Moreover, hearsay and general opinions are often admitted as trustworthy evidence. Critical study of International Criminal Law must be expanded because a complete study of the ultra-liberal evidentiary rules applied in the international courts and their implications on the fairness of proceedings would be required to prevent injustice in the future.

## The Future

David Jacobs' homage to Michael Mandel shows how the International Criminal Law movement has helped to change the rules in international relations. This change has virtually eradicated the principle of the sovereign equality of nations. The fundamental principle of the Nuremberg judgment, namely that the crime against peace is the greatest international crime, has been replaced by superpower intervention by military might under the doctrine of the Responsibility to Protect (R2P), and by political and judicial interventionism. Therefore, it is necessary to reinforce the United Nations with the fundamental principles on which it was created, namely the sovereign equality of nations and the non-intervention by a country in the internal affairs of a sovereign nation. With these reforms completed based on these principles adapted to the early twenty-first century, it is possible that a fair International Criminal Court may be born, just as the international community had hoped at the end of the Second World War.

History will determine the future of International Criminal Law. There is a live debate among the critics. Can it be reformed or will it die a slow death? We believe that it has not brought justice and fundamental changes are required for it do so in the future. But above all, the world should not rely on International Criminal Law as a substitute for politically negotiated solution to its problems.

## Notes

1.  *La Presse*, August 19, 2014 at 07:31, updated on August 19, 08:43.
2.  David Hoile, *Justice Denied: The Reality of the International Criminal Court,* The Africa Research Centre, July 2014.
3.  Réseau Voltaire, "Rectificatif : Saleem al-Saqqa déclare maintenir la plainte palestinienne devant la CPI," *Voltairenet.org*, August 9, 2014, http://www.voltairenet.org/article185036.html.
4.  Public Testimony, *The Prosecutor v. Protais Zigiranyirazo,* ICTR, March 1, 2006, pp. 30-38 (public transcripts).
5.  See, John Philpot, *Le tribunal pénal international pour le Rwanda - La justice trahie, Études internationales*, vol. 27, n° 4, 1996, pp. 827-840.

# Contributors

**Joseph Bukeye** is a member of the executive committee of the Rwandan opposition party FDU INKINGI. In this capacity, he followed day by day the political trial of Mrs. Victoire Ingabire. Economist and former diplomat before, during and after the so-called October war, Mr. Bukeye fled Rwanda after the 1994 genocide and sought asylum in Belgium.

**Sébastien Chartrand** has worked primarily in international criminal law since becoming member of the Quebec Bar in 2011. He has been legal defence assistant in cases before the International Criminal Tribunals for Rwanda and the Former Yugoslavia. He earned his law degree at the Université du Québec à Montréal and also holds a degree in Political Science and Philosophy from the Université de Montréal. He lives in Montreal.

**Michel Chossudovsky** is professor *emeritus* of Economics at the University of Ottawa. He has been advisor to governments of several developing countries and his books include *The Globalization of Poverty and the New World Order* (2003) and *Towards a World War III Scenario: The Dangers of Nuclear War* (2011). He is the founder and director of the Centre for Research on Globalization that hosts one of the world's most important alternative media websites, GlobalResearch.ca, as well as Mondialisation.ca (in French). He lives in Montreal.

**David P. Jacobs** is a partner at Watson Jacobs McCreary LLP with over thirty years' experience in professional regulation, labour relations, international criminal law, human rights, employment law, health law, civil litigation, insolvency, constitutional law and administrative law. He has represented clients before tribunals and courts at all levels in Canada, and has acted as lead defence counsel before the Trial and Appeal Chambers of the ICTR. David is a lecturer, writer, and media commentator on international, administrative, labour, human rights, constitutional, criminal, and other legal issues. He is Past Chair of the Constitutional and Civil Liberties Section of the Canadian Bar Association (Ontario) and author of a section in the leading publication Macaulay's Practice and Procedure Before Administrative Tribunals.

**Glen Ford** has more than forty years' experience in broadcast, print, and Internet journalism. A former Washington Bureau Chief and White House, Capitol Hill, and State Department correspondent, he co-founded and hosted *America's Black Forum*, the first nationally syndicated Black news interview program on commercial television. He has edited or served as staff reporter for three newspapers and was national political columnist for *Encore American & Worldwide News* magazine. He co-founded *BlackCommentator.com* in 2002 and *BlackAgendaReport.com* in 2006 where he is currently executive editor. He also co-hosts online radio programs that air on some forty radio stations. Glen Ford is author of *The Big Lie: An Analysis of U.S. Media Coverage of the Grenada Invasion*, IOJ, 1985.

**Fannie Lafontaine**, Lawyer, Associate Professor, Canada Research Chair on International Criminal Justice and Human Rights, Founder and Director of the International Criminal and Humanitarian Law Clinic, Law Faculty, Université Laval, Quebec City, Canada. Some excerpts of this essay are taken from Fannie Lafontaine & Alain-Guy Tachou Sipowo, "The contribution of international criminal justice to sustainable peace and development" in Sébastien Jodoin & Marie-Claire Cordonier Segger, eds, *Sustainable Development, International Criminal Justice, and Treaty Implementation* (Cambridge: Cambridge University Press, 2013), at Chapter 11.

**Philippe Larochelle** has been a member of the Quebec Bar since 1998, and is a partner at Roy, Larochelle. He practices in international criminal law before Canadian Courts, the ICTR, the ICC, and the STL. Amongst other cases, he also represented Leon Mugesera in Expulsion proceedings, and Regent Boily in his case before the Committee against torture and Jacques Dery before the Supreme Court of Canada.

**Léopold Nsengiyumva** holds a Master's degree in law from Michigan State University; an LLB degree from the University of South Africa; and a Licence with distinction from the National University of Rwanda. He lectured shortly at the National University of Rwanda and joined the United Nations International Criminal court for Rwanda (UNICTR) in May 2000 where he worked as a defence investigator and/or legal assistant on cases including *Prosecutor v. Edouard Karemera et al; The Prosecutor v. Augustin Ndindiliyimana et al;* and *The Prosecutor v. Ildephonse Nizeyimana.* He also wrote expert reports on cases in the UK and Canada.

**Beth S. Lyons** has been a Defence Counsel at the ICTR since 2004. In February 2014, she and Lead Counsel Chief Charles A. Taku (with their defense team) won the acquittal of their client, Major F.X. Nzuwonemeye, by the Appeals Chamber, in the *Ndindiliyimana et al.* ("Military II") case. She also worked with Lead Counsel Maître Sadikou Ayo Alao, representing Mr. Aloys Simba. She served on the Bureau of the Association of Defense Attorneys at Arusha (ADAD), and has been an Alternate Representative to the U.N. for the International Association of Democratic Lawyers (IADL) since 1997. Beth may be contacted at bethlyons@aol.com.

**Jordi Palou-Loverdos,** lawyer, conflict mediator, and consultant living in Catalonia (Spain), holds a Master's degree in Criminal Law and Criminal Law Science from the University of Barcelona, and is a member of the International Criminal Bar. Accredited at the ICC, he is also a member of the Human Rights Institute of the International Bar Association. He has a Master's in Conflict Mediation and Resolution and was co-facilitator in charge of the Intra-Rwandan Dialogue process. He is legal representative of more than thirty Spanish, Rwandan, and Congolese victims before the Spanish courts together with international NGO's and public institutions under the International Forum for Truth and Justice in Africa of the Great Lakes region (www.veritasrwandaforum.org).

**John Philpot** has thirty years' experience as a criminal defence lawyer including twenty years in international criminal justice. He has represented clients before the International Criminal Tribunal for Rwanda, including the Appeal Court in The Hague, and the International Criminal Court. He was chief organiser of three international criminal law conferences. John Philpot earned his law degree at the Université de Montréal and also holds an MA in History from the University of Toronto and an MSc in Mathematics from Sussex University in the UK. He lives in Montreal and is a member of the Quebec Bar.

**Théogène Rudasingwa** is a medical doctor former diplomat who served as Rwandan Ambassador to the United States, Mexico, Argentina, and Brazil and represented Rwanda at the UN, the World Bank, IMF, and the African Union. As a leader of the Rwanda National Congress (RNC), he is currently involved in working with all Rwandans to embrace truth telling, forgiveness, and reconciliation. Dr. Rudasingwa has a medical degree from Makerere University, in Uganda, an MA in International Relations from the Fletcher School of Law and Diplomacy, Tufts University, and an honorary PhD from Trinity College of Vermont.

**André Sirois** is a consultant to international tribunals and organisations, legal counsel to unions of international organizations, and lecturer in international administrative law and legal translation. He has been active in creating a bar association for lawyers working in international organizations and tribunals and in the reform of the internal UN justice system. André Sirois ranked first, over 4000 candidates, at the UN translation competition, and was the first Canadian to be hired as an official of UN linguistic services. He was also among the first employees of the ICTR. When he subsequently denounced the mismanagement he became one of the first whistleblowers in UN history. He has worked for several UN offices, missions, and tribunals.

**Érick Sullivan**, Lawyer, Deputy Director of the International Criminal and Humanitarian Law Clinic, Law Faculty, Université Laval, Quebec City, Canada.

**Chief Charles Taku** was Lead Counsel at the International Criminal Tribunal for Rwanda from October 1999 to February 2014, the Special Court for Sierra Leone from July 2005 to May 2013 and the International Criminal Court (continuing investigation in the Situation in the Republic of Kenya) from March 2012 to October 2013. Chief Taku and Co-counsel Beth Lyons won an acquittal in the Military II case on appeal at the ICTR. He is the author of "*Contextual Foundations of International Criminal Jurisprudence*, Authorhouse, 2012.

**Phil Taylor** has been a defence investigator at the ICTR since trials began in Arusha, Tanzania in 1997. He has more than twenty-five years of experience as a defence investigator for the late Charles Roach, internationally renowned human rights lawyer. Phil Taylor is also a broadcaster and host of widely listened to radio program *The Taylor Report* at CIUT 89.5 FM, Toronto.

# Acknowledgements

This book would not have appeared were it not for the help, encouragement, advice, and contributions of many people. Thanks are due first to the authors who contributed their knowledge, their time, and their skills to produce a book with such a broad scope

Over close to two decades of work in international criminal law, many counsel, investigators, and legal assistants have made this work possible and helped solve the countless problems that arise when working in defence in international criminal law. A few names must be mentioned; those whose names may have been admitted receive our full apologies. Counsel and defence team collaborators at the International Criminal Tribunal for Rwanda and in France include Raphael Constant, Philippe Meilhac, Peter Zaduk, Ken Ogetto, Gershom Otachi Bw'Omanwa, Evans Monari, Beth Lyons, Peter Robinson, Paul Skolnik, John Floyd, Abbe Jolles, Tiphaine Dickson, Carmelle Marchessault, André Tremblay, Peter Erlinder, Gilles St Laurent, Michelyne St Laurent, Fabien Sagatwa, Seydou Doumbia, Michel Marchand, Benoit Henry, Caroline Buisman, Lennox Hinds, Stefan Kirsch, Chris Black, Alexandra Marcil, Sylvia Geraghty, Chris Gosnell, Innocent Nzabona, Dick Prudence Munyeshuli, Léopold Nsengyumva, Valens Hahirwa, Melissa Kanas, Allison Turner, and Myriam Bouazdi. David Jacobs, who wrote the homage to Michael Mandel, would also like to thank Karen Golden, Michael Mandel's widow, for her comments and for allowing him to consult Michael's unpublished papers and also Harry Glasbeek for his comments.

Thanks also go to Chris de Beule, the late Antoine Nyetera, Gaspard Musabyimana, Helmut Strizek, and the late Michael Hourigan, Barrie Collins, Charles Ndereyehe, Pierre Péan, et Bernard Lugan to mention only a few, who are always sources of reliable information and documentation.

At the ICTR, we have had the pleasure of collaborating closely with Pascal Besnier, former defence counsel who became Deputy

Registrar, Rosette Muzigo-Morrison of the Appeal's Registry, and Laurent Wastelain of the Defence Counsel Section.

As defence counsel, we are also grateful for the support and for the dignified approach to their defence of our clients and their families throughout difficult trials and appeals: Jean Paul Akayesu and his sister Rita Loiseau, Protais Zigiranyirazo and his brother Seraphin Rwabukumba, and Ildephonse Nizeyimana. A special thanks is due to the late Jean-Bosco Barayagwiza whose legal writings contributed to the defense of many.

Between 2009 and 2012, defence counsel at the ICTR held three conferences: The Hague on November 14-15, 2009, Brussels on May 22-23, 2010, and Montreal on September 28, 2012. Many of the papers presented at those conferences are available at the French and English-language website at http://www.ictrlegacydefenseperspective.org/En.html. Thanks are due to all organisers but special thanks go to Professor André Tremblay without whom none of this work would have been possible. These conferences inspired us to write this book. Thanks also to Dr. Olivier Nyirubugara who is responsible for our website.

We would also like to thank Robin Philpot of Baraka Books who provided important advice and support which allowed us to complete this book. Thanks also to Maja Romano for the thorough proofreading and Josée Lalancette for book design.

Finally, a very special mention must be made about Ramsay Clark, former Attorney General of the United States and defence counsel at the ICTR for the late Pastor Elizaphan Ntakirutimana. He has been a constant inspiration for our work in international criminal law. Similarly, Phil Taylor, defence investigator, broadcaster, and contributor to this volume, has provided invaluable guidance thanks to his vast understanding of Rwanda, Africa, and US foreign policy.

Sébastien Chartrand and John Philpot, September 15, 2014

MORE NONFICTION FROM BARAKA BOOKS

*Dying to Live*
*A Rwandan Family's Five-Year Flight Across the Congo*
Pierre-Claver Ndacyayisenga

*Slouching Towards Sirte*
*NATO's War on Libya and Africa*
Maximilian Forte

*Rwanda and the New Scramble for Africa: From Tragedy*
*to Useful Imperial Fiction*
Robin Philpot

*Challenging the Mississippi Firebombers*
*Memories of Mississippi 1964-65*
Jim Dann

*Barack Obama and the Jim Crow Media*
*The Return of the Nigger Breakers*
Ishmael Reed

*Going Too Far*
*Essays about America's Nervous Breakdown*
Ishmael Reed

*The Question of Separatism*
*Quebec and the Struggle over Sovereignty*
Jane Jacobs

*The History of Montréal*
*The Story of a Great North American City*
Paul-André Linteau